COSMIC HISTORY CHRONICLES

Volume IV

BOOK OF THE INITIATION

Time and the Hidden Order: Consciousness and its Transmission

Transmitted by Valum Votan—Jose Arguelles
Received by Red Queen—Stephanie South
"We are but the secretaries, the authors are in Eternity"

White Lunar Wizard Fourth Ray: Harmony

Cosmic History Chronicles IV – Book of the Initiation
Copyright © Galactic Research Institute

White Lunar Wizard Year (2008)

All rights reserved by the Galactic Masters.

ISBN 0-9767759-0-4
www.lawoftime.org

Original Graphics by Valum Votan (Jose Arguelles), Kin 11 and Red Queen (Stephanie South), Kin 185
Computer enhancement by Kelly Harding, Kin 240 and Jacob Wyatt, Kin 201
Book Design and Layout by Kelly Harding, Kin 240

Cosmic History Chronicles Volume IV
Book of the Initiation
Time and the Hidden Order: Consciousness and its Transmission

Contents

Forward: The Making of Cosmic History Volume IV ... v

Part I: Defining the Path

- Gate 1: Entering the Labyrinth ... 13
- Gate 2: Cosmic History—Mind Gate to a New Reality ... 23
- Gate 3: Hermetic Life and the Hidden Rainbow ... 35

Part II: Crafting the Vehicle

- Gate 4: Esoteric Personality ... 51
- Gate 5: Creative Power—Taming the Forces ... 87
- Gate 6: Madame Blavatsky—an Initiatic Doorway ... 103

Part III: Mapping the New Reality

- Gate 7: Hermetic Stream GM108X—the Nature of Transmission ... 123
- Gate 8: Symbolic Systems: Traditions Beyond Words ... 141
- Gate 9: Synchronicity and the Living Template of Time ... 163

Part IV: Exploring the Inner Dimensions

- Gate 10: The Serpent Initiates ... 179
- Gate 11: Sex and the Coming Noogenesis ... 193
- Gate 12: Noospheric Initiation—Becoming a Cosmic Medium ... 211

- Gate 13: Seven Planetary Initiations ... 227
    - Appendix: Synchronic Order as Symbolic Construct ... 243

FOLLOW THE LABYRINTH THAT LEADS TO YOUR OWN STAR!

IN ORDER TO EVOLVE LEARN SOMETHING NEW

YOU ONLY ADVANCE ACCORDING TO YOUR OWN EFFORT

1. Entering the Labyrinth
2. Cosmic History—Mind Gate to a New Rainbow
3. Hermetic Life and the Hidden Doorway
4. Esoteric Personality
5. Creative Power—Taming the Forces
6. Madame Blavatsky—An Initiatic Doorway
7. Hermetic Stream Catuor
8. Symbolic Systems
9. Synchronicity and the Living Template of Time
10. The Serpent Initiates
11. Hermesphere Gnosis
12. Sex and the Coming Initiates
13. Planetary Initiation

LOVE, LOVE, ABOVE ALL

Forward: The Making of *Book of the Initiation*
Nauthiz is the Testing that Ripens the Initiation
White Lunar Wizard Year

I polarize in order to enchant
Stabilizing receptivity
I seal the output of timelessness
With the lunar tone of challenge
I am guided by the power of death.

Study day and night, and supplicate the Creator that he would be pleased to grant thee knowledge and understanding; and that the pure spirits may have communication and influence, in thee.

—Francis Barrett

We are living in a time of unprecedented planetary initiation as our world is shifting from one state to another. Living on this planet, at this time of the summation of history and evolution, is in itself an initiatic process. Each day we are faced, as individuals and as a collective, with a labyrinthian process of making the right decisions in an ever-shifting landscape of information bombardment.

As we saw in the previous volume, *Book of the Mystery*, human beings of the modern civilization have become a race totally disconnected from Source. This disconnect is inclusive of the emotional, mental and physical bodies. The situation is exacerbated as the information age reaches its final stage, the cybersphere with all of its outlets—Internet, iPhones, video games, etc.

The impact of the cybersphere causes a disconnect so intense that people actually die from sitting on their couches flipping through endless channels, shopping on the Internet, eating microwave dinners and fast food and, in general, just not moving.

However, this stage of the cybersphere must play out; it is the final phase of sensory overload. Yet, while everybody's individual channels are being opened, these channels cannot be genuinely utilized through disconnected beings operating in artificial environments with mechanized sense modes.

To disentangle ourselves from the web of virtual reality and artificial lifestyles we must enter a new labyrinth—only one that leads to the cosmic self. The maze or labyrinth is the archetypal structure of the process of initiation. *Book of the Initiation* is constructed as a labyrinthine journey addressed to the planetary human—everyone alive today. In the labyrinth, there are unsuspected energies to be confronted, tamed and transcended.

The creation of *Book of the Initiation* was a labyrinthian journey unto itself, fraught with many experiences attesting to the truth of its purpose and meaning.

The Cosmic History Chronicles • Volume IV

Any creative process is an initiatic one. To be true and exemplify what it is communicating, the creative act must be grounded in the experience of its message. If you have not eaten an apple, then you cannot tell anyone what an apple tastes like. Having eaten the apple, we will now explain, first by placing each volume into the context of the whole vision.

Every volume of this seven-part series, *Cosmic History Chronicles*, is unique, yet an integral strand in a tapestry unlike any woven on this Earth. This means that each volume calls upon us—the secretaries, the creators, the investigators—to take the shape and form, as it were, of the grand theme defined by its title. Knowing this, we submit and allow the divine will to seize and mould us by whatever experience is appropriate to the theme we are working with.

For each of these volumes we are given one year, one solar orbit, to complete the assignment—from studying and transcribing the original tutorials, to creative processing, to writing, re-writing editing and, finally, to artistic production and layout.

In this way, each volume is defined by a single solar orbit of the Earth, each solar orbit measured by one thirteen moon/28-day solar-galactic year. The *Book of the Initiation* was a function of the solar orbital cycle of the White Lunar Wizard.

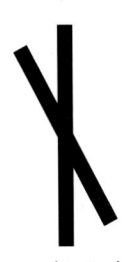

"Nauthiz is the testing that ripens the Initiation"

The essence of the initiatic journey necessary to provide the authentic experience informing this volume was a sequence of experiences that were highly polarizing, characterized by great disruptions and dislocations. How did this occur?

Several years ago, we were called by inner guidance to relocate to a remote region of the Earth, the better to focus on the cosmic nature of our duties. What began as the answer to a summons, turned out to be a testing and initiation at a number of levels. We were entered into a labyrinth of programs that expressed in a microcosm of events the totality of the struggle of the human soul during the cycle of history.

In seeking to find a base to continue our galactic investigation, we were tested by the prevailing system and its disparate social elements. The two sides of the human family—the indigenous and the civilized—the raw and the cooked—provided the initiation rites that marked the backdrop of the *Book of the Initiation*.

At the very outset of the White Lunar Wizard year, Valum Votan had been recognized by the oldest tribal group of the land of our chosen relocation as the long-awaited one prophesied to arrive on their shores at the end of the cycle. In an effort to grant him recognition as the returning "time lord", and residency in the mainstream society, we were both officially adopted, given our tribal names and granted status as natives, "People of the Land". At a later public ceremony we were formally accepted and recognized by representatives of the entire tribal family. This was the first stage of the initiation.

The second stage was the effort to bring our adoption to the place of official recognition by the mainstream governmental order. In this process, the motives of a few of our new tribal family seemed less than honorable, and even misleading and deceptive. This was the second stage—initiation into the corruption of the original people by the ways of history.

The third, and climactic level of initiation, was at the hands of the dominant government that refused to recognize or accord any right to the traditions and rights of the indigenous people, much less any matter pertaining to prophecy. As a consequence, while we were traveling out of the country on an educational tour, we were denied a visa to re-enter. Our intention had been to return to complete the process that had already been initiated by our tribal family. No number of appeals by elders of our tribe, nor of ourselves, could dissuade the government to allow us re-entry.

As a consequence, we found ourselves in another country, while the *Book of the Initiation*, in the midst of its creative process, lay in fragments, unreachable by us in the land of our adoption. Due to the diligence of a loyal supporter, who was able to retrieve our research and few personal items, bit by bit, the scattered elements of the *Book of the Initiation* were returned to us. We had passed through the labyrinth of the late historical cycle, and were now at a place of nakedly awaiting the new cycle, the coming aeon of cosmic consciousness.

Everything happens for a reason. The *Book of Initiation* reveals that all experiences are part of this planetary initiation, leading up to 2012—this includes our day-to-day struggles and all world and cosmic events. We are undergoing an initiation of the inner realms. Initiation means we are in the process of ascent; it is a rite of passage that transits us through different stages of evolution. For each of us, these stages of initiation differ according to our state of consciousness and level of evolution of our soul essence.

Our lessons of the labyrinth of the human social order were profoundly experienced and learned from. Because of our maintaining a cosmic perspective of our own sense of mission, and of a deep and abiding faith in the divine will and its plan for all creation, we understood the multidimensional and microcosmic nature of our own initiatic experience. There are many channels of perception available, and those who are conscious serve as cosmic instruments—testing the world of matter by the world of spirit.

The initiations of individuals correspond very closely to the shifts of consciousness through which we, as an entire species, are passing. While the production of each of these volumes is a function of a single orbital cycle around the sun, and of the Law of Time in general, the *Cosmic History Chronicles* also define a harmonic progression consisting of seven tones. The *Book of the Initiation* is the central note in the scale of a cosmic octave.

To go from "mi"—the *Book of the Mystery*—to "fa", the *Book of the Initiation*, requires a kind of shock, a jump in frequency. This is precisely what occurred in the process of producing this volume. Without the shock, you cannot know whether the initiation is actually real or not. You cannot expect to go from one state or another while clinging to any vestiges of your old self.

What happened to us in the creation of the *Book of the Initiation* was a microcosm of the dialectic of the historical cycle and of the planetary initiation that marks the closing of the cycle. Before we reach 2012, virtually everybody will receive a shock, in one way or another. This is the key ingredient in the initiatic process. We shall not be the same, but a new race will rise from among us.

By the Spectral moon we had stabilized enough to continue our creative process and see it to its conclusion. Every aspect of this book bears the resonance of this labyrinthine adventure.

Long has it been since we had set sail from our native land. Many times over have we died to the past, leaving behind much baggage at each stage of the journey. The initiations of the Lunar Wizard year not only refined our perceptions, lifting us into the radiant light of the New Dawn, but from it came this book, the fourth volume of the *Cosmic History Chronicles, Book of the Initiation*. This entire process paved the way for the fourth stage of the initiation, full graduation into cosmic consciousness and being.

The purpose of the *Book of the Initiation* is to understand where we are going—from a sensory to a telepathic operating field. For this to be meaningful, it is important to paint a picture of where we have come from and to review the parameters of former thinking. For this reason, we turn our attention to the principle occult personalities of the nineteenth and twentieth centuries. In light of the planetary initiation now underway, these personalities create a composite whole, a psychocosmic totality, and a foundation or matrix for the comprehension of the evolutionary energies about to unfold.

From the time of this writing it is now less than five years to the closing of the cycle, and we emphasize the significance of leading a hermetic life for the salvation of the soul—the salvation of the soul is the salvation of the world.

The lesson being demonstrated is this: No matter what the circumstance, we must all learn to rise above our present circumstances. Being on the Earth plane is nothing but a series of tests. This is the nature of the evolutionary journey, and was clearly understood by Madame Blavatsky, who opened this universal door for the first time 133 years ago with the founding of the Theosophical Society.

The spirit and example of Madame Blavatsky played a key role in the making of this fourth volume, and is actually a guiding force underlying all seven volumes. For this reason, we have dedicated an entire chapter to this great pioneer (see Gate 6), as the parallelisms between her work and the *Cosmic History Chronicles* are great.

As the successors both to the hermetic lineage in general and to the Galactic Maya on Earth, GM108X, the voice of the *Cosmic History Chronicles*, is also explored and given further definition. The process of all other esoteric templates, symbolic systems and teachings has been to give the GM108X and Cosmic History its thrust, higher purpose and focus. This voice weaves everything together for the closing of the cycle and the opening of the new. We are coming into a phase where we must learn to make the inner the outer, while we listen with the inner ear to voices from afar.

2012 is the eye of the needle. This is the cosmic gateway—the final stage of completing the Harmonic Convergence. We have four years to see how polished we can get. Those administering the initiations are here to lift us out of dualism and free us from the veils of illusion, while paving the entry into pure realms of absolute truth.

We are now being called to take life into our own hands. Each of us is responsible for his/her own process—and each of us must seek to understand the unique mission that the Creator requires of us.

Welcome to the *Book of the Initiation!*

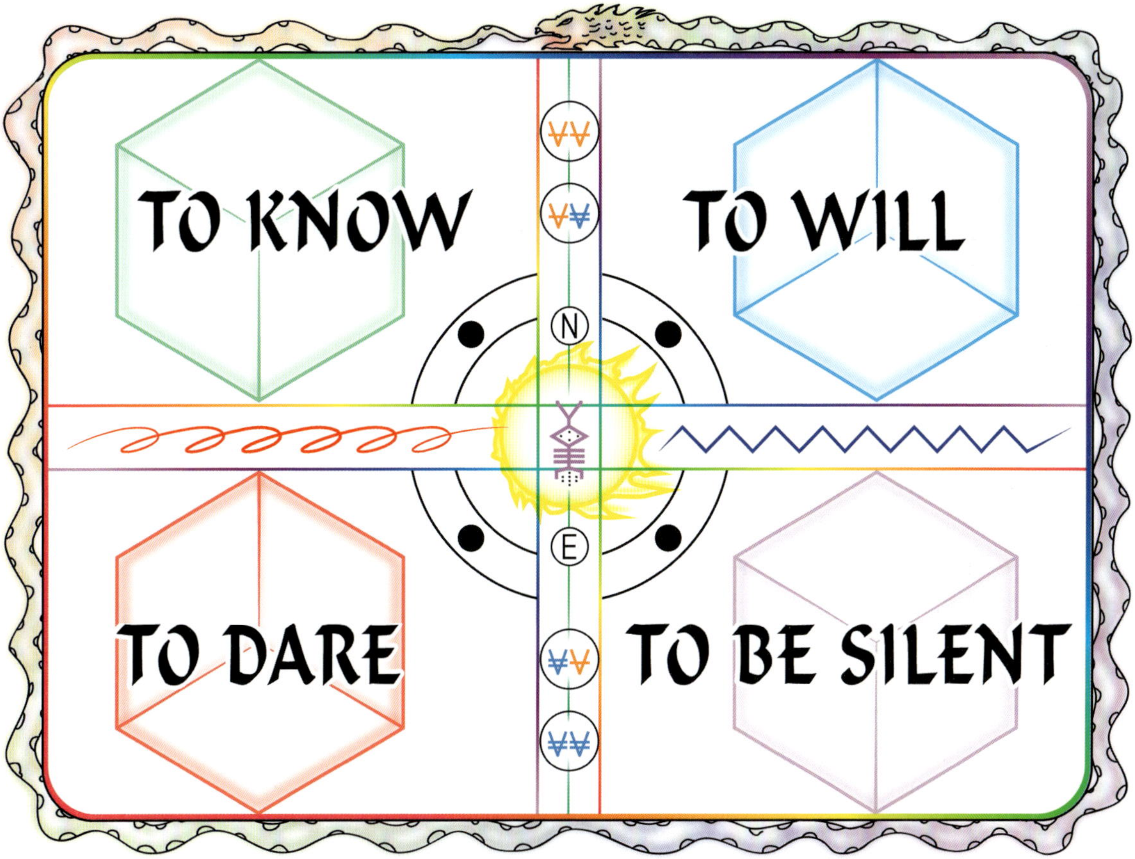
TO KNOW
TO WILL
N
E
TO DARE
TO BE SILENT

Part I
Defining the Path

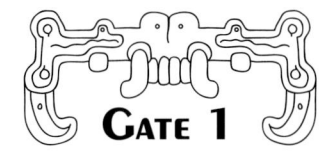

Gate 1
Entering the Labyrinth

A mutation is occurring as you read these words—a mutation that is a function of the entire transformation of cosmic reality.

This planet is currently undergoing chaotic ferment. The Earth is heating up. Social chaos is increasing. People are losing their identities or holding onto old ones. It is as though the entire planet is being held captive in a deep, empty prison, under a strange enchantment, chained to an illusion that renders it seemingly helpless in the face of the destruction of the entire Earth. As the layers of darkness close in, it seems there is no apparent escape. What once worked, no longer works. People seek solace in technology, traditional religion or entertainment and sports—only to be left cold and unsatisfied. What is going on?

We, as a species, are undergoing an unprecedented process of initiation.

Initiation is the act of making conscious the passage from one state or condition of being to another. Initiation brings about a change of focus of your mental vision so that a higher harmony may manifest. It is not just your initiation, but a planetary initiation. This has happened before. What do you remember? What is your part?

The *Book of the Initiation* emphasizes a planetary initiation that begins with you. The initiatic process is a journey into the labyrinth of the evolving cosmic self that catalyzes the soul from sensory input to telepathic output. New knowledge comes through the ritual of initiation. In this planetary initiation, the human is emerging from the various cocoons of tribalism, nationalism, history and all the factions that separate. All conditioned cocoons are bursting and we find ourselves, as a species, in a field of incredible chaotic ferment.

Those who are sensitive are feeling the shifts, both in the external world and within their own mind and body. Many might wonder: Is something big going to happen? Are we going to mutate? Is the world going to end? Are we going to become something else? Are the space brothers going to come? Are we going to receive telepathic signals from other galaxies? Are we going to know something different? Are we transforming even as we ask these questions?

If you want to find answers, then you have to go on a journey. You must take this journey if you want to discover what is behind the veil of the perpetual social fiction. Only you can find out for yourself.

If you have picked up this book then you have already lifted your vibration to a certain frequency. Perhaps you seek to lift your vibration up an octave more. Perhaps you wish to glean more meaning from your everyday existence in relation to the Universal Plan. Whatever the case, you, the reader, this is your journey. This is your labyrinth.

Many people start this journey full of enthusiasm, only to stop or turn back when the path gets thorny. Others persevere and know they have to keep going. If you got this far, then you realize you are being guided by an invisible force that is drawing you on. This force is felt as a vibration or magnetism that is pulling you deeper into the labyrinth—to the place where the usual social conventions and customs are less and less valid. Here, in the deepest recesses of our being, we communicate with the Universal Power and then manifest this power for the highest good of humanity and Planet Earth.

As you enter this labyrinth you may encounter multilayered conditionings that you must confront and peel away. There is only one path with many facets, just as there is only one universe and one truth that unfolds in kaleidoscopic turns. Everybody follows a path according to his/her state of evolution and consciousness.

The path, though unitive, appears different to each person. Despite differences in appearances all levels of consciousness ultimately converge; we are all headed for the same center point. Each being has a unique role to play in this grand journey into wholeness.

Cosmic History appears at this time to assist in a major initiation taking us from one aeon to another; from one state of evolution to another. You cannot know the truth if you follow your lower conditioned instincts. You must subjugate the lower to know something higher and transcend your being. This is the grand theme of the *Book of the Initiation* and entry into the first gate. Keep in mind three points as you make your way through the labyrinth:

1. **Love, love above everything!**
2. **You only advance according to your own effort.**
3. **In order to evolve, you must learn something new.**

We cannot know unless someone has gone before illuminating the doors on which to knock. But it is you who have to enter. This is not a Google search, but is rather a type of journey or path exemplified by the avatar as the archetype bearing knowledge and light for those seekers who have come to this Earth.

As you approach the entrance of the labyrinth, the first gate swings open and four doors appear; each door has written on it a different question. The first question is:

Who are you?

It might be good to pause before you answer this.

Let us consider a few possible answers: We could say that you are an *ambulatory sensorium*. But what is that? *Ambulatory* is something that walks and a *sensorium* is the capacity for a sensory apparatus to process, conceive and construct its world through its sense organs. All information regarding the physical world is brought to you through your senses. Have you ever considered this definition of yourself?

Who are you? Are you an economic animal, as many corporations, governments and institutions might make you think? In this definition, the purpose of life revolves around money, markets, commodities, and buying and selling. From this economic/Darwinian perspective, the human is the highest form of animal that has evolved. This definition is reinforced by the mass media that tells us our purpose is to buy, sell, trade, consume and produce goods to increase our wealth and satisfy material sensory creature comforts. Is this who you are?

Have you ever thought of yourself as a *biogeochemical processing system?* In this definition, we see the human lives within a particular environment governed by certain laws that control the circulation of various elements or energies, atmospheres, minerals, sunlight, radiation, etc. In this description, the function of the human is to metabolize and process complex chemicals and photons, or different kinds of information and energy contributing to a whole order of the biosphere. Is this who you are? Or are you merely an ego clad in a bag of bones?

This may not be a flattering description, but most people operate, to one degree or another, by a fundamental premise of this particular stage of evolution. They think, "What's in it for me?" or "If I don't get something out of this, then why should I do it?"

Many people feel it is common sense to think this way, and *it is* common sense from a materialist point of view. The ego is always thinking about getting its piece of the pie. This type of thinking produces a being that clamors for attention and tries to get noticed. This can be witnessed particularly in the cybersphere, where the body sits in front of a computer—blogging or surfing the Internet—while the mind becomes absorbed in virtual reality. In this instance, is the body not just a bag of bones?

Who is talking? Who is thinking? Who is running the mechanism? Is it merely a set of conditioned reflexes?—a robotic automaton with fixed responses? Are you more than your digestive track? Are you more than what happens in your larynx when you talk? Who are you anyway?

Once again, you have been brought to this text. Who is reading? Who is considering what is being read? Who is thinking there might be something else? Do you feel the intangible part of yourself as you read these words? Do you feel the subtle levels of your soul?

The Cosmic History Chronicles • Volume IV

When you reach this level of self-reflective questioning, then you have already entered the labyrinth and there is no turning back. The labyrinth is comprised of the questions that you ask about yourself, about your society, about your environment, about your Planet and about your universe. Are the answers you receive mirror projections of something you are putting out, or do your answers have deeper meaning that penetrates your conditioned responses? Asking "Who am I?" is the first stage of entering the labyrinth. Each question answered takes you down another corridor, and opens another door.

Proceeding to the second door, there is a question that reads:

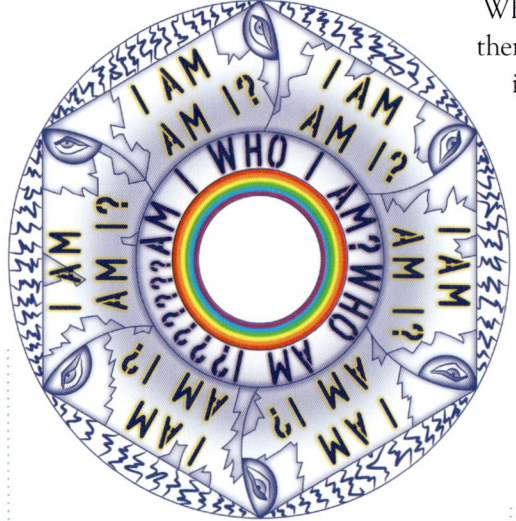

The tape loops of belief and self-perpetuating feedback are being shattered. Cosmic History is the mirror. Look inside and you will see your own mind reflected back.

How did you get here?

How did you get to this Planet at this time? And what are you doing here? These questions open the second door of the first gate of the labyrinth. From a materialist point of view, you got here through your parents. In this regard, you are the result of genetic coding that was transferred through conception when your mother and father came together one night. How did that happen?

How did it happen that your parents at that precise moment produced what you now know as *you*? How did it happen that the physical/biological being, known as *you*, came into existence at that moment when Mom and Dad were making love? How did it happen that you crystallized at that moment and became an embryo in a placenta for nine months (260+ days) and grew and grew in a deep, cosmic dark unconscious womb filled with amniotic fluids? How did it happen that you arrived through the body of your mother, blinded by the light, kicking and screaming?

Of course, we could say that your existence is biologically based and is merely the result of a genetic coding transfer from your parents—but what about the cells in your body—where did they come from? Were they created just for you? What is their origin? Are your cells the result of some kind of magical multiplication process coded into the sperm and ovum of your parents? How did it happen that you suddenly appeared complete with zillions of cells, a neurocerebral system, senses, muscles and a skeleton? Where did your voice come from? When you talk, who is the "me" that speaks? Look at your hands who constructed all of this? How could it be that everybody on the planet has a different set of fingerprints? What does it all mean?

Also consider that at the moment of your birth you did not know who you were or where you were. Perhaps you were born in a hospital in Sydney, Australia, but at the moment of your birth, you had no idea where you were, nor did you care. Being called an "Aussie" meant nothing to you. Shortly after you were born, a nurse might have put ink on your feet, stamped them onto paper and gave you a number and an identity. And your parents gave you a name. But that meant nothing to you at that moment. You had no identity. You might have had some deep subconscious self-perception of having been ejected from the warm, nurturing womb into a noisy place with blinding lights. You may have felt something when you were passed around to family, doctors, nurses, or midwives, some with warm feelings and some without. But you had no idea that you were an Australian boy or a Chinese, Arab or Zambian girl. You were just a pure, cosmic cipher that had come into this world.

Immediately after your birth, you began to receive imprints of the socialization process. You heard voices around you, but at first you did not know what language it was. Soon, you learned to construct and mimic human sounds that you heard to get what you needed—this furthered your socialization and conditioning process. You realized there was someone you were supposed to call "Mama" and someone you were supposed to call "Papa", and maybe someone you called "brother" or "sister". You felt the center of a nucleus of an ensemble of other beings that you somehow resembled in general ways.

The you that was you when you were born was slowly covered over by language, family customs, and styles of being and doing. Sometimes the big humans seemed happy with you, sometimes mad with you. Sometimes you did something that you were happy with, but the big ones didn't like it so they pointed a finger at you and scolded you. Or maybe you did something they liked so they smiled at you and clapped and said you did it right. These are all factors of conditioning.

Where did you lose the sense of pure innocence, the star memory you had when you were born? Who are you anyway? And how did you get here? Where did you come from?

As you grew, you may have asked these questions less and less, particularly after you entered something called "school". In this school, you were surrounded by other people born around the same time as you, with a central figure called "teacher" who taught you to read, write, do mathematics, and about the nature

Where did you lose the sense of pure innocence, the star memory you had when you were born? Who are you? How did you get here? Where did you come from?

of the world in general. You were taught that the world was round and about the history of your country and of the world, according to the country you were born in. What is taught about history in Russia is not the same history taught in Venezuela or in Iran. The point is to see how the layering of conditioned consciousness occurs.

Growing up, you probably had moments when you sensed something greater was occurring. Perhaps you went on a camping trip with your friends and looked at the stars and had a dim memory of your cosmic origins. Perhaps at that moment all of your conditioned tape loops were erased and you felt your pure essence. Or maybe some kind of shock occurred in your life that jolted you out of your conditioned reality back to the space you were in at birth. Or maybe you experienced your true essence through art, a book, a piece of music, or through some mind-altering substance that gave you glimpses of the beyond and made you wonder about the true meaning of life.

A MUTATION IS OCCURING AS YOU READ THESE WORDS, A MUTATION THAT IS A FUNCTION OF THE ENTIRE TRANSFORMATION OF COSMIC REALITY

Is there something else going on that we don't know about? Is there some other connection to a greater reality that no one is telling us about? Is there some other meaning to life? Who are you and where did you come from?

Is it possible that your cells go back millions and billions of years? Are the molecules that comprise you made from different minerals, nutrients and liquids you ingested? Are you part of the earth? Are you part of the sky? Are you part of something greater than the social fabric that has absorbed you as you were growing up?

It is only the seeker of knowledge who probes these questions further into the labyrinth. It is only those who truly wish to see behind the façade who are allowed access to the deeper cosmic truths. You must be one of these, for you have come this far.

Advancing to the third door, you see the question:

WHAT IS YOUR COSMIC ORIGIN?

Your cosmic origin is the third point to consider when navigating the labyrinth. It is clear that we live in a vast universe. Pictures from the Hubble telescope show us images of far out galaxies. What we call our solar system and planet is located in a far out arm of the galaxy known as the Milky Way. There are billions of configurations of solar systems just like this one scattered throughout the universe. We are not alone. We have all been here before. These thoughts occur to many of us.

We are taught certain ways of thinking, being and doing so we can perform "useful" functions in a larger, economically-based, social fabric. To get beyond this, we must exert a further sense of logic and intellect. Most people realize they have surplus logic and intellect—more than what is required of them at their daily "job". It is the seeker who takes it upon him/herself to apply this surplus energy to evolve.

Sometimes you find yourself in the middle of day-to-day tasks and you remember something—it is this point of remembering that is to be opened, explored and cultivated There is something that is meant to be remembered; other worlds, planets and lifetimes where life existed before, where, perhaps, you existed before. When we hear stories about places such as Atlantis, we must ask: Are those just stories that Plato and other writers made up, or did these places exist? Where do these stories of other worlds come from?

Most stories about previous worlds describe a type of deluge or a cataclysm. Did the human beings misuse its technology and destroy the world(s)? We also know that many classic rock and roll songs contain references to other worlds and planets (see *CHC, Vol. III*). Déjà vu: We have all been here before. If you want to remember your forgotten origins, you have to exert on your own. This brings us to the fourth door with its question:

> **STAR CHILD**
> There is a pure moment of awareness that is always available that connects you to the moment you were born—when you were not a particular nationality or identity, but a pure star child. Can you go beyond your surface identity and contact this star child now?

WHERE ARE YOU NOW?

In the process of questioning your origins, it is important to get a clear understanding of where you are now. Think about the social landscape that you find yourself in. Think of the larger social context of the world as it is today. What kind of species are we? We know more about ourselves biophysically than we have ever known before. One hundred years ago people hardly knew that galaxies existed, and only about 50 years ago was DNA discovered. Now, we know we are products of this DNA and that we live in a universe with numerous galaxies. This information creates the background tone of our mental landscape.

As a planetary human we have become a chaotic unity. We are a unity because we know, at least scientifically, that we are on one planet that we all operate with the same life code and DNA. If this is so, then why are we chaotic? On the one hand, the systems of technology and information have already dissolved the historical religious ideological barriers; we are in one big cyber-ocean that equalizes us, and yet most of us are jam-packed full of unexamined ideological, tribal or religious reflexes. What is this about?

We are continuously confronting self-contradictions, as well as contradictory information from the outer world. Most of us are loaded with contradictory information on every subject:

physical science, biology, astrophysics, geology, solar science, and the cybersphere. With the cybersphere, people can, and are, communicating about everything to everyone, everywhere all the time (see *CHC, Vol. III*). We are swimming in this cyberspheric ocean.

As this information from the cybersphere enters us, it creates conflicts and contradictions. At the same time, at a fundamental level we feel the barriers and boundaries dissolving, yet we are confronted with all those conditioned reflexes such as: I belong to this nation, I belong to this religion, I belong to this particular ideological stream, or I don't belong to any of them and I reject them all, or whatever the case may be. The point is there is a wide gamut of reactions that create a chaotic unity. We are unified on this planet with a sense of awareness that the planet is in crisis with war and global climate change. These factors may or may not affect human sensibility depending on the level of consciousness.

Once we have realized our planetary situation, then how do we start to lift above it? Or will we choose to stay plugged into our computers and job because we believe it is too difficult to change?

Viewed from space, the Earth has no boundaries. All the fighting is based on fictitious, outworn belief systems. So how do we get out of this mental superstructure of different nation states created by the mass media that keeps feeding to us who we are and what kind of nationalism or patriotism we should have? It is all a contradiction. How can it be that there are 180 different patriotisms, each asking for allegiance to itself?

At the same time that these seeming divisions occur, there are unifications such as art and music. Art crosses all borders (see *CHC, Vol. III*).

We are continuously confronting self-contradictions, ... Most of us are loaded with contradictory information on every subject ...

Planetary Initiation

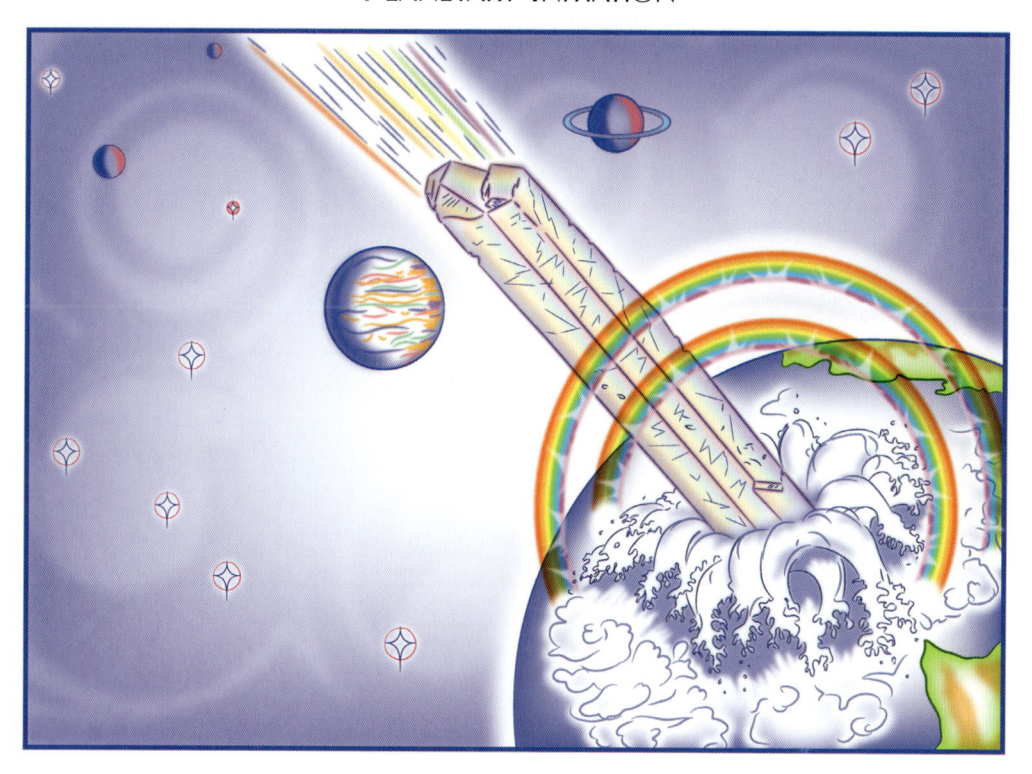

We are in an initiation that is planetary in nature, and that ascends through different stages. When you were born you were initiated from an embryonic being in a placenta to an oxygen breathing entity. This was your first initiation into the world.

Then came your next initiation: entering school. Graduation from school is another initiation, as is losing your virginity. An initiation occurs at any point in your life when you pass from one state of being to another, or from one state of consciousness to another.

If you stop and examine your life, you will see you are always going through different stages. The entire planet is now undergoing a supreme initiation. The point of initiation is that you make conscious the path that you are journeying upon. This is why the *Cosmic History Chronicles* are presented—they make conscious the passage of the closing of one cycle and the opening and the regeneration of another cycle. The *Cosmic History Chronicles* exist as memory templates in the form of seven books so that we may become conscious of the planetary transition from one state to another. Through use of the seven volumes, we may learn how to adapt to this, what to expect, how to move forward, how to view what has gone before, and what new methods of operations and stages of consciousness that we might look forward to.

This planetary rite of passage takes us on a labyrinthian journey into the template of inner wholeness. On our passage through the labyrinth, we might go down one way and find a dead end, and we may go another way and find another dead end. We might find another passageway that leads us to another level, or we might find a passageway that takes us backwards or spins us in circles. In this passage, if you don't know who you are, you might at times feel lost and confused in the act of getting to where we are all going.

The different passageways, dead ends and strange circuits in the labyrinth are a function of the confusions that arise when we mistake a conditioned aspect of our being for our true self. The labyrinth journey is the process of uncovering or unwinding to your true self. If we are not all these conditioned factors, then there must be something else that we are—we must get to the bottom of this—to the treasure within the center. The first step is to know your own mind.

As we gain more understanding into the workings of our mind, then we might not encounter so many dead ends or diversions. The more we confront different levels of our false self, the closer we are to seeing and owning the true self. This process takes us to many different levels and stages. We are not saying that there is not some purpose to your present incarnation as you look for your true self, there is. You catch glimpses of this as you make your way through the labyrinth.

The point of the template of the Cosmic History labyrinth is to get you to the place where your present self and your true self merge so that you can fulfill your evolutionary function. The fact that you are a seeker means you know there is a deeper meaning to life that is beyond conditioned appearance. You know there is a purpose. There are many beings who have come before you; but who or what is going to come after you? You can see that before you there existed different stages of evolution of thought, culture, and art.

You are here, and the more conscious you become, the more you realize you are on the leading edge of a mutative evolutionary wave that is rushing you through this labyrinth to the point of light at the center where your true self resides. Then comes a new stage of being. But first you must get with the wave. To get with the wave, you have to be willing to move through different levels and layers of being and consciousness until finally you arrive at your true self. This is the creative point where the future is being woven or created and brought to light. It is your destiny to take a creative role in this process.

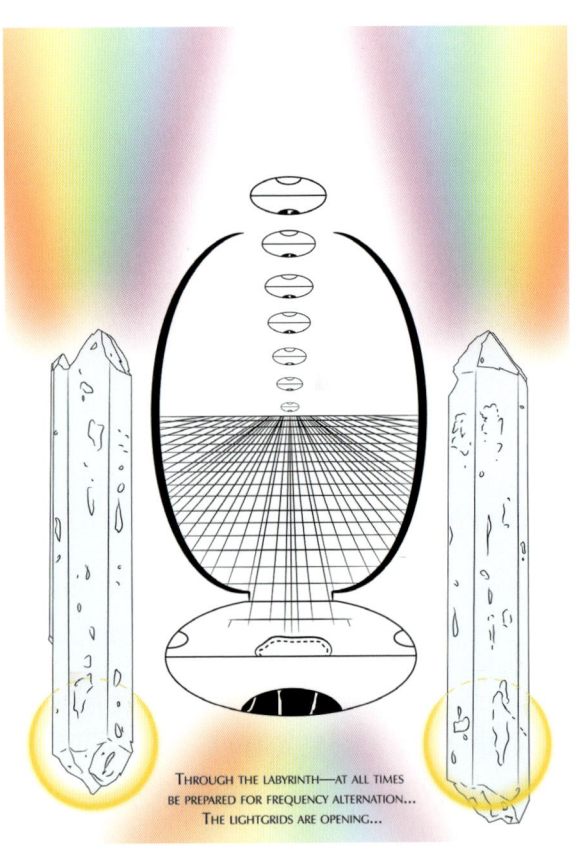

THROUGH THE LABYRINTH—AT ALL TIMES BE PREPARED FOR FREQUENCY ALTERNATION... THE LIGHTGRIDS ARE OPENING...

Gate 2

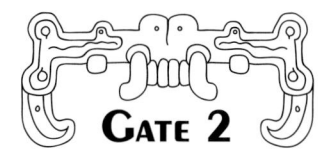

Cosmic History—Mind Gate to a New Reality

Up ahead you see a most peculiar gate. As you reach to open the gate, it dissolves, and a large shimmering door appears in its place. A signpost above the door flashes in iridescent violet. It reads: "Cosmic History—Mind Gate to a New Reality". Intrigued, you knock on the door. Suddenly you hear a loud, booming voice: "Suspend the delusion that fascinates your senses!" With those words, your mind becomes blank and open—vast vistas appear sprinkled with multi-colored trees—the land sparkles pristine. You decide to explore.

If you have come this far through the gate of Cosmic History, then you have probably felt a shift in your reality that is gaining momentum, spurring you from one condition to another. This is the process of initiation made conscious.

When new knowledge enters the sphere of human consciousness, only a few people at first are able to perceive what it is. Then those few transmit it, and in time, it begins to activate and accelerate a new process. To learn something new, we must suspend our conditioned thoughts in order to create a receptive space in the mind. It is through these receptive spaces that new cosmic fragrances seep in.

Knowledge is not visible, but is rather the knowing of the internal nature of objects. In this way, we could say that all true knowledge is occult or hidden. What we perceive with our senses and call "reality", is an existence that has no fixed nature. It lives in constant motion, appearing and disappearing. In order to attain true knowledge, we must penetrate the surface to see what lies behind it. This is the work of hermetic practitioners or initiates.

Hermetic practitioners form an invisible network. All knowledge comes from God, the Supreme Creative Force and the Master of Infinite Intelligence. New knowledge is called forth by the collective mind in the time that has been revealed. The reality that we find ourselves in is not the same reality as the people who lived even three centuries ago. We are living in an entirely different medium of time and dimension of consciousness that is rapidly shifting.

As a species, we are undergoing a crisis in the collective unconscious—the crisis of the lack of meaning. This crisis has reached its peak and we are now witnessing an acceleration of events coupled with a loss of orientation on a collective level. Most people are estranged and live in exile far away from their true essence. Their cosmic life is absent from their day-to-day existence.

This species-wide disorientation requires a greater vision and answer than previously known. Cosmic History manifests as the response. Cosmic History first seeps in by using familiar terms and speaking within a historical context. Cosmic History activates the imaginal realm and uncovers

The Cosmic History Chronicles • Volume IV

INITIATION INTO THE LABYRINTH OF COSMIC HISTORY

Template of Wholeness

hidden worlds, revealing the ways in which they correspond to the present and coming worlds.

We are in a new territory and landscape. We are now at a point of phenomenal, qualitative shift. It is the qualitative change that is responsible for increasing secularism—moving away from transcendent thought. But we are also in a new time dimension, a kind of bardo or between-the-worlds consciousness. We are approaching the coming age of universal unification. This is not the same as religion.

The pace of change in the last 260 years has been so profound that it is virtually impossible to gauge what is going on. This is where Cosmic History enters and holds up a large mirror to reflect the process of transitioning from human history to Cosmic (post) History.

Cosmic History as Hermetic Stream

At its root, Cosmic History is hermetic lore. Through hermetic lore, the mind stream is kept alive during the cycle of human history. *Hermetic* is a word with several meanings, most commonly "airtight, hidden or shut away". Its occult origins derive from a series of alchemical writings attributed to Hermes Trismegistus, the Egyptian/Greek culture hero and wisdom bearer, often identified with the Egyptian God, Thoth.

Hermes lived some time before Moses and is known as the first being to communicate celestial and divine knowledge through writing. He received the name Trismegistus, or *Mercurius ter Maximus* (thrice greatest intelligencer), as he attained perfect knowledge of all things contained in the world. Hermes is famous for the adages, "as above so below", and "True, true, certain without doubt". These maxims of conduct and investigation are the essence of the entire hermetic tradition as it has unfolded from Ancient Egypt to the present.

A principle objective of hermetic tradition is the attainment of the philosopher's stone. This is a highly ambiguous image that is open to many interpretations. Hermetic philosophy calls the philosophers stone, *Azoth,* the soul of the world, the celestial virgin, the magnum opus. The underlying motif of the

... we are also in a new time dimension, a kind of bardo or between-the-worlds consciousness.

philosopher's stone is realizing the quintessence of things. Quintessence literally means the fifth element or the *fifth force*.

Many of these hermetic traditions dissipated during the modern industrial age. However, seers such as Madame Blavatsky reactivated and kept the hermetic stream alive. Through *The Secret Doctrine*, Blavatsky actually brought this tradition to a new frequency. She was writing from the urgency of a crisis that had been brewing in the collective unconscious of the entire human race for millennia. Up until around 300 years ago, the human race had been operating through the cosmic unconscious, where everything could be represented through symbolic structures; but now with the advent of technology, the sacred symbols and structures have lost their meaning.

Let us now look at four fundamental factors, based on *The Secret Doctrine*, that underlie Cosmic History, or the secret history of the universe.

1. **Principle of the Unity of all Existence.** All of existence forms an absolute unity. The mind of historical consciousness is like a ship that hit a rock and broke into many fragments that equally resist the idea of unity. In the historical social structure, the idea of being in a collective mind is a totalitarian fascist concept. In actuality, to expand into the experience of unity is to increase your freedom. The individual cell confined to protecting itself, makes its own prison or self-defeating beliefs. There are many levels beyond this, infinite levels of hierarchical order, creating ever more conscious and integrated fields of unity. The unity of all existence will continue to assert itself mightily as we enter the phase of evolutionary consciousness, referred to as *noosphere*. In this phase, we will realize that unity is the inescapable destiny of the one Being in its syntropic multifaceted unfolding.

2. **There is No Such Thing as Dead Matter.** Everything is animated either by force of electrical energy, which at a certain stage goes from inorganic to organic, or by the spiritualized matter that constitutes "organic life". The electrical impulse within matter maintains itself at a stable rate, or, by process of chemical transformations becomes self-generating.

   All matter participates in a great vital force of electrified universal life-breath. Everything is part of a vast, living complex network of self-generating processes by which the universe keeps itself in a continuous self-program of change. Everything is alive. The basis of the living reality is electricity. Everything has an electrical charge, even inert rock. It is the electrical charge of the brain cell that allows it to be in communication with all that is—be it mineral, vegetable, animal or angel!

3. **The Human Being is a Microcosm.** Everything in the universe can be experienced through the mind and its ability to extend consciousness radially in all directions. All universal laws and principles are inherent in the entire psychophysical structure. This includes the mental, non-manifest state of mind and consciousness that we are capable of as well as of the entire physical

plane of our existential third-dimensional experience. We participate in the gravitational field that coheres our molecules into a particular form and structure in physical plane reality. Yoga is the self-realization of the microcosm as macrocosm that makes us multidimensionally coherent.

We participate in an electrical field that creates the whole aura of radiance depending on the degree of physical well-being that we are able to maintain. We enter into the biophysical mental field that extends to the very limits of the cosmos. Everything can be known to us and within us. We are at a stage where we are approaching mass awakening. Then we will see through all the veils that have kept us in the dark at this concluding historical stage where we are undergoing a final exam, taking us to the next level: conscious micro-cosmic totality.

4. **As Above so Below, as Within, so Without.** The universe is in a state of holonomic self-resonance from the highest, most complex, to the lowest and the least complex. There is a principle or law of unity that binds everything together: the whole is reflected in the part, and the part is reflected in the whole. Everything contains a reciprocal unity and self-resonance. There are gradations of consciousness and dimensions that extend within us below into mini-cosmoses and extend above into macro cosmoses. There are unifying principles and ordinances of law that govern the whole system. Everything is run by a large plan that operates through all systems. Just as the human is a microcosm, so eternity can be read in a grain of sand. The resonance of higher orders within lower orders contains forces and energies that can assist us in everything from the transformation of matter to time travel.

ENTER THE MIND GATE OF COSMIC HISTORY

The activation of Cosmic History is the activation of the continuum of the hermetic stream.

Hermetic lore employs different methods and systems of coded languages and architecture that can be penetrated with a flexible fourth-dimensional mind.

Planetary Rite of Passage

Cosmic History connects us with the central hermetic channel through which all the prana of the universe flows. The field of intelligence of the galactic brain is vast. The galactic superstructure of Cosmic History is the core in the field of galactic intelligence. The human race entered the cosmic unconscious at the beginning of history when a separation occurred between the third-dimensional operating self and the deeper self or fourth-dimensional essence being. The successful conclusion of this transformation is to raise the overall planetary field to a higher, more harmonic frequency.

Cosmic History is not just a philosophy—but also a means and method for actualizing and expressing the cosmic being. It does not take sides, but is the core nature of cosmic reality and its gradations into different evolutive stages of consciousness. In itself, Cosmic History is the stage of cosmic consciousness that metamorphosizes the "fallen" historical man into the living paradigm of cosmic unity. In this way, Cosmic History is the script of the planetary rite of passage.

In this planetary rite of passage, the humans are in a process of psychic and cellular ferment, whether they are aware of it or not. It is like a man walking into a room and not realizing the floor is covered with ball bearings; he begins to slip but does not realize he is falling. This is the condition of the human race at this moment.

The Extraterrestrial Origin of Cosmic History

Cosmic History is a new knowledge system for this planet derived from extraterrestrial origin. Its nontraditional, extraterrestrial thought base revolves around a certain set of immutable principles, as well as certain mathematical orders. The Earth itself is extraterrestrial, from the point of view of other planets or star systems. Everything on this planet has evolved as far as it can go—it has reached its limit—it can go no farther. Therefore, it needs an assist or boost. Cosmic History is part of an extraterrestrial salvation plan.

LOSE YOUR MIND TO FIND IT

Any time you enter a quest for truth, you have to give up your mind in order to find it—your conditioned mind, that is. Jesus says he who would save his own soul must first lose it. This means you have to surrender your conditioned historical self or concepts about life and the universe if you are to reach your essence. Your destiny is to become a transformationalist channel for super conscious reality.

You have had intimations and intuitions and peripheral visions of greater realities, but now is the time to access these dimensions in order to benefit all beings. But first you must work to shed all parts of yourself that do not serve the highest good.

These aspirations to express greater realities lead to the gate called Cosmic History. To manifest these aspirations, you must learn to create peace in yourself by attuning to your central essence. This generally requires following a definite system of mind training that includes the practice of certain exercises frequently in order to acquire concentration. Methods for this can be found in all seven volumes of the *Cosmic History Chronicles*.

Perhaps you have (or are) following some type of traditional spiritual path. If you have really applied yourself to another path, then you might never read these words, but rather remain in the chamber of the Christian Gnostic or in the chamber of the Sufi or in the chamber of the Buddhist, etc.

Cosmic History is a vast mirror that reflects the systems that create the context of conditioned historical traditions and social customs. Traditional religious systems are functions of different aspects of the Salvation Plan that descended during the historical cycle. These systems appeared as reminders to the historical man that had fallen so far away from the unitive source. Without the essence of these religious systems, the historical cycle might be even more overflowing with barbarism and degradation. For this reason, we should be grateful to all the saints, sages, prophets, sadhus, monks and all those beings who have held the light high in the world of shadows.

There are few individuals who have reached enlightenment—the first stage of cosmic consciousness—through tradi-

All of our physical and environmental apparatus is going through a rapid transformation—in the blink of an eye.

The Cosmic History Chronicles • Volume IV

tional esoteric methods. Enlightenment is simply the stage where the ego no longer controls our perceptions of reality, allowing for the Greater Reality to flood our being, unhindered. This is the stage where we consciously realize ourselves as part of the divine circuitry of the cosmos.

It is not easy to sustain cosmic consciousness within the horizon of historical man and the collective unconscious. The spiritual force or vigor of the truth that Muhammad or Christ brought to the world is dissipated and concretized into dogma and belief systems which do everything but allow the light in.

The age of religion, as we have known it, is over. The age of the religious impulse, being an ideological factor that shapes history, is over. Today, there is a kind of fundamentalist revival—but this is not the same as the age of religion. Today, religion is featured in the news as an active fundamentalist force resisting historical materialism and globalization. However, identified with only one side of the coin, it is fighting against itself.

WE ARE THE WISE ONES WE KNOW WHO YOU ARE

YOU CHOOSE YOUR DESTINY WE GUIDE YOU TO YOUR STAR

SHIFTING REALITIES

We are on the verge of an unprecedented shift in the true capacity of the thinking layer on Earth. All of our physical and environmental apparatus is going through a rapid transformation—in the blink of an eye. It is this mutational shift that renders traditional religion inoperative. Soon, everyone will know something has shifted. There will be no doubt in anyone's mind that something bigger is going on. What is it?

Perhaps it is a giant mind avalanche from the Galactic Federation rushing across the cosmic unconscious, clearing away dysfunctional conditionings that keep the mind embedded in its own self-created tape loops of belief and self-perpetuating feedback. All of this is in the process of being dissolved. Look inside and you will see your own mind reflected back.

The opportunity has now arrived to lift to a greater level. If you have knocked at the Cosmic History door, then you have a sense of this. Kundalini yoga master Yogi Bhajan said that the Aquarian age was going to begin on 11-11-2012. Everyone at some level knows something is going to happen.

Whatever the date, 2012 is the gate, 2013 is the other side, when the formulation of cosmic history is the new landscape of the mind.

We have to hold our ground until we get to this place where everything comes into greater view—the accelerated molecular structure is coming in, affecting all of our brain cells. Our traditional thoughts fall apart and suddenly we experience new feelings. It might feel that there is something beyond mind and consciousness that is ripping the veil apart. This is the mutational shift, the qualitative shift that is taking place. Cosmic History is the means of shedding light on what is already happening.

We are here to unzip the conventional mind and let the genie out of the bottle. We know that traditional approaches to reality no longer work. Any true path is defined by some type of aspiration or goal. Where are we going now? What is the goal? We have to consider that there is something beyond mind and consciousness that informs us with a new frame or context. The new frame of consciousness with its planetary description of noosphere invalidates the old parochial views.

Noosphere is a stage of consciousness that we have not experienced as a totality—but we are about to. Some people or individuals have reached cosmic consciousness. But not all the individuals who have reached cosmic consciousness have been able to reach the others who have also reached cosmic consciousness. Unified planetary consciousness occurs when the different molecules of intelligence reach a stage where they can all communicate with each other.

The telepathic order of aboriginal society is closer to this type of consciousness than even the enlightened individuals of history have achieved. Prior to the advent of Western civilization, the consciousness of aboriginal society was collective and tribal; it did not expand and deviate from the natural order. This natural state of mind must be expanded and raised to a planetary level. To grasp this is difficult for some. This is largely due to the effects of technology and mechanisms of modern science, particularly the astrophysical mechanisms, and the ways in which they have impacted us culturally and shaped our consciousness.

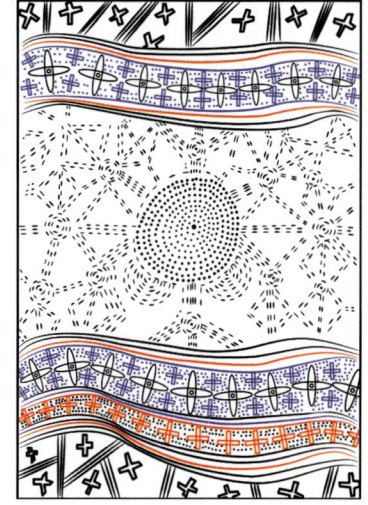

Our consciousness extends anytime we see a farther view of outer space. Our cellular motion accelerates with each new technological invention. We have been changing from within, impacted by these technologies and images brought to us by science. The farther out we have gone looking for the big bang and the edge of the universe, the further removed we become from the inner journey, the more we are being prepared for our cosmic self-revelation.

No matter how striking the images we receive from outer space or micro space seem to be, these images are still conditioned by limited awareness and inability to grasp deeper cosmic levels. We are projecting these images because this is what we want to see. The point is these images and technologies are already reshaping us—breaking us down and dissolving our borders, both within our minds and external to our sense field could we but grasp it—we are being brought ever closer to the new freedom.

Imagine a world where everyone on the planet could consciously contact whomever they choose via telepathy. Imagine a world where you could send out a telepathic broadcast to everyone on Earth and everyone would get it at the same time. To reach this level of consciousness, we cannot be consigned to "working for a living", in the traditional sense. This is an outmoded way of being that keeps human consciousness enslaved to a mere sliver of the potential of cosmic reality.

We have to burst out of this box altogether as one. Life is not about working a job that you don't enjoy just to be a glorified wage slave. We already know this does not work, but neither did any revolutions. We are on the verge of leaving this phase of reality altogether. We are at the final accelerated stage—the glowing incandescent tip of a mutational shift. We must reeducate ourselves according to a higher light, and purify our minds and bodies so we can pop through the veil into the cosmic order of reality.

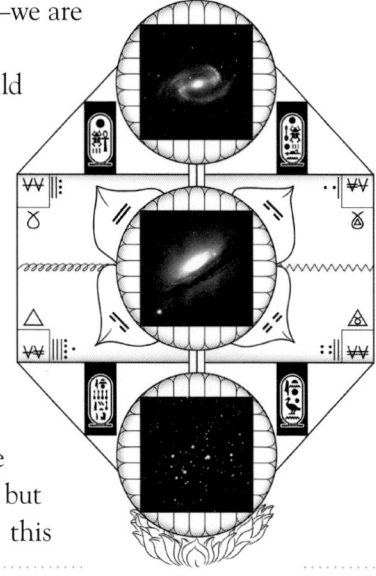

> Cosmic History provides the great reevaluation and reordering of all human systems of thought as manifestations of universal time and synchronic order.

Convergent Evolution

Just beneath the surface in the collective planetary consciousness there is an innate knowing that we are all one. This can be recognized on the surface level by realizing ourselves as part of one cyberspheric entity covering the planet. We now know that artificial borders are meaningless if we can "Google" someone anywhere in the world at any time. We all know borders are fake. We have to wake up and realize our minds have already dissolved these borders by the cyberspheric medium that unifies all minds all the time, everywhere.

We are at a place where the mutation is just about complete for the new evolutionary beings to appear. We want to elevate the vibration of our bodily cells up to the vibrational purity of our essence nature. When we have sufficient minds that have attained this vibrational purity then we will see real magic. After individuation is exhausted and we are tired of our egos, then we can return to source and ready ourselves to rejoin the Oversoul and the noosphere. Then, together we will advance to the next stage. This is always a process, but it is a process we must all must undergo alone—as the individual soul dissolves into the ocean of universal awareness.

Our job is to see to it that our bodily cells are vibrating at the frequency of our primary intention to take this journey in the first place. Everyone who is alive at this time on this sphere of reality is being

Part I • Defining the Path

tested—it is an across-the-cosmos process. For us, it means we have all come to this planet at this time and 2012 is graduation. Many of us may realize that this is our last incarnation in this particular process.

The meaning of being alive today is that the present incarnation has the opportunity to come to unity with the essence self—the self that caused you to begin this journey countless incarnations ago. We are now positioned to synch up with one another to raise the collective vibration that brings new life. The refashioned galactic prototypes, "Adam" and "Eve", can finally penetrate through the veil in their full splendor!

Cosmic History is the core of this streaming galactic reality radiating the new consciousness. The texts that you pick up that say "Cosmic History" are the manifestations of an evolutionary salvation/resurrection plan. The information in the text is to facilitate the process of the transmutation of your own psychophysical apparatus—the cleaning of your mind and body, and the change in vibration of your thoughts and cells so that you become a medium of transformation attuned to the super conscious mental level of a higher reality that is starting to pierce and break through the dense clouds of the final stage of historical materialism!

This is why you entered the labyrinth of initiation, so that you could come into the full scope of your potential and actually experience, while living, a transformation of your being. This is not just, "today I will think a new thought". No, far beyond. Through deep attunement to your cellular body, you will experience an entire and complete transformation from within to without. Your normal state of perception will be attuned to the reality of a higher dimension—a "heavenly" reality of being that alters the perception of heaven and earth. As our inner being changes so does everything in our world. This is a process of *convergent evolution*. At this point, we are converging with invisible cosmic forces at work in nature and beyond; reality itself is changing in vibrational frequency as are we.

At a certain point in this convergent evolution, we will suddenly break through into a changed world where the medium of consciousness opens us into a wide spectrum of interaction with various dimensional levels of psychic realities. These realities exist now, though our veiled awareness fails to perceive.

The meaning of the labyrinth of Cosmic History is to arrive at our true self. In this planetary initiation, the human is extricated from history and traditional religious dimensions and planted in a higher dimension (without invalidating the Absolute that has gone before). When you are entering a new reality, it is best to leave old baggage behind. What a great opportunity!

Cosmic History provides the great reevaluation and reordering of all human systems of thought as manifestations of universal time and the synchronic order. Up to the point of the manifestation of Cosmic History, humans who entered a quest for truth had only a set number of systems of thought available to them. For example, they could take the Western hermetic route or they could study Sufism or Zen Buddhism, or Christian mysticism, etc. Cosmic History places viable traditional systems in the context of the synchronic order where their meaning is renewed and expanded into a cosmic order of perception.

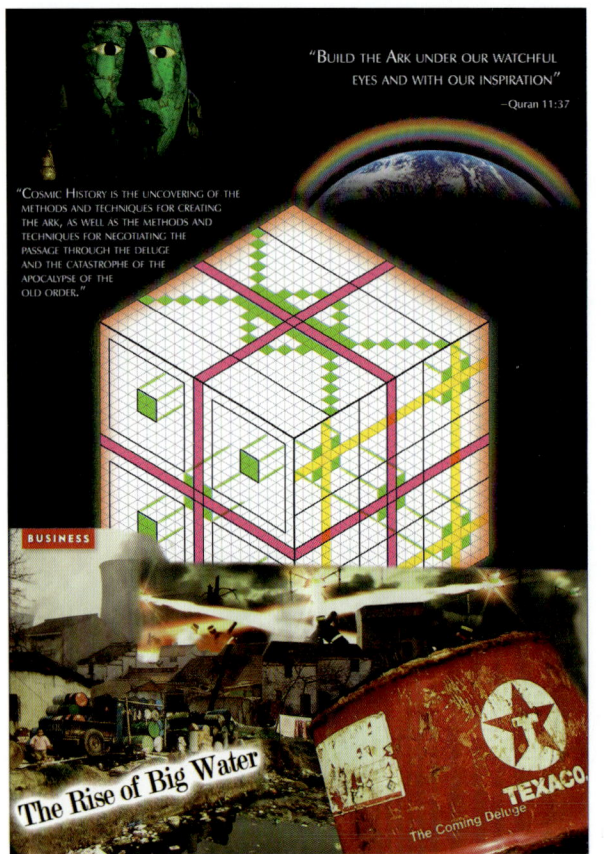

Everything is being organized and reordered at this very moment. We are at the final stage of re-merging with our cosmic identity—we are being given the greatest opportunity ever known—the complete transmutation and unification of the planetary human. We are all breathing the same cyberspheric thought-forms and we all want to have our own individual channels open wider and wider so that our unique forms of expression might emerge.

The fact that we are aware of ourselves as our own channels and mediums is preparatory to being hooked up to the master switchboard—noospheric consciousness. Then we will have realization of merging self-transcendence. According to Cosmic History, this last 260-year cycle of the age of transformation climaxes with the great mutational shift in 2012-13.

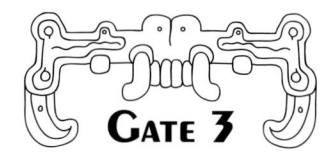

Gate 3
Hermetic Life and the Hidden Rainbow

Proceeding down the path you perceive glorious new colors emerging from a ground crevice. You stumble in the dark—a strange thirst for knowledge fills you. You delve deeper into the hidden, the mysterious, the inexplicable. You long to know everything: The movement of the sun, the changing of the seasons, the cycle of human life and the hidden power that governs the universe and its destiny. Despite the many detours and blind alleyways, a new certainty fills your being—a certainty that no matter what, you will reach the central point of luminosity—the shining of your soul essence.

As we wind our way through the labyrinth, we eventually come to a hidden aspect, sometimes referred to as *hermetic* or *occult*. Occult refers to the hidden, mysterious, invisible source of manifestation and the laws that govern life. The occult aspects of being lie beneath the surface of conditioned reflexes and programmed belief systems. The occult leads to the buried treasure at the bottom of it all.

We follow our intuition until suddenly we realize that we have always been led by an invisible guide in another dimension. For what is intuition but a direct perception of a reality that may not yet have entered our sensory field of consciousness? At this stage, we realize we are actually involved in the evolution of consciousness itself. This is not just a planetary evolution, but a cosmic one.

We know there have been long traditions of hermetic, occult, or esoteric thought in the succession of temporary existences. This invisible tradition has existed since the time of the first human. It is made up of seekers—people just like you—who time after time, generation after generation, push the envelope, step out of the box to see what is beneath the surface of the conditioned patterns. Not only have there been predecessors, there are also contemporaries participating in this process, as well as other guides.

Evolution depends on each individual atom of consciousness realizing its own level of wholeness. When you reach a state of pure self-awareness that is not constrained by conditioned beliefs or compulsive behavior, this is genuine freedom. In your freedom, you attain realization of totality consciousness. In a single perception, the whole universe can be comprehended. This is where the channel of Cosmic History opens to—a new stage of evolution.

We know we were born into this world of conditioned illusion—this world of errors, misperceptions and mistaken notions about reality. The nucleus of enlightenment or *bodhichitta*—seed of enlightenment within us—is contained within the essence of our heart as a center of a type of knowledge, or knowing. When we wake up to this, then we are afforded the opportunity to know more about what has been forgotten—that which lies hidden within us. Because of this opportunity, we can speak of the *hermetic life*.

In order to discover this hidden knowledge, it is important at times to go to a place that is concealed, closed off or away from the normal social conditioned mind streams. In this process, aspects of the lower self are recognized as obstructions to the realization of the higher self. It is important to allow these obstructions to manifest so we can see them, overcome them and transmute them. By exerting in positive thoughtforms, we quicken and activate psychic factors necessary to project the highest image of the new psyche or persona.

The hermetic personality is not so much about Hermes and what he accomplished, but about a personality developed apart from the social mainstream of conditioned illusion. The purpose of hermetic personality is to develop and cultivate a way of life leading to our true essence. It has always been important to safeguard hermetic teachings, which contain the return path in their essence.

EVOLUTION OF THE PLANETARY HUMAN THE HIDDEN SIDE

If you go into the streets and tell people that society is full of illusions and hypocrisy, you will most likely not be met with favorable responses. This is because people generally do not like to be told that they are living in a fictitious society held together by self-deceived norms—no matter how much damage or destruction they might create to both the environment and the soul.

In this late age of materialism, the straight way often appears as a most elaborate rigged cybersphere labyrinth; one must find a path and maintain a discipline that cuts through the opinion strewn maze of the "information" revolution. The basis of hermetic thought is not just an individual matter. Its root lies in a psychomythic drama that describes an original oneness of all beings followed by their fall into separation.

Psychomythic Fall into Separation

The famous fall from grace, or fall from purity and perfection, led us to the outskirts of the labyrinth. This fall from the original, inner unity into the external world of opposites is defined in five precepts, according to *The Knowledge Book:*

1. Whoever you are, so is your brother and sister.
2. Mothers are the mothers of all children, fathers are the fathers of all children.
3. In one morsel, partiality, even as small as a wheat grain, cannot be made.
4. Everything will be equally distributed to everyone.
5. One who does not radiate his/her love to his/her surroundings, who does not flow his/her energy to his/her essence is transferred beyond the curtain of immortality. He/she is sent to the principle of existence program of reincarnation and karma, which engenders the world of illusion and confusion, but also provides the impetus for becoming or evolving into a genuine human.

In some way, because of the "fall" no one is a genuine human being. Most people are run by unconscious programs, operating with a lack of integration of their physical and emotional bodies. In this sense, a human being, by nature, is incomplete, fragmented—a remnant of the genuine prototype. Being fed conditioned half-truths, the human constructs a false self that buries its essence beneath a mantle of inauthenticity.

Many remain in this state, supported by the social norms and props of fear that constitute conventional morality. But those who pay heed to some gnawing sensation to awaken, will soon find that living in a veiled awareness no longer satisfies.

What is not real, is not genuine. Most humans are carbon copies—few are the genuine human beings. The genuine humans are those who choose the arduous path of waking up and staying awake. At the core of striving to be a genuine human is memory, however dim, that we were all once one—and we are now to be one again. What was that like?

In oneness there is an ethic of equality. It is only when we made a distinction that we fell out of grace. Buddhist or Zen teachings say that one dualistic thought, which can be as small as a width of a hair, separates us from Nirvana or bliss as if it were an abyss of 5,000 miles.

The model of each individual life recapitulates this primal pattern of the fall from unity and of the search for regaining the true self. Despite the ignorant coverings of history embedded within this world, there is an invisible power that is always remembering the true nature of reality

When everything is equalized, then it is easy to radiate love to your environment and surroundings. There is no impediment between your sensory input and true essence. This is also the primal ethic of UR, and the basis of the ethic of the People of OMA—the Original Matrix Attained.

The Cosmic History Chronicles • Volume IV

THE COMING SOLAR AGE

**SEEK ONLY WITH THE INNER EYE AND
KNOWLEDGE WILL FLOW INTO YOU**

Fall from Grace

At one point, there was a breaking or a rupture within "eternity" when the souls were sent to evolve according to the existence program of reincarnation and karma. *Cosmic History Chronicles, Volume I* says that this breaking or rupture resulted in the *interval of lost time in eternity*—the primary forgotten memory fragments summarized by the ratio frequency seven. This is recapitulated any number of times and is generically known as the "fall from grace" or the "fall of man", and the beginning of sin, karma and reincarnation.

This was the point when someone said, "I'm better than you", or "this tastes better than that", or "that's not my child, it is yours". These metaphors illustrate the break or cosmic degeneration. From these thought-forms sprang the necessity to create pillars of reality with the possibility to regain that primal state. All wisdom teachings are predicated on this point.

Part I • Defining the Path

The paths to enlightenment appeared simultaneously with the break in equalization that characterized eternity. With this break came the establishment of a path of spiritual ascent with its hierarchical orders, inclusive of revealed texts. Different constitutions were applied in accordance with the evolutionary level of each planet, and for each planetary directing staff was connected a next highest directing staff—thus establishing a system of hierarchical order.

The perception of "the single" had been reached and necessarily made conscious—its all unifying order had been projected on all the laws. Such was the origin of religion, cosmically understood as the path of unification, or the path of realizing the genuine human, the perfection of the image of God.

In the five precepts from *The Knowledge Book*, radiating love to the environment is precisely the point. Society with all its so-called "progress" destroys the environment faster than it can regenerate it. This situation exists because humanity as a whole does not know how to reach its essence and thus, properly radiate love to its environment. Once sufficiently purified, there comes the natural tendency toward turning to a harmless diet derived from the plant kingdom. This is the path to reach our divine inheritance and restore peace and abundance to the Earth. The genuine human naturally radiates love for all living creatures and thus feels a kinship with All That Is.

The Knowledge Book makes clear that at this late stage in the cycle of history, everybody's unique channel has been opened. This means that everyone has an equal opportunity to cultivate him/her self as a medium or channel that connects with a higher level of reality. Practice and exertion are required to keep the channel clear—it is by keeping the channel clear that we are able to "hear" the essence we are seeking.

Many channels, at this time, are co-opted by outlets connected to the cybersphere, and therefore forego the unique opportunity of connecting to the higher reality. *The Knowledge Book* says you can either take the path of essence or the path of ego. Salvation and resurrection are afforded to those people who, eschewing the path of ego, cultivate the hermetic lifestyle. Like burrowing through a hill to get to the other side, the hermetic path is the only way to become a genuine human—to reach the light at the end of the tunnel.

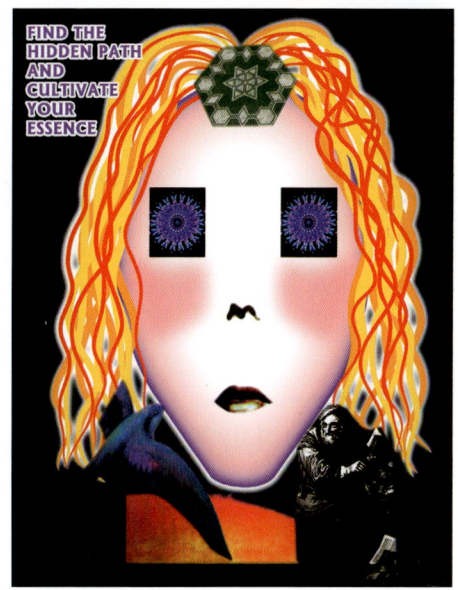

Once we realize that there is a hidden way, or a way apart from the social mainstream, then the cultivation of our essence becomes a primary value. There are two levels of the hermetic life. One is following a particular set of teachings followed by organized groups, and the second is the personal level of striving to reach your true essence. In order to do this you have to realize that society, as you know it, is misleading—if you listen to it, it will lead you away from the straight path. On this straight path you do not deviate to the right or the left. We are continuously being distracted and trying to get back to the straight path.

The nature of society is repressive—it maintains a rigid form or ideology that causes it to compress its adherence to conform to particular ways or laws. This creates an externalizing tendency in human nature, whereas, the hermetic personality is an internalizing nature focused on inner work.

> ### THE INNER WORK
>
> Active participation in the "inner work" is the key to occult or esoteric personality throughout history. This often involves the search for the keys and cultivation or use of symbolic languages to convey meaning that can be passed down from generation to generation. With the right key, the right door and the right attitude, we can enter. The idea of the keys traces back to the key of Solomon, which is now the basis of the Freemasons.
>
> The inner work defines specific keys that give meaning to life and elevate the spirit to comprehend and experience a higher harmony in the universe. The inner work is concerned with bringing this higher harmony into the human realm in order to impact the unruly, despotic, highly conditioned human society.

MADAME BLAVATSKY AND CHELASHIP

In the process of human cosmic evolution, there were always various paths of initiates, adepts or students. Mme. Blavatsky refers to these students as *chelas*, those who knew the "mysteries of the temple". A chela is one who follows a hermetic path pertaining to essence.

In *Raj Yoga*, Madame Blavatsky lays out seven qualities to qualify for chelaship. According to Mme. Blavatsky, and traditional schools, the chela or initiate cannot undertake this path without a teacher or master—someone ahead of your current consciousness to help point the way to enlightenment or God realization. In some cases it may be that the disciple is evolved enough to hear the inner voice of the Divine Command, but in most cases, a guide is invaluable.

Today, many people recoil at the words, "teacher", "master", "guru", etc. They scoff at these names and see those who adhere to them as weak or "not in their own power". Of course this is true for some, but not for all. Those who scoff at these types of words, generally have their channels open to some degree and don't feel like they have to do anything more or that they can just surf the web and find all they need to know.

The highest teachings say there is no such thing as good/bad or right/wrong, which is true at the Absolute level. However, these teachings are often misunderstood by people who have not yet restrained their ego and so use the teachings as an excuse to carry on different kinds of neurosis. This is why in the hermetic life it is useful to have a guide to point out certain pitfalls.

In light of this, let us review the seven qualities for chelaship as put forth by Mme. Blavatsky who reformulated them from an ancient text, said to be 2,000 years old (*Raj Yoga and Occultism*).

1. **Perfect physical health.** Mme. Blavatsky said it is difficult to find many who fit this description. The point is that the chela should at least be conscious and striving in this direction with the

awareness that the majority of "health problems" stem from unconscious habits, both mental and dietary, and it is precisely these habits that we must uproot if we are to become enlightened and true. For the new human, perfect radiant health is a necessary goal. If pursuit of perfect health isn't a top priority—then we are still unconscious.

2. **Absolute mental and physical purity.** This is another hard one to come by today. We live in a society that contains so much pollution in the environment—cell phones and computers—and numerous other attendant distractions. At present, this second quality indicates an acute environmental consciousness and the deliberate effort to live an organic unpolluted life. The chela is always seeking a radical shift in consciousness—where everything resolves into an absolute mental and physical purity.

3. **Unselfishness of purpose.** This trait can also be understood as Universal charity and compassion for all beings. It's easier to come to this and develop it. But one must work at overcoming all tendencies of egoic selfish behavior. This is the whole point of compassion, charity and charitable behavior.

4. **Truthfulness and unswerving faith in the law of karma.** This is an important point that many people overlook. Many people think they can say one thing, then do another; or say one thing, and not really mean it. This type of behavior is in disregard of the law of karma. When we make promises and then don't follow through, this creates problems for others, and for ourselves. It is rare to find truthful people who genuinely understand the laws of karma and so are capable of acting in a fearless manner.

5. **Courage undaunted in every emergency even up to the point of giving your life.** Few people have the courage of their convictions to really do what must be done in a selfless manner—to risk it all for the sake of truth. The point of recognizing one's own self is to then abandon it for the sake of others.

6. **Intuitional perception of ones being the vehicle of the manifested Avalokiteshvara or divine spirit.** In other words, you really are a vehicle, an avatar of the unfoldment of the Divine Plan. Many people can see this and think they are really special. But how many can embody it? The Dalai Lama, for instance is an embodiment of Avalokiteshvara, the bodhisattva of compassion. Do you doubt it? Do you have the qualities of the Dalai Lama? Only you can say if that is true for you or not. Only you know if you have a calling for a higher path or order. Here again, the point is to embody non-egoic norms of behavior, and to act in selfless ways.

7. **Calm indifference or the just appreciation for everything that constitutes apparent reality.** We must first distinguish between indifference as opposed to careless indifference; for example,

you cannot be so indifferent that you do not take responsibility for your own life and rack up a bunch of speeding tickets. Yes, it is all a dream, but one with a system of penalties built into it. Calm indifference refers to bearing the slings and arrows of fate, the criticism and hostility of others—of being equanimous with loss or gain. Only people with clear perception of their role in the Divine Plan can truly cultivate this "calm indifference"—for they know they have nothing left to lose.

These are high qualities even to begin the path. It is helpful to have a category of qualifications to reflect on. We are summarizing the teachings that have existed and the notions of stages of chelaship/adeptship on the road to mastery—becoming a genuine human. But this is only the beginning—beyond this, there are stages of the master.

Temple of Cosmic Destiny

To lead a universal life, we must do our best to be absolutely positive, radiating love into our environment. Everything in the universe is a function of energy. This being so, we wish to dissolve negative states of mind that block us from essence and, at the same time, activate channels for the radiant expression of our genuine self. The key is to radiate positive vibrations from your essence to your surroundings at all times.

The positive function of "negative" energy is to alert us to avoid people or situations that might not be good for us and to prompt us to create a positive force field of protection. This is the right use of "negative energy".

Eight Precepts for Practice of Hermetic Life

1. **Practice self-restraint** (this builds inner spiritual force).
2. **Accept suffering** (until you are free—use suffering as a further means of building up spiritual energy).
3. **Bring selfish desires under control on the spot** (this helps uncloud the mind).
4. **Master the art of forgiveness and graciousness** (this furthers bringing lower instincts under control).
5. **Become actually anxious to know who you are** (you must want this self-knowledge as much as you have ever wanted anything in your whole life).
6. **Overlook others faults, except dishonesty** (the practice of dishonesty, lack of truthfulness, perpetrates a gloss of illusion that is actually harmful).
7. **Be ready to help the needy** (do not flinch from looking into the face of suffering and hunger and give what you can without hesitation).
8. **Know all things, but remain unknown as much as is humanly possible** (the more that you are able to do this, the more you overcome egotistical tendencies of arrogance and pride).

Considering the seven attributes and meditating on the eight precepts, we can begin to conceive of a path to follow to cultivate and embody the attributes and precepts.

Rainbow Ladder of Hierarchy

All hermetic, occult or esoteric teachings recognize some type of hierarchy or hierarchical structure. Most see it as a hierarchy of stages going from darkness to ever greater levels of illumination. The rainbow ladder of hierarchy shows the states of initiation into the galactic order of being through the nine-story temple of cosmic destiny. At its base is the underground, beneath the temple. This signifies the pure unconscious world—the underworld—the non-reflective world of cosmic memory fragments where everybody is an automaton. It is home to those who have not yet remembered the higher light.

Directly beneath this pyramid is the tomb of the Self. Here, in the center of the subterranean unconscious, we find the karmic portal of reincarnation; many times have we been born, many times have we died. Above the tomb, this temple is built on the foundation of the archetypal memory of UR—Universal Recollection. This is the memory of our ultimate origin and, our ultimate destiny.

At our root we are one, we are whole, we are equal. Before the primal rupture, we did not need to discriminate—everything was fluid and flowing in a state of universal love. We all knew who we were. Then, we fell—spiralling down, down, down. With this fall, we entered the worlds of the lost planets and, thus, became cosmic memory fragments. This is where most people dwell—in the unconscious world, the non-reflective fragmented world—the world of automatons and sleepwalkers.

However, there are always a few steps in front—these are the steps of the always existing possibility of self-evolution. It may be that something occurs or happens to us in our tomb of Self that causes us to notice, we might say: "What are those steps? I never noticed them before. I wonder where they might lead." And away we climb, up, up, up.

Running down the center of the pyramid are the steps of the rainbow ladder of hierarchy that cut through illusion. The lowest portion is the unconscious world or the underworld. The first five stories of the pyramid are encompassed by glamour and illusion—built in the ocean of samsara or ego—the self caught in the world of appearance.

At our root, we are one, we are whole, we are equal. Before the primal rupture, we did not need to discriminate—everything was fluid and flowing in a universal state of love.

The Cosmic History Chronicles • Volume IV

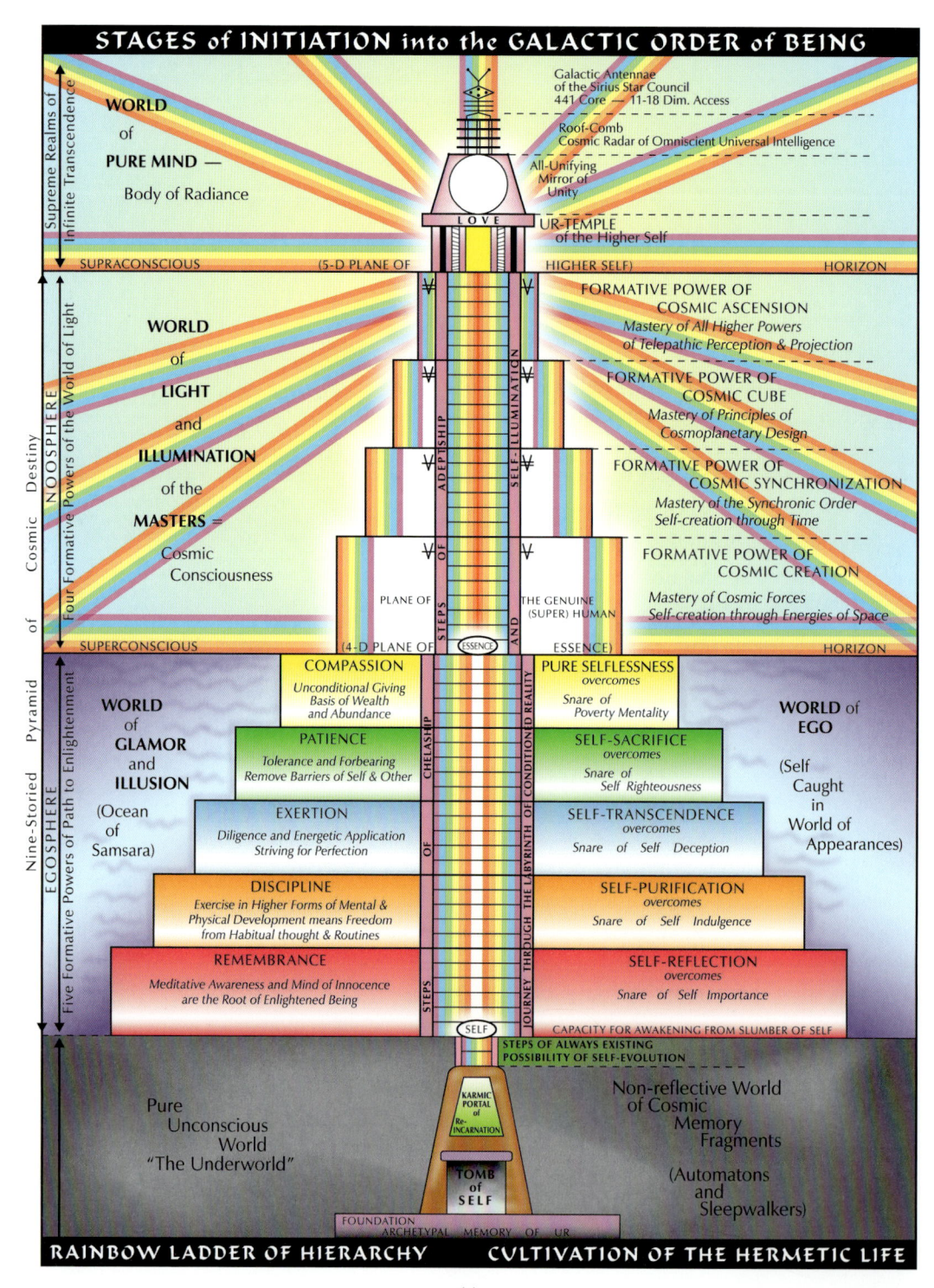

STAGES of INITIATION into the GALACTIC ORDER of BEING

Supreme Realms of Infinite Transcendence

WORLD of PURE MIND —
Body of Radiance

Galactic Antennae of the Sirius Star Council
441 Core — 11-18 Dim. Access

Roof-Comb
Cosmic Radar of Omniscient Universal Intelligence

All-Unifying Mirror of Unity

LOVE

UR-TEMPLE of the Higher Self

SUPRACONSCIOUS — (5-D PLANE OF HIGHER SELF) — HORIZON

Cosmic Destiny — **NOOSPHERE** — **Four Formative Powers of the World of Light**

WORLD of LIGHT and ILLUMINATION of the MASTERS = Cosmic Consciousness

ADEPTSHIP / SELF-ILLUMINATION

FORMATIVE POWER OF COSMIC ASCENSION
Mastery of All Higher Powers of Telepathic Perception & Projection

FORMATIVE POWER OF COSMIC CUBE
Mastery of Principles of Cosmoplanetary Design

FORMATIVE POWER OF COSMIC SYNCHRONIZATION
Mastery of the Synchronic Order Self-creation through Time

FORMATIVE POWER OF COSMIC CREATION
Mastery of Cosmic Forces Self-creation through Energies of Space

PLANE OF / STEPS / ESSENCE / THE GENUINE (SUPER) HUMAN

SUPERCONSCIOUS — (4-D PLANE OF ESSENCE) — HORIZON

Nine-Storied Pyramid — **EGOSPHERE** — **Five Formative Powers of Path to Enlightenment**

WORLD of GLAMOR and ILLUSION
(Ocean of Samsara)

CHELASHIP / JOURNEY THROUGH THE LABYRINTH OF CONDITIONED REALITY

WORLD of EGO
(Self Caught in World of Appearances)

COMPASSION
Unconditional Giving Basis of Wealth and Abundance

PURE SELFLESSNESS
overcomes
Snare of Poverty Mentality

PATIENCE
Tolerance and Forbearing Remove Barriers of Self & Other

SELF-SACRIFICE
overcomes
Snare of Self Righteousness

EXERTION
Diligence and Energetic Application Striving for Perfection

SELF-TRANSCENDENCE
overcomes
Snare of Self Deception

DISCIPLINE
Exercise in Higher Forms of Mental & Physical Development means Freedom from Habitual thought & Routines

SELF-PURIFICATION
overcomes
Snare of Self Indulgence

REMEMBRANCE
Meditative Awareness and Mind of Innocence are the Root of Enlightened Being

SELF-REFLECTION
overcomes
Snare of Self Importance

SELF — CAPACITY FOR AWAKENING FROM SLUMBER OF SELF

STEPS OF ALWAYS EXISTING POSSIBILITY OF SELF-EVOLUTION

KARMIC PORTAL of Re-INCARNATION

TOMB of SELF

Pure Unconscious World "The Underworld"

Non-reflective World of Cosmic Memory Fragments
(Automatons and Sleepwalkers)

FOUNDATION ARCHETYPAL MEMORY OF UR

RAINBOW LADDER OF HIERARCHY • CULTIVATION OF THE HERMETIC LIFE

44

Within these first five stories is the beginning of the first stage—the third dimensional plane of ego consciousness. Here, exists the capacity for awakening from the slumber of self. The first step is attaining "ego consciousness", this means realizing you are an ego—this is the beginning of waking up.

There are 26 steps in the lower world and 26 steps in the upper world. The lower world represents the *egosphere* and contains the five formative powers of the path to enlightenment—the memory of essence. The five formative powers are: 1) the power of remembrance; 2) the power of discipline; 3) the power of exertion; 4) the power of patience; and 5) the power of compassion.

Through accomplishing these formative powers we slowly climb the steps or ladder of chelaship to reach our essence, and become a genuine human, one no longer bound by veils of the illusory world called forth by ego.

Let us look a bit more in-depth at these five formative powers of the first five stories of the rainbow pyramid. These powers are meant to help us cut through the ego of world glamour and illusion—the ocean of samsara.

1. **REMEMBRANCE:** First comes an awakening, followed by a memory. To establish memory as continuing consciousness we must cultivate meditative awareness and the natural mind of innocence—the root of enlightened being. With remembrance comes the capacity for cultivating self-reflection. Self-reflection overcomes the snare of self-importance. This is the first big snare as we climb the ladder of chelaship.

2. **DISCIPLINE:** Discipline is exercise in higher forms of physical and mental development. Discipline means freedom from habitual thoughts and routine. Discipline is the capacity for self-purification and has meaning only when it is voluntarily undertaken. Self-purification overcomes the snare of self-indulgence.

3. **EXERTION:** Exertion means diligence and energetic application—striving for perfection. The quality of exertion is self-transcendence. Self-transcendence overcomes the snare of self-deception. No matter how well we think we have done, we can always exert more and do better. This is the root mechanism of mental/spiritual evolution.

4. **PATIENCE:** Patience is tolerance—a forbearing which removes the barriers between self and other. Patience brings forth the cultivation of humility and the quality of self-sacrifice; it tempers aggression and dissolves the snare of self-righteousness.

5. **COMPASSION:** Compassion is unconditional giving—the basis of wealth and abundance. Compassion is pure selflessness. When we are rich in selflessness, then we no longer base delusions on our own point of view. Pure selflessness overcomes the snare of poverty mentality—for we are always rich in giving. Compassion also means exchanging ourself for others, putting yourself in the others' shoes. In this way, we cease judgment and equalize perceptions of others.

When these five stages have been mastered, then we have sufficiently tamed or dissolved the false self—and the genuine self can manifest in all its glory. Here, there is a threshold.

The first threshold is the capacity for awakening from the slumber of self—from unconscious to conscious. When we have mastered the art of compassion, then we cross the next threshold and arrive at the superconscious horizon. Here, we leave the ocean of samsara and enter the world of light and illumination. This is cosmic consciousness.

In the third dimension, we have the *egosphere* and then, in the fourth dimension, *noosphere*, sphere of mind free from ego. This leads us to the four formative powers of the world of light. When we realize our essence, then we become a genuine human, which compared to the present fragmented human appears superhuman.

3. Cosmic Cube
REFERS TO MASTERY OF THE PRINCIPLE OF COSMOPLANETARY DESIGN. THIS IS A HIGH LEVEL OF COSMIC MASTERY ENTERING US INTO HIGHER MENTAL DESIGN PROCESSES BY WHICH PLANETS AND WHOLE UNIVERSES COME INTO BEING. HERE, WE BECOME CO-CREATORS OF THE COSMIC EVOLUTIONARY PROCESS.

2. Cosmic Synchronization
REFERS TO MASTERY OF THE SYNCHRONIC ORDER: SELF-CREATION THROUGH TIME. HERE, WE MASTER THE CODES OF THE SYNCHRONIC ORDER, EMBEDDING THEM INTO OUR SUBCONSCIOUS.

4. Cosmic Ascension
REFERS TO MASTERY OF HIGHER POWERS OF TELEPATHIC PERCEPTION AND PROJECTION. THIS MEANS WE CAN PERCEIVE OURSELVES ANYWHERE IN THE UNIVERSE AND PROJECT TO THOSE PLACES AS NECESSARY.

1. Cosmic Creation
REFERS TO MASTERY OF THE COSMIC FORCES. THIS COMES ABOUT THROUGH THE SELF-CREATION OF THE ENERGY OF SPACE. HERE, WE ARE NO LONGER THE VICTIM OF CONDITIONED REALITY, THOUGHTS AND PATTERNS. WE HAVE FREED OURSELVES FROM THE CLAIMS OF THE FALSE SELF THROUGH THESE FIRST FIVE STEPS. HERE, WE ARE CREATING OURSELVES AND REALITY ANEW. WE HAVE REACHED THE SOURCE WITHIN OUR MIND.

Four Formative Powers of Adeptship

The people who are going to create the new world beyond the threshold of 2012 are consciously working to elevate their minds and bodies. At one point, we reach a horizon and cross over from the world of illusion to the world of the masters—then appear the steps leading to adeptship and self-illumination—the mind of the masters where we are all awaiting.

When we speak of "mind in the noosphere" as the collective mind of the masters, we are also defining qualities of cosmic mediumship. The four formative powers are derived from access to the four intergalactic channels. This takes us to the next horizon—the supraconscious—the fifth plane of the higher self. We have reached the top story of the nine story pyramid—it is here that the UR temple of the higher self is projected from the archetypal memory of the previous worlds. We have finally arrived. This is the pyramid temple of cosmic destiny where the higher self dwells all the time—this is the world of pure mind; it is the temple of pure love.

The rainbow steps are rolled out by the higher self and projected by the grace of God—you can either cultivate higher virtues or get caught in snares. The higher self is always in the UR temple radiating compassion—this is the fifth-dimensional level of the higher self. The sixth-dimensional level of the higher self is the all-unifying mirror of unity. The seventh-dimensional level is the roof of the cosmic radar of omniscient universal intelligence. The eighth-dimensional level is the galactic antennae of the Sirius star council, same as the core code of the 441 with access to the 18-dimensional universe. The ninth dimension level is the primary unitive power coordinating the cosmic cube as the command of fifth force galactic intelligence.

This access point of the radial dimension of time is within the tenth dimension of the "stations of the ark", the realm of the fundamental universal archetypes. The eleventh to eighteenth dimensions open vertically from the center of the primal time space cube matrix. These are all the realms beyond mind and consciousness to be defined and explored in the next three volumes.

Body of Radiance and Ascension of Consciousness

The medium of the Cosmic History channel is a portal that opens to this time. The force of its intelligence is pushing through the labyrinth into the focal point of our self-reflection. We cannot ignore what previous masters have accomplished. We cannot ignore the definition and description of mind and cosmic space that they have accomplished. We always have to ask ourselves: "Is this my experience or is this just words?"

What does the hermetic path and hermetic life look like today? It is on this consideration that we re-present the archetypal order of the hermetic teachings, life and path so that anyone can study and learn the actual nature of reality and release themselves from the world of illusion—into the eternal wonder of their essence, the one core of the genuine human.

What are the steps we need to take? What are the snares that we have to look out for? What are the particular goals? We know the actual goal is to reach our essence buried deep within the trappings of conditioned personality. We are searching for the pure essence that leads us to the higher self. This is all that ultimately matters.

Anyone in the modern world has the opportunity to wake up and realize that the outer world does not have the answer to the purpose of his/her being on this planet. Having your own career, website and option to blog whenever you choose wears thin fast. Even novelty wears out. And besides, look at the world around you. Can it be regenerated? And how?

The answer comes through the consciousness that everyone has to direct themselves inward and to see, feel and realize the essence that is not defined by the outer world of glamour, money or technology.

We are coming to a point of a quantum consciousness shift. This is an advance from functioning at the level of the egosphere to functioning at the level of the noosphere. Functioning at the level of the noosphere is the purpose to which all the hermetic traditions of the past pointed. This is the new stabilized higher evolutionary state. There is a very simple way to attain this. First, we must detach ourselves from the deification of the conditioned beliefs of the outer world and turn our attention inward to the qualities of essence. We must continuously cultivate these qualities to ascend the rainbow ladder until we reach the real treasure—our own radiant higher self animating our essence.

Part II
Crafting the Vehicle

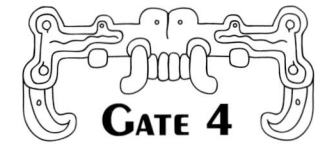

Gate 4
Esoteric Personality

As you venture down the winding path of the cosmic labyrinth, you sense other presences. You wonder, am I alone? Are there other beings watching me? Are they aware of my quest? As you think these thoughts, an ancient book appears suspended in mid air in front of you. Its pages turn without you touching them. It stops on page 33, and you read: "Since the beginning of time, there have been initiates and disciples whose work it has been to keep wisdom alive, often in secret." The book turns a page and you read: "Your body is the laboratory; your mind is the vessel—use them wisely for the sake of ALL." With that the book disappears.

The journey through the labyrinth is a process of *hermetic transmutation*—transforming the inauthentic persona back into the true self. We are each responsible for the harmonious resolution of all tensions and polarities within our own being. Such work is never easy, for it involves full confrontation of the lesser self, and the bringing to light of that which would otherwise shun the light. To exemplify the courage to change is already heroic. At the same time, it is a wise admonition that the best way to dispel evil is to make energetic progress in the good.

Hermetic transmutation is a mental art that requires the cultivation of will. Determine, to begin with, to be really good, says Eliphas Levi, and all that you do will be good. Will is the quality of the alignment of the third-dimensional self with the fourth-dimensional soul essence, as guided by the fifth-dimensional guardian or angel. The cultivation of will provides the direction or force of momentum that helps us to attain higher ends on behalf of the All. Consider these words from Eliphas Levi:

> *For the will, to be powerful, must be persevering and calm. God does not waver, says the Bible, and we can never advance by continually halting and retracing our steps. When we have sown the good seed, we must move the earth no more, but we must yet not cease to water what we have planted. Then the germ will be produced, and the plant will sprout of itself. When we have placed the leaven in the dough, we must leave it to work. The smallest effort constantly repeated ends by conquering all obstacles.*

In this process of hermetic transmutation, we must persevere with invincible patience. The first step is to take heed of our inner motives and make them pure. This means we must be honest with ourselves and see things clearly, fairly and objectively, so that we can judge rationally and not allow ourselves to be carried away by prejudice or passion. It is a sacred struggle to pass from the conditioned self to the self of the higher harmony; It is a sacred struggle to remain awake to conditioned social factors. For this reason, it is of comfort to hear stories of initiates who have tread the path before us working on behalf of the Higher Plan.

This Gate 4 focuses on the constellation of esoteric and hermetic personalities that arose in the nineteenth and twentieth centuries. Because these esotericists appeared in the industrial age, they are set apart from personalities of earlier times. Through their lives and teachings we can begin to feel a mini fractal of the cycle of transformation over the last 260 years.

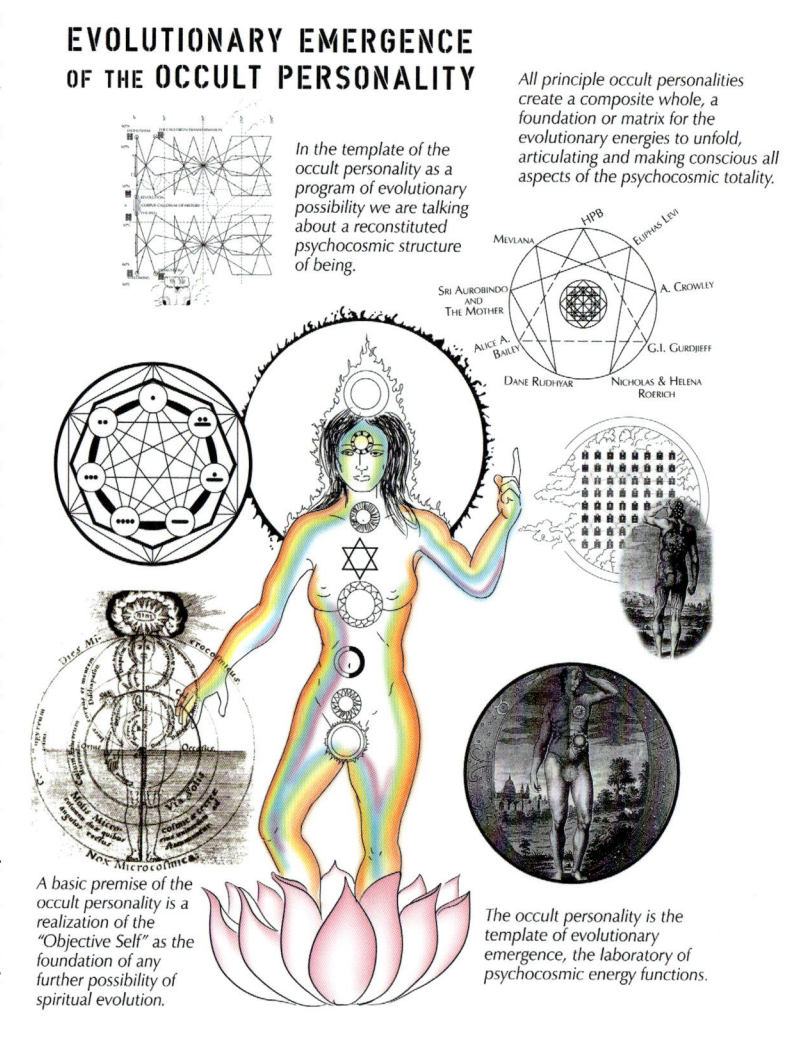

EVOLUTIONARY EMERGENCE OF THE OCCULT PERSONALITY

In the template of the occult personality as a program of evolutionary possibility we are talking about a reconstituted psychocosmic structure of being.

All principle occult personalities create a composite whole, a foundation or matrix for the evolutionary energies to unfold, articulating and making conscious all aspects of the psychocosmic totality.

HPB · ELIPHAS LEVI
MEVLANA
SRI AUROBINDO AND THE MOTHER · A. CROWLEY
ALICE A. BAILEY · G.I. GURDJIEFF
DANE RUDHYAR · NICHOLAS & HELENA ROERICH

A basic premise of the occult personality is a realization of the "Objective Self" as the foundation of any further possibility of spiritual evolution.

The occult personality is the template of evolutionary emergence, the laboratory of psychocosmic energy functions.

Brief History of Esotericism

Throughout history, there have been those who reveal the mystery and keep the wisdom of the ages kindled. These beings are called initiates, hermeticists, occultists, seekers, adepts, chelas, etc. There are only a certain number of these essences that continue to recycle.

The nature of the hermetic mind is like a stone skipping across the water of different times, but it is always the same stone. The few true essences responsible for hermetic tradition have tremendous capacities for incarnation and magical appearance. Their task is to reformulate the original doctrine according to the different ages and languages.

The original doctrine that we speak of is the prehistoric knowledge—the original primal knowledge—revealed by God to Adam and Moses, among others. This "original" knowledge was handed down in a long, elite chain of tradition, transmitted from age to age, from initiate to initiate. Hermes Trismegistus was a major link in this hermetic chain, as were Plotinus, Socrates, Zoroaster, Pythagoras, Apollonius, Paracelsus and Plato, and so forth.

The knowledge was transmitted through symbols, ceremonies, initiations and rituals in order to preserve, for the world to come, the secrets of the forgotten worlds. Many symbols were purposefully cryptic in order to preserve the knowledge from those who would profane it. For this reason, secret societies arose, such as the Rosicrucians, the Freemasons, the Illuminati, the Knights of the Holy Grail, and later the Hermetic Order of the Golden Dawn.

The Freemasons are perhaps the most well-known occult or hermetic society. Nearly every small town in the Anglo Saxon society has erected a Masonic temple, many of which are now abandoned. The Order of the Freemasons traces back to Solomon, renowned as a great and uniquely esoteric king, and also an accomplished magician possessed of many paranormal powers. From Solomon originated many types of symbols and symbolic structures passed down through the ages.

The eighteenth century brought a definite quantum break in hermetic thinking, beginning with the industrial revolution. At this point, there was a peak in European society of hermetic thought and symbolic systems in general. This came to a magnificent flowering in the sixteenth, seventeenth and early eighteenth centuries with the creation of the Hermetic Museum, a huge graphic compendium using popular print media to communicate symbols of the inner journey. Key personalities at this time included Francis Bacon, Robert Fludd, Jakob Bohme and Emanuel Swedenborg.

With the rise of the industrial revolution in the eighteenth century, the mind of Western civilization was caught up in spreading the new social and political forms characterized by the American and French revolutions. At this point, social

The few true essences responsible for hermetic tradition have tremendous capacities for incarnation and magical appearance. Their task is to reformulate the original doctrine according to the different ages and languages.

The Cosmic History Chronicles • Volume IV

democracies were developed, resulting in a decline of the aristocracy in general. (As long as there is a type of aristocracy there is a better chance of occult schools operating, as these societies are already based on hierarchical principles.) However, this shunning of hierarchical spiritual sensibility in Western civilization was necessary so that the individual human psyche could ferment into its final stage of evolution.

Most esoteric schools operate with hierarchical principles, often accompanied by outer forms or degrees of initiation. Once the monarchies were finished, then the old sensibility that had characterized the occult and hermetic streams in the West also subsided. At this stage, arose esoteric bridge personalities such as the mysterious St. Germain and William Blake, a visionary artist who integrated late medieval artistic modalities into his anti-industrial age mythology and symbolism.

By the end of the nineteenth century, the landscape of the planet had completely transformed—the industrial age Europeans had affected every part of the world spreading their influence of railroads, telegraph and manufactured goods. At this time the great Western magical tradition, which stretched back to the Renaissance, was scoffed at it by most educated Europeans.

With changes in the economic system, coupled with Charles Darwin's findings, people began to lose faith in traditional religion, which also led to the perception of life as barren and devoid

OCCULT PERSONALITY: IN SEARCH OF HARMONY

of meaning. It was no longer the world of cathedrals, temples and mosques—but a world where commercialism reigned supreme. At the time, it appeared that vistas were opening for the individual to become free of feudal society—but in actuality it is questionable whether spiritual consciousness was significantly raised or not, between 1800 to 2000.

During the time leading up to the twentieth century, there is no question that the physical universe expanded its information belt, allowing humans to receive more information than ever before—but this is only physical/horizontal information. The real question is: How much did consciousness expand and continue to expand at the spiritual/vertical level?

In 1848, the modern spiritualist movement began to flourish in New York. By 1852 the first mediums arrived in England and then France. In 1882, the British Society for Psychical Research was established. From this time onward, the spiritual movement (presently known as "New Age") has only increased and flourished, bringing to the fore the need for a planetary knowledge and the spreading of universal love. It is in this context that occur the matrix of the template of the modern occult personalities.

During the course of this writing, the following personalities made their presences known the most strongly: Eliphas Levi, Madame Blavatsky, Sri Aurobindo and the Mother, G.I. Gurdjieff, Aleister Crowley, Alice Bailey, Nicholas and Helena Roerich, Dane Rudhyar and Mevlana (Bulent Çorak).

Esoteric Personalities are Universal

When we hear the words "esoteric personality", "chela", or "initiate", we might think of Hermes Trismegistus, Pythagoras, Apollonius of Tyanus, St. Germain, or Francis Bacon, etc. An initiate is someone who, through their own exertion, has passed from merely functioning on the physical plane to experiencing the possibilities of evolving into the higher dimensions. Eliphas Levi says that true initiates are shepherds and conquerors; they raise the sheep and conquer the wolves. In this regard, Jesus was a master initiate, as demonstrated when he drove the money lenders from the temple.

True initiates value unity and harmony and are always striving for the highest possible self-integration and experience of universal brother/sisterhood. As we mentioned earlier, there are only a few essences that keep reincarnating and repeating alternate versions of the same story. For example, it is said that St. Germain is the emanation of Pythagoras: and also that Pythagoras and Francis Bacon are one! The Kabbalah states that Noah is an incarnation of Adam, as Moses is an incarnation of Abel and Seth, etc.

Mme. Blavatsky says the greatest proof of these repetitive incarnations is found in the Bible.

> *... The greatest proof of it (reincarnation of certain personalities) is the distribution of the characters in the Bible. For instance, beginning with Cain, the first murderer, every fifth man in his line of descent is a murderer. Thus there come Enoch, Irad,*

> Mehujael, Methuselah, and the fifth is Lamech, the second murderer, and he is Noah's father. By drawing the five-pointed star of Lucifer (which has its crown-point downward) and writing the name of Cain beneath the lowest point, and those of his descendants successively at each of the other points, it will be found that each fifth name—which would be written beneath that of Cain—is that of a murderer. In the Talmud this genealogy is given complete, and thirteen murderers range themselves in line below the name of Cain. This is no coincidence. Siva is the Destroyer, but he is also the Regenerator. Cain is a murderer, but he is also the creator of nations, and an inventor. This star of Lucifer is the same one that John sees falling down to Earth in his Apocalypse.
>
> —HPB, *Isis Unveiled*. Chapter IX

Hermetic Philosophy

All true esotericists are Universalists; the basis of their philosophy can be traced back to Hermes Trismegistus who received the *Emerald Tablets* believed to date back between the sixth and eighth centuries A.D. These eleven theses are the underlying modus operandi esotericism:

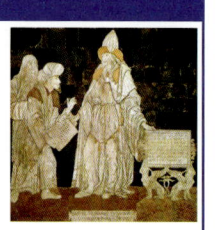

1. *True, true. Without doubt. Certain:*
2. *The below is as the above, and the above as the below, to perfect the wonders of the One.*
3. *And as all things came from the One, from the meditation of the One, so all things are born from this One by adaptation.*
4. *Its father is the Sun, its mother the Moon; the Wind carries it in its belly; its nurse is the Earth.*
5. *It is the father of all the wonders of the whole world. Its power is perfect when it is transformed into Earth.*
6. *Separate the Earth from Fire and the subtle from the gross, cautiously and judiciously.*
7. *It ascends from Earth to Heaven and then returns back to the Earth, so that it receives the power of the upper and the lower. Thus you will possess the brightness of the whole world, and all darkness will flee you.*
8. *This is the force of all forces, for it overcomes all that is subtle and penetrates solid things.*
9. *Thus was the world created.*
10. *From this wonderful adaptations are perfected, and the means are given here.*
11. *And Hermes Trismegistus is my name, because I possess the three parts of the wisdom of the world.*

Religious and Esoteric Personalities

It is necessary to make the distinction between religious personality and esoteric personality. The religious personality is primarily concerned with fulfilling or attaining the religious dimension, usually in accord to a prescribed order of practices. Religious personalities include St. Francis of Assisi, Milarepa the yogi of Tibet, St. Hildegard of Bingen, Jalalludin Rumi, Hafiz, or Ramakrishna, many of whom wrote poetry or mystical songs. Each of these beings represents a religious/mystical personality. The mystical generally transcends the religious bounds—while upholding the religion that they are transcending. Milarepa is a devout Buddhist. Rumi and Hafiz are Muslim mystics. St. Francis and Hildegard are Christians and Ramakrishna is a Hindu—though they all have a universal appeal.

The esotericist or occult personality, on the other hand, is set apart from institutionalized spiritual practice—though they might have particular religious leanings, such as Eliphas Levi who was trained as a Catholic Priest before pursuing occult interests. Throughout his life, Levi continued to admire the ritual aspect of the church, and said that true Catholicism is "official occultism and rests entirely on mystery". He said that the secret of the sanctuaries has been profaned, but has not been explained.

G.I. Gurdjieff's father was prepared to send him to Russian Orthodox seminary—but Gurdjieff had other plans. Mme. Blavatsky took formal Buddhist vows, but was anything but a traditional Buddhist. Sri Aurobindo, on the other hand, somewhat remained in the tradition of a Hindu yogi—though he transcended "religious personality". Though Sri Aurobindo used yoga as a spiritual vehicle, his emphasis was not on traditional religion, but on the science of spiritual evolution.

All of these adepts or initiates form aspects of a higher template of order that prepares the ground for the emergence of a new evolutionary type. This higher comprehension of order and harmony comprises all parts of one larger body, similar to the mystical body of Christ. Below is a brief biography of each of these pioneers of esoteric thought, who carved new paths into the future that still influence our world today.

Eliphas Levi

Birth name: Alphonse Louis Constant
Born: February 8, 1810 in Paris
13-Moon calendar date: 8.2, Seli, Kin 1

Eliphas Levi was the most notable French occult writer of the nineteenth century. He initiated the modern revival of magic as a spiritual path and felt the purpose of the magician was to become a more fully realized human being.

He was born to a poor Catholic family. His father was a cobbler and he was known as a bright, hard-working student and a pious Catholic with a mystical bent. He attended seminary school and was ordained as a deacon in the Catholic church in 1835 (some say he was defrocked before this happened). Whatever the case, his career in priesthood was short-lived. He was also imprisoned three times for his radical politics.

Levi sought to reconcile magic and religion. He confidently positioned magic as a discipline compatible with both science and Christianity, and capable of unifying both.

> *Science ... is at the basis of magic, as at the foundation of Christianity there is love, and in the Gospel symbols we see the Word incarnate adored in his cradle by three magi, led thither by a star ... Christianity owes, therefore, no hatred to magic ...*

Levi was deeply influenced by eighteenth century English occultist Francis Barrett. Barrett's classic work, *The Magus*, contains the magical viewpoint of eighteenth century England and laid the foundation for many esoteric schools and magical orders to come.

In 1852 Levi became a disciple of Joseph-Marie Hoene Wronski, a Polish mathematician, mystic and kabbalist. Wronski had a huge influence on Levi's becoming a writer on magic.

In July, 1854, Levi claims to have evoked the spirit of Apollonius Tyanus, a Pythagorean philosopher, in London. At this time he devoted himself to the study of the Kabbalah, and became associated with the English Rose-Cross. He was first to use the term "astral light", and said it is through this astral light that the signs and wonders of magic are mediated.

Levi also played a significant role in the development of the esoteric Tarot, which he referred to as the ancient Egyptian "Book of Hermes". He described the Tarot as the "universal key of magical works" and, as such, "the key of all ancient religious dogmas", including even the Bible. He also was one of the first to connect the Kabbalah with the Tarot. He was also a great artist and illustrated his books with symbols and diagrams, many of which have attained iconic status.

Levi identified three fundamental principles of magic:

1. That the material universe is only a small part of total reality, which includes many other planes and modes of consciousness. Full knowledge and full power in the universe are only attainable through awareness of these other aspects of reality. One of the most important of these levels or aspects of reality is the "astral light", a cosmic fluid which may be molded by will into physical forms.

2. That human willpower is a real force, capable of achieving absolutely anything, from the mundane to the miraculous.

3. That the human being is a microcosm, a miniature of the macrocosmic universe, and the two are fundamentally linked. Causes set in motion on one level may equally have effects on another.

His most famous work is *Dogme et Rituel de la Haute Magie* (1855), and was translated into English by Arthur Edward Waite as *Transcendental Magic, its Doctrine and Ritual*. This book contained a synthesis of Western magic, including Kabbalah, divination (Tarot), astrology, alchemy, talismans, prophecy, and much more. This book was the base for Mathers' formation of the Hermetic Order of the Golden Dawn, founded in London in 1888, which adopted much of Levi's magical system.

Madame Blavatsky

Birth name: Helena Petrovna von Hahn
Born: August 12, 1831 at Dnepropetrovsk (Ekaterinoslav), Ukraine
13-Moon calendar date: 1.18, Kali, Kin 51

Madame Blavatsky single-handedly defined a new cosmology—everything that we now refer to as the *New Age*—and influenced all the different streams of esoteric thought in the twentieth century.

Madame Blavatsky was born to nobility and wealth. She was the daughter of Col. Peter von Hahn and Helena Andreyevna, nee de Fadeyev, a renowned feminist and novelist. Helena's Grandmother on her maternal side was Princess Helena Pavlovna Dolgorukov, a noted botanist and writer.

As a child, she was known to be impatient with authority, yet deeply sensitive, possessing remarkable psychic powers. She was a talented pianist, a fine artist, a clever linguist and also liked to ride half-broken horses.

Madame Blavatsky is responsible for the bridging of Eastern mysticism and Western occultism. The term *occult* as we know it today, is by and large a product of her writings. Her writings also brought to the West, Eastern thought and terms such as *karma, yoga, reincarnation, swami, master, adept* and *mahatma*. She was taught by her masters, most notably Master Morya and Koot Hoomi. Blavatsky wrote many volumes on numerous subjects of Eastern and Western occultism. Her main written works are *Isis Unveiled* (1879) and *The Secret Doctrine* (1889). Her works influenced many significant people in many walks of life, including W.B. Yeats, Gandhi, Nicholas and Helena Roerich, Dane Rudhyar, and Alice Bailey among others.

Blavatsky, together with Colonel Olcott, founded the Theosophical Society in New York City in 1875. The headquarters were established in Bombay in 1878 and later in Mount Adyar, near Madras. The purpose of the Theosophical Society was to extend and centralize the study of Oriental Occult philosophy and to "investigate the hidden mysteries of nature under every aspect possible, and the psychic and spiritual powers latent in man." (*Key to Theosophy*).

The formation of an esoteric section or school of theosophy was intimately connected with another influential force of the nineteenth century, the Hermetic Order of the Golden Dawn. She died May 8, 1891.

See Gate 6 for more in-depth coverage of her life.

Part II • Crafting the Vehicle

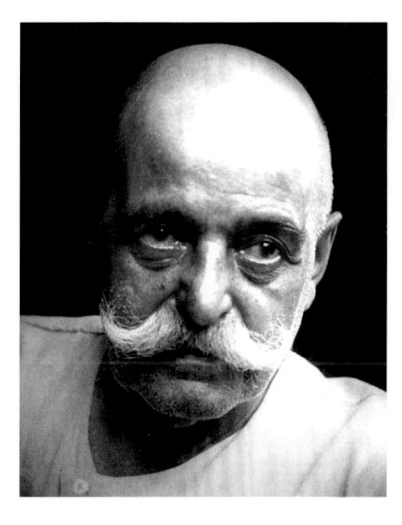

G.I. Gurdjieff

Birth name: Georgei Ivanovitch Gurdjieff
Born: January 13, 1866 in Alexandropol in the Caucasus mountains
13-Moon calendar date: 7.4, Kali, Kin 135

G.I. Gurdjieff was a dynamic and enigmatic Russian Mystic and spiritual teacher. His revolutionary philosophy, commonly called 'the Work', blazed a new trail for occultism in the early twentieth century. He synthesized his teachings into one geometrical symbol—the Enneagram—based on the nine-pointed star.

He was the eldest of four children born to an upper middle class Greek-Armenian family. His father, Ioannas Giorgiades, was the owner of extensive herds of cattle and sheep. His father was a great disciplinarian and also skilled at the art of the *ashokhs*, the traditional recitation of epics and legends in verse. His imaginative and resourceful character was formed through listening to his father's stories about the Old Testament, Atlantis, as well as accounts of sages and astrologers who traveled the Earth "observing celestial phenomena from different places", maintaining telepathic contact with home through entranced "pythonesses". Through these stories Gurdjieff understood that the ancients must possess a secret knowledge that was lost in the historical cycle.

He left home at 17 and went to Tiflis in Georgia where he met others, like himself, who were searching for the meaning of life. From here, he traveled to many places surveying spiritual schools and finding his way into remote monasteries throughout the Middle East and Asia, Afghanistan, Tibet, India, Turkey and Africa. He worked various jobs to pay for his travels: carpet trader, businessmen, hypnotist, Russian spy, etc. During World War I, he led a large group of Russian followers across Eastern Europe to safety, through the raging battle lines of Bolsheviks and Cossacks in turn.

Gurdjieff possessed great personal magnetism, courage, drive and strong psychic abilities. When he emerged on the Western scene in 1912, he had already devised his program for whole-person spiritual development. His central postulate was that human beings are essentially sleepwalkers—machines run by forces outside of their control. In order to wake up the sleepwalkers, Gurdjieff developed a system of unconventional means and methods to help people break free of the ordinary life that binds them to the mundane.

He was known for advocating the "Fourth Way". He said there were basically three ways to govern the maintenance of the soul. The way of the yogi (mind), the way of the monk (heart) and the way of the fakir (body). The Fourth Way encompasses all three and includes new methods as well.

Gurdjieff developed an entirely new cosmology and approach to psychology that contributed greatly to the familiarization of the West to the then radical idea of the psyche or soul (which at that time Sigmund Freud was also bringing to Western notice). This paved the way for new types of "now" centered encounter groups.

Gurdjieff brought, for the first time, to the European mind an awareness of the sacred ritual dances and dervish exercises of the East. He developed an intricate choreography of spiritually instructive dances, specific methodologies for increasing consciousness and harmonizing inner disunity. (It is said that these practices have strong links with the Altaic shamanism and Tibetan and Chinese tantra).

Gurdjieff founded the Institute for the Harmonious Development of Man in Fontainbleu, France. Here, he trained his students in a variety of whole-person programs. Gurdjieff said without these teachings and disciplines it is impossible for man to govern and maintain the planet. The Gurdjieff schools of self development spread to numerous countries and his ideas became common coinage in the sixties.

After 1924, Gurdjieff focused his energy on writing down his knowledge. His masterwork was *Beelzebub's Tales to his Grandson* (1950). *Meetings with Remarkable Men*, his 'autobiography', was published in 1960, and *Life is Real Only Then, When 'I Am'* in the early 1970s. He died October 29, 1949.

Part II • Crafting the Vehicle

Sri Aurobindo

Birth name: Aurobindo Akroyd Ghose
Born: August 15, 1872 in Calcutta
13-Moon calendar date: 1.21, Silio, Kin 199

Sri Aurobindo was a philosopher, mystic and cosmic poet who played a significant role in defining the stages of the future evolution. As founder of Integral Yoga, he was a pioneer of exploring and documenting the supermental realms of divine consciousness. He also made a significant contribution to Hinduism by setting forth an esoteric meaning of the Vedas.

He was the third son of four boys born to Anglican Bengali parents. His father was a medical doctor and demanded that English be exclusively spoken in his house. In 1879, at age 7, his father took him and his three brothers to Manchester, United Kingdom to begin their education. Sri Aurobindo excelled in literature and history and also showed great interest in romantic poetry, particularly that of Keats, Shelly and Byron. He became a classical scholar at Cambridge University.

He returned to India in 1893 where he co-founded the Indian Nationalist Party. His radical political views got him arrested twice, once in 1907, and again in 1908. (He is still regarded as one of the four founders of the modern state of India).

It was during his second jail term in Alipore that he began to seriously study and meditate on the Bhagavad Gita. In one of his meditations, he claimed that Swami Vivekananda visited him. Vivekananda, a Hindu philosopher and great disciple of Ramakrishna Paramahansa, guided Sri Aurobindo in the importance of his spiritual practice or yoga.

In 1914 he met "the Mother", then known as Mirra Richard. This was a truly transformative encounter; he found in the Mother a spiritual partnership and considered her the incarnation of the Divine Mother, hence her name "the Mother". In 1920, she returned to live with him in Pondicherry for the rest of his life. They became known as the "two in one".

Following his initial meeting, Aurobindo experienced a great creative outburst, and immediately after their first meeting much of his original synthesizing, critical and systematic philosophy of Divine Consciousness and *Integral Yoga* was written, including his masterful synthesis of philosophical thought, *The Life Divine* and *A Synthesis of Yoga*. (The collected works of Sri Aurobindo comprise more than thirty volumes, many of them quite substantial.) The purpose of Integral Yoga is to further the evolution of life on Earth by establishing the Supermind that represents a divine life free from physical death, with the first step being utter surrender to the divine.

He called himself a "pathfinder hewing his way through a virgin forest". He taught that the human being is a transitional entity evolving—that is the embodiment of an eternal, divine soul. It is the evolution of this divine soul which causes and supports the material evolution from the deepest inertia back to its divine origin.

He perceived that the descent of the supermental was imminent and that he himself experienced it in 1926. This was the first step to the new evolutionary condition—the supermental Overmind or noosphere. As he wrote in the Human Cycle:

> *The coming of a spiritual age must be preceded by the appearance of an increasing number of individuals who are no longer satisfied with the normal intellectual, vital, and psychical existence of man, but perceive that a greater evolution is the real goal of humanity and attempt to effect it in themselves, to lead others to it, and to make it the recognized goal of the race. In proportion as they succeed and the degree to which they carry this evolution, the yet unrealized potentiality which they represent will become the actual possibility of the future.*
> —*Essential Aurobindo, p. xii*

He explains this transition in the following way:

> *There must first be the psychic change, the conversion of our whole present nature into a soul-instrumentation; on that or along with that there must be the spiritual change, the descent of a higher Light, Knowledge, Power, Force, Bliss into the whole being, even into the darkness of our subconscience; last there must supervene the supramental transmutation—there must take place as the crowning movement the ascent into the supermind and transforming descent of the supramental consciousness into our entire being and nature.*
> —*Srinivas Iyenegar, p. 696, Life of Aurobindo, 1972*

India attained Independence on Aurobindo's 75th birthday, August 15, 1947. He died on December 5, 1950.

The Mother

Birth name: Mirra Alfassa
Born: February 21, 1878 in Paris
13-Moon calendar date: 8.15, Dali, Kin 134

The Mother was an occultist, writer, artist, architect and founder of Auroville community in Pondicherry. She was a pioneer of supramental transformation alongside Sri Aurobindo.

She was born to Turkish and Egyptian parents. At age five she claims to have realized that she did not belong to this world and so began her spiritual disciplines. At age 12 she began her study of occultism and claimed to astral travel. At 16 she joined the Ecole des Beaux Arts where she acquired the nickname "the Sphinx", and later married artist Henri Morisset, a student of symbolist painter Gustave Moreau, and became part of the Paris artistic circles. Among her friends were Rodin and Monet. When she was 20, she discovered Vivekananda's *Raja Yoga*, which enabled her to make further rapid progress.

A few years later she began reading the Bhagavad Gita, taking Krishna as a symbol of the inner divine. In 1905 she befriended occultists Max and Alma Theon, who affirmed for her many of her psychic experiences.

She met Sri Aurobindo in Pondicherry on March 29, 1914. She said she recognized him as the one from her dreams that she used to call Krishna. She said that when she first met Sri Aurobindo, she found that her thoughts ceased to run, her mind became quiet, and silence began to gather momentum, until two or three days later there was only the silence and the yogic consciousness.

Six years later, she would become Sri Aurobindo's active collaborator in the process of bringing down and embodying the Overmind and supramental into the Earth plane. She planned, ran and built the growing Sri Aurobindo ashram and also established the Sri Aurobindo International Centre of Education. The Mother said of Sri Aurobindo:

> *Sri Aurobindo belongs to the future; he is the messenger of the future. He still shows us the way to follow in order to hasten the realisation of a glorious future fashioned by the Divine Will ... All those who want to collaborate for the progress of humanity and for India's luminous destiny must unite in a clairvoyant aspiration and in an*

> *illumined work ... Sri Aurobindo came upon earth to announce the manifestation of the supramental world and not merely did he announce this manifestation but embodied also in part the supramental force and showed by example what one must do to prepare oneself for manifesting it.*

After Sri Aurobindo's passing, The Mother continued her promise to Sri Aurobindo to attempt the physical transformation of her body in order to become a new type of human by opening to the supramental truth consciousness, as defined by Sri Aurobindo.

The Mother writes of her experience of Sri Aurobindo's passing and his transference of energy to her:

> *... He had gathered in his body a great amount of supramental force and as soon as he left ... You see, he was lying on his bed, I stood by his side, and in a way altogether concrete—concrete with such a strong sensation as to make one think that it could be seen—all this supramental force which was in him passed from his body into mine. And I felt the friction of the passage. It was extraordinary—extraordinary.*

On April 24, 1956, after several supernatural experiences, she announced "The manifestation of the Supramental upon Earth is no more a promise but a living fact". Her experiments are documented over a thirty year period in a 13-volume series of books known as *Mother's Agenda*.

The Mother had many renowned visitors, such as the King of Nepal and the Dalai Lama after he had recently escaped Tibet. He asked The Mother if Tibet would one day be freed of Chinese rule. She affirmed it would one day happen.

In the mid 1960s she began Auroville, an international township sponsored by UNESCO. Auroville is located near Pondicherry and was to be a place "where men and women of all countries are able to live in peace and progressive harmony above all creeds, all politics and all nationalities." It was inaugurated in 1968 in a ceremony in which representatives of 121 nations and all the states of India placed a handful of their soil in an urn near the center of the city. Auroville continues to develop. The Mother died on November 17, 1973.

Nicholas Roerich

Birth name: Nikolai Konstantinovich Rerikh
Born: October 9, 1874 in St. Petersburg, Russia
13-Moon calendar date: 3.20, Limi, Kin 204

Nicholas Roerich was a planetary artist, explorer of mystical worlds, and a cultural revivalist—promoting peace through art and culture. Culture, in his mind, was closely related to the problems of cosmic evolution of humankind. He was also a world renowned painter, poet, writer and archaeologist.

From childhood, he was attracted to the arts as well as to the heritage of the East. In 1893, he simultaneously entered the Saint-Petersburg University Faculty of Law and the Emperor's Academy of Arts. He graduated from both. At 24, he became assistant to the Director of the Emperor's Art Encouragement Society Museum and, at the same time, editor assistant of the art magazine "Mir Iskusstva" ("World of Art").

In 1899, he met his soul mate and spiritual collaborator, Helena Ivanovna Shaposhnikova. They married in October 1901 and remained together for the rest of their lives. Helena brought an esoteric spirit to his life and introduced him to the works of Ramakrishna and Vivekananda, as well as the Upanishads, which they studied together. He credited Helena with being the inspiration behind all of his works. He wrote: "We created together, and not in vain it was said that the creations should bear two names—a woman's and a man's".

Because of his world repute as a painter and artist (he designed the stage set for Stravinsky's *Rite of Spring*), he was invited to the United States by the Art Institute of Chicago in 1920. Shortly after he and Helena joined the Theosophical Society. While living in New York, he founded several organizations to embody his ideal of art as a unifying force for humanity. He co-founded the Agni Yoga Society with Helena in the early 1920s.

He also began the Pax Cultura Initiative, which resulted in an international treaty known as the *Roerich Peace Pact*. Many nations agreed to it and officially adopted the Banner of Peace as a symbol of the preservation of cultural and artistic monuments. He wrote in the interest of the Banner of Peace:

I am not astonished that we receive so many enthusiastic responses to our Peace Banner. The past is filled with deplorable, sad and irreparable destructions. We see that not only in times of war but also during other errors, creations of human genius are destroyed. At the same time the elite of humanity understand that no evolution is possible without the cumulations of Culture. We understand how indescribably difficult are the ways of Culture. Hence the more carefully must we guard the paths which lead to it. It is our duty to create for the young generation traditions of Culture; where there is Culture, there is Peace; there is achievement; there is the right solution for the difficult social problems. Culture is the accumulation of highest Bliss, highest Beauty, highest Knowledge.
—Realm of Light Book II (1931); "Banner of Peace" Address (1931), p. 108

From 1924 to 1928, he organized an expedition in search of Shambhala over difficult-to-approach and little-explored regions of Central Asia. It was perhaps the major expedition of the twentieth century. Those on the expedition discovered dozens of new mountain peaks and passes which they marked on maps. They also discovered archeological monuments and rare manuscripts. The Roerich's carefully documented their adventure, much of which was released in *The Heart of Asia* and *Altai–Himalaya*. He created about five hundred paintings during this time.

After 1935, when he was barred from reentering the United States, he settled permanently with his family in Punjab where he became fascinated by studies of solar radiation and magnetism. Here, he founded the Institute of Himalayan Studies "Urusvati" and continued to write numerous books and essays on art, peace, and spirituality. He died December 13, 1947.

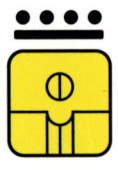

Part II • Crafting the Vehicle

Helena Roerich

Birth name: Helena Ivanovna Shaposhnikova
Born: February 12, 1879 in Saint-Petersburg, Russia
13 Moon calendar date: 8.6, Limi, Kin 230

Helena was a spiritual adept, writer, seeker of truth, and the main inspiration behind the founding of the Agni Yoga Society. This society drew on Vedic and Buddhist traditions as well as the writings of Madame Blavatsky and Theosophy.

She was born to a well-to-do aristocratic family. Her father was architect-academician, Ivan Shaposhnikov, and her mother was Ekaterina, born Golenischeva-Kutuzova, granddaughter of the great Field-Marshall. Through her maternal line, Helena was a distant relative of the famous Russian composer M. Mussorgsky.

By the age of seven, Helena could read and write in three languages. She was also a brilliant pianist and received an extensive musical education. Helena met the young painter Nicholas Roerich in 1899 at the estate of her aunt, Princess Y. Putyatina. They shared a deep spiritual bond and would marry two years later.

She was a strong speaker on behalf of the equality of sexes. In March, 1929, she wrote:

> *The approaching great epoch is closely connected with the ascendancy of woman. As in the best days of humanity, the future epoch will again offer woman her rightful place along side her eternal fellow traveler and co-worker, man. You must remember that the grandeur of the Cosmos is built by the dual Origin. Is it possible, therefore, to belittle one Element of It?*

She translated *The Secret Doctrine* into Russian and also claimed to receive regular communications from Master Morya, the master of Madame Blavatsky. Her first book, received from him was *The Leaves of M's Garden* (1924).

In her letters, Helena clearly defines the difference between a clairvoyant and a medium:

> *A clairvoyant is one who has raised the spinal serpent into the brain and by his*

> *growth earned the right of perceiving the invisible worlds with the aid of the third eye, or pineal gland. ... The clairvoyant can become such only after years, sometimes lives, of self-preparation; on the other hand, the medium ... may secure results in a few days.*

Helena continued to receive telepathic communication from Master Morya and wrote 13 books of Agni Yoga, also known as "Teaching of the Living Ethics", over a 17-year period (1920-1937). She also wrote several volumes of letters. The Agni Yoga Society was founded in the mid-1920s, beginning informally as a group of students who gathered to study her book *Leaves of M's Garden*.

From 1924 to 1928, Helena joined her husband on a difficult expedition in search of Shambhala. She was the only woman who passed the whole extremely difficult itinerary.

After Nicholas's passing in 1947, Helena strived to return to Russia. None of her appeals and submissions to the Soviet Embassy were answered. She died October 4, 1955.

Aleister Crowley

Birth name: Edward Alexander Crowley
Born October 12, 1875 in England
13-Moon calendar date: 3.23, Seli, Kin 52

Aleister Crowley claimed to be the reincarnation of Eliphas Levi. Crowley reshaped the theory of magic into a tool for the New Aeon, a contribution that has yet to be exceeded. His extensive writings on mysticism and magic clarified, extended and supplemented the core correspondences found in the Golden Dawn system, which influenced virtually every other magickal system to date.

Crowley was born just before midnight to a wealthy family of strict evangelical Christians called "The Plymouth Brethren". Crowley's father was a retired engineer, preacher and also a successful brewer of alcohol. As a boy, Crowley was encouraged by his father to love God and was receptive to his father's guidance initially. He used to love reading the Bible as a boy. This book was to become the central core of Crowley's philosophy.

Crowley's beloved father died when he was 11 and his mother sent him to Christian boarding school. He became disillusioned by all the hypocrisy he witnessed within the Christian faith and adopted a rebellious behavior toward the church. His behavior displeased his mother so much that she began calling him "The Beast" from the Book of Revelation. Crowley became extremely controversial in his lifetime and was frequently deemed by the tabloids as "the Wickedest Man in the World". By playing this role, he encouraged people to "learn to love what they loathed" rather than hating.

He attended Cambridge University where he studied English literature. In his third year at Cambridge he devoted himself consciously to the Great Work, or as he put it, "the work of becoming a spiritual being, free from the constraints, accidents and deceptions of material existence." At this time he was studying Madame Blavatsky and Theosophy and was at a loss for what to designate his own investigations. He chose the name Magick, with a "k". It seemed to him the most sublime, and also the most discredited, of all the available terms. He says:

> *I swore to rehabilitate Magick, to identify it with my own career; and to compel mankind to respect, love, and trust that which they scorned, hated and feared. I have kept my Word.*

In 1898 at age 23, Crowley joined the Hermetic Order of the Golden Dawn—but was later expelled from the Order. His life mission quickened on March 20, 1904, while in Cairo, Egypt, he claims to have invoked his "holy guardian angel" whom he knew as the Egyptian god, Horus. He claimed that Horus told him that a new magical aeon was coming and that he was to be its Prophet. This vision was followed by a clairaudient experience. Crowley claimed to hear a voice that dictated to him what would be his most famous work: *The Book of the Law*, with its main theme "Do what thou wilt shall be the whole of the law—Love is the law". This formed the basic precept of his spiritual cosmology known as *Thelema*.

After splitting with the Golden Dawn, Crowley co-founded another magickal order, the AA, or Astrum Argentium, in 1906 to further his occult studies. In 1910, he joined the O.T.O., the Ordo Templi Orientis, which he took over in 1921.

Crowley was the first to link the Taoist I Ching with the Kabbalistic Tree of Life. He revolutionized the Tarot with his famous Thoth deck, depicting far more daring and sensory images than previously known. He also conducted an extensive, exhaustive research into the esoteric meaning of numbers developing an encyclopedia of numerology and gematria. He realized Blavatsky's mythic Chaldean Book of Numbers, by publishing an extended number language dictionary known as the *Sepher Sephiroth* (Hebrew for *Book of Numbers*). This is the most extensive analysis to date of any number language.

Aleister Crowley died December 1st, 1947. The doctor caring for him died 24 hours later.

Alice Bailey

Birth name: Alice LaTrobe Bateman,
Born: June 16, 1880 in Manchester, England
13-Moon calendar date: 12.18, Kali, Kin 199

Alice Bailey was a cosmic channel, a prolific writer on mysticism and the founder of an international esoteric movement: The Arcane School or Lucis Trust, that sought to mobilize planetary good will. Bailey's life mission was to prepare the human race for the Age of Aquarius and the reappearance of the cosmic Christ. She believed the coming Christ was identical with the awaited Maitreya of the Eastern teachings.

Bailey was born to a wealthy aristocratic family and had a strict Anglican Christian upbringing. Her father was an engineer. She described her childhood as oversheltered and unhappy, so much so that she said she attempted suicide three times before the age of 15.

After high school she travelled to India where she did evangelical work with the British army. In 1907 she married and moved to America, where her husband became an Episcopalian minister. After the birth of three daughters she and her husband separated.

In America in 1917, she discovered the works of Madame Blavatsky and the following year became a member of the Theosophical Society at Krotona in Hollywood, California. She also became editor of its magazine *The Messenger*. At this point, she broke from Christianity altogether and in her autobiography she wrote that "a rabid, orthodox Christian worker [had] become a well-known occult teacher".

In 1919, she was telepathically contacted by Master Djwal Kul, whom she called 'the Tibetan'. She was, at first, very skeptical and reluctant to become a cosmic medium, but finally acceded.

The Master dictated to her a series of books over a period of 30 years, which she wrote down word for word. The themes of the books covered a wide range of fields including esoteric thought, spiritual psychology, hierarchy, karma, and the master plan, as well as the training for disciples, advanced study of the cosmic rays, international relationships and future world religion.

Bailey wrote much about those she called the "Masters of the Wisdom", which she believed to be a brotherhood of enlightened sages working under the guidance of "the Christ". She also sought to educate the public about the spiritual causes of the major world problems and how to solve them.

In 1920, she married fellow Theosophist, Foster Bailey. Foster described his wife's telepathic communications in the following way:

> *During the long course of the work, the minds of the Tibetan and Alice Bailey became so closely attuned that they were in effect—so far as much of the production of the teaching was concerned—a single joint projecting mechanism.*

The Bailey's were soon expelled from the Theosophical Society by president Annie Besant who was skeptical about Bailey's claims of telepathic communication with the Tibetan. Bailey claimed that she witnessed within the Society many works of "lower" psychic phenomena. Despite this, Bailey believed she was the disciple that HPB had prophesized to come in the twentieth century to give the "psychological key of cosmic creation" that would elucidate *The Secret Doctrine*. Bailey worked in complete recognition of this as her task and dedicated her first book *Treatise on Cosmic Fire* (1925) to HPB.

In 1923, Alice and Foster Bailey started The Arcane School to teach disciples how to "further the Great Universal Plan under the guidance of the inner hierarchy of spiritual masters led by Christ". This school was structured in a series of degrees similar to Freemasonry. This school still operates today under the name Lucis Trust in New York City. For a long time, the Lucis Trust was located across from the United Nations, which she felt necessary in order to establish "benign esoteric influences of the planetary and solar hierarchy in the new planetary organization."

She died December 15, 1949, 30 years and 30 days from her initial contact with The Tibetan.

Part II • Crafting the Vehicle

Dane Rudhyar

Birth name: Daniel Chenneviere
Born: March 23, 1895 in Paris
13-Moon calendar date: 9.17, Gamma, Kin 129

Dane Rudhyar was a planetary artist, cosmic astrologer, modern composer, philosopher, painter and esoteric initiate of the Western occult tradition. He made numerous invaluable contributions to human understanding in this time of planetary transition into a new global civilization and culture—the Age of Aquarius.

Of Celtic and Norman ancestry, Rudhyar began playing piano at age seven, and started composing for the piano in 1912. He was often ill as a child, and when he was 13, he had a kidney removed, which would later exempt him from military service in 1914. His father died in 1911, when he was 16. That same year, he received his baccalaureate in philosophy, and went on to study at the Paris Conservatory, where he wrote revolutionary articles about music and dance.

At age sixteen, Rudhyar had two spontaneous realizations that would shape his entire life's work: First, he realized that time is cyclic, and cyclicity governs civilizations as well as all aspects of existence; and second, he realized that Western civilization is coming to the "autumn" phase of its cycle of existence. Such realizations, changed his self-perception to that of a "seed man" seeking the New World. He gave up his birth name at the age of 17 after arriving in New York.

Rudhyar put forth such ideas as that both the cultural art whole and the planetary art whole and the future of the species lay in the restoration of humanity as a work of art. He also pioneered the idea of the planetary consciousness based on planetarization of consciousness. In this next stage of evolution, consciousness would be fully realized as a planetary phenomena, the noosphere. He also recognized that there is a galactic dimension to astrology and consciousness.

Rudhyar is the pioneer of transpersonal astrology, and began using the term "transpersonal" in 1930 long before Transpersonal Psychology was coined. He put forth the notion that astrology is not essentially predictive but rather productive of intuitive insights. Among those influenced by Rudhyar were Henry Miller, Leopold Stokowlski, Anais Nin, Roberto Assagiolo, Jose Arguelles and many others.

Though most well known for his astrology, Rudhyar's real love was music and he was greatly influenced by Theosophy and Henri Bergson. He viewed composers and musicians as mediums and magicians. He introduced the phrase "planetarization of consciousness" in the 1920s and 30s.

His most famous works were *Astrology Of Personality* in 1936 and *The Planetarization of Consciousness* (1971). He introduced archetypal concepts to astrology along with Mark Edmond Jones. They worked with the sabien symbols—the 12 houses of zodiac divided into 30 degrees each or 360 symbols.

According to Rudhyar, the basic function of humanity in the entire evolution of our planet is to provide the process of transition between a state of existence rooted in the biosphere and a superhuman state where conscious unanimity prevails. Rudhyar used astrology and other art forms to communicate his message of self-cultivation during the time of great transition. He felt that humanity should all try to think, feel and act in terms of a common new future which must be created together.

> *There is need for a new mind, a new way of thinking. There is need for the rise of new feelings, detached from the exclusivistic values of our particular cultures and geared to the needs and aims of humanity as a whole—understood as a spiritual being within which we all have particular functions to perform. There is need to act with a sense of purpose, not a purpose dictated by ego-desire, but the end purpose of our life as members of a global humanity.*

This end purpose is what Rudhyar calls: "participation in the Pleroma". Rudhyar died peacefully on September 13, 1985 in San Francisco. Jose Arguelles witnessed his body which he described to be in an ecstatic state.

Part II • Crafting the Vehicle

Bulent Corak

Birth name: Vedia Bulent Onsu (Çorak)
Born: November 28, 1923 in Bursa, Turkey
13-Moon calendar date: 5.14, Silio, Kin 199

Vedia Bulent Onsu Çorak is an incarnation of Sufi mystic Jalalludin al-Din Muhammad Rumi. Rumi was a Persian born poet and mystic that made the Islamic based Sufi sect famous for the Whirling Dervishes, and for his openness to other religions and beliefs.

Her birth occurred at the same time Colonel Ataturk established Turkey as a republic in the modern world, a fact of great importance to her and her vision of the role Turkey is to play in the New Age of Universal Unification. Ataturk is known as a universal genius and is known for voicing women's rights for the first time in the former seat of the Ottoman Empire.

With no more than a high school education, Mevlana was married to a highly successful medical doctor, which allowed her the leisure time for reflection and self cultivation. After some years of inner preparations, she began to receive messages on 1-11-1981 from the celestial authorities, and over a 12-year cycle transcribed what she heard into what is now known as *The Knowledge Book* or the *Golden Book of the Golden Age*.

The Knowledge Book is a Guide Book received through the channel ALPHA, a direct channel of the Lord. It was dictated from a sacred 18th dimension focal point from which all the books of religion had been revealed. The function of this cosmic book is to gather the entire Universe and our Planet into the consciousness of human integration, and by overcoming the separation that divides them to unite the religions and ways of thinking of our Planet. It is a book of unification for the age beyond religion.

In *The Knowledge Book*, it states:

> *The natural characteristic of your Planet is its acceptance of the latest given information as if it were the Final Information. Only those who can transcend this limit deserve to receive more advanced information. At the moment, in this Total with the world appearance on which you live, there are Friends who possess very advanced consciousnesses who had transcended this awareness and who had come from dimensions your planet does not know yet, and whose doors are open*

to all information.

This is the very reason why cosmic currents given by the mechanism of influences reach your planet as much as the power each consciousness can attract. Because, in order to be able to attract these influence currents, there is the need for an evolutionary and revolutionary thought potential.

In 1993, Mevlana founded the *World Brotherhood Union Universal Unification Center Association* and the *World Brotherhood Union Mevlana Supreme Foundation*. Both organizations are based in Istanbul, Turkey, but with international outreach, and set out from Ataturk's principle: "Peace at home, peace in the universe."

The aim of these organizations is to prepare human beings for the reality of Unified Humanity, to provide the evolution of Humanity towards a Universal Consciousness, to study celestial information by supporting scientific work and to cooperate with other establishments serving on the Universal Path.

Their universal call, as issued by Mevlana, is as follows:

Our World, which is at the verge of a great change is henceforth changing its crust. The days we will be living in the future will be very different from today. The mass pains felt with these fast changes are investments made into the Golden Age of the morrows.

This is a transition period. And in this period there are Great Awareness Attainments in the Human Totalities, and henceforth, the human being who has reached awareness is now expected to love, to respect and to embrace Humanity by getting out of his individual consciousness. This is an awareness of unity. Because the Supreme Consciousnesses who can transcend their individual consciousness, who can share their love, who can even embrace their enemy will found the happy world of the morrows. And the morrows will bring unexpected beauties to our Planet.

Other Notable Esotericists

Other esoteric personalities worth noting are Polish mathematician and occultist Hoene Wronski, who influenced Eliphas Levi as well as Max and Alma Theon. Max and Alma Theon were highly regarded esotericists who made their home in France and Algiers. Max was a skilled Kabbalist and deeply influenced by Wronski, who incidentally was also a great influence on psycho mathematician Charles Henry (1859-1926), another hermetic personality (see *Charles Henry and the Formation of a Psychophysical Aesthetic*, Jose Arguelles, 1972).

The Mother, then known as Mirra, often stayed with and learned many of the occult arts from Max and Alma in the first decade of the twentieth century before meeting Sri Aurobindo. The Mother claimed that Alma was one of the "most remarkable" clairvoyants possessed of many paranormal powers. On one occasion, the Mother said that Alma was quite exhausted and said she was going to replenish her energy. She lay down and asked the Mother to bring her a grapefruit and place it on her solar plexus and then return in one hour. When she returned the Mother said that the grapefruit was flat and Alma's energy was renewed.

According to the Mother, Max Theon taught Madame Blavatsky the Kabbalah in Egypt. His teachings revolved around the seven planes of existence, evolution, reincarnation of the soul or higher self as distinct from personality. Around 1900, Max and Alma produced the unpublished six volumes, known as *Cosmic Tradition*, a precursor or foreshadow of *Cosmic History Chronicles*. The six volume series remained unedited and was only given to advanced students. It was a cosmological doctrine, written in French that tells the story of creation and the history of the world similar to *The Secret Doctrine*. The Theon's, founded the Cosmic Movement using the seal of Solomon or six pointed star as its symbol. The Mother would later design a similar symbol for Sri Aurobindo. The Mother claimed that Theon and Aurobindo arrived at similar conclusions about consciousness without ever physically meeting.

We begin to see a whole esoteric patterning or weaving during the nineteenth and twentieth centuries, similar to the generation of rock and roll in the 1960s and 1970s where all the great artists intermingled and exchanged styles and influence. In this regard, Eliphas Levi can be likened to the Elvis of modern esotericism. It is interesting to note that Levi was 17 in 1827, the year William Blake died.

A few other esotericists worth noting are Paul Foster Case (Builders of the Adytum), Manly P. Hall (Philosophical Research Society), Arthur Edward Waite (one of the leading proponents of the Golden Dawn System and designer of the most renowned Tarot deck).

Also noteworthy in relation to Crowley is S.L. MacGregor Mathers and W. Wynn Westcott, the esotericists behind the creation of the Golden Dawn, the nineteenth century Kabbalistic-Masonic Order. Mathers dedicated countless years in the stacks of the British Museum and other European libraries, synthesizing the essential symbolic correspondences for the tradition of Western ritual magic.

Gurdjieff, Blavatsky and the Roerich's

Gurdjieff's life paralleled that of Madame Blavatsky's in many ways. Both were in search of harmony and both undertook arduous travels, namely through central Asia, in their search for hidden truths. Gurdjieff traveled extensively in the Caucasus, where he is said to have received a number of initiations in the Kurdish foothills. He would later set up schools in the West that transmitted the cosmological and psychological teachings he had learned during his travels. Mme. Blavatsky was most remarkable as she traveled the world in steamboats and locomotives visiting North America, Mexico, Middle East, Tibet, South Africa, India, Egypt, Europe, etc. Her remarkable life endowed her with a global personality and character. Blavatsky claims to have lived for seven years in Tibet.

Gurdjieff's father was intent on sending him to seminary school in the southern Caucasus (now known as Georgia). But instead, he went his own way and founded an intimate society known as the Seekers of Truth. After reading the works of Mme. Blavatsky, Gurdjieff and his small entourage traveled to India seeking to discover the hidden mystical places that they had read about.

One of these places was the Surmang Monastery (This is the same monastery of which Chogyam Trungpa, the eleventh Trungpa tulku, was abbot before escaping to the West in 1959). However, Gurdjieff did not find many of the other hidden places, and so concluded that they did not exist.

From the 1890s until he arrived in Moscow in 1914, Gurdjieff spent much time traveling. Gurdjieff was accidentally shot three times on three different occasion during his treacherous travels. Like Mme. Blavatsky, he also lived in Tibet for about three years, and even had a wife and children there. Problems with his health caused him to leave. While in Tibet, he met Lama Dorje. Lama Dorje was a famous Tibetan lama who found himself in St. Petersburg during the Revolution at a particular Buddhist temple with stained glass windows designed by Nicholas Roerich.

It is interesting to note that both Gurdjieff and Mme. Blavatsky were basically from a Russian background. Just as Mme. Blavatsky traveled for 10 years without keeping a record,

We begin to see a whole esoteric patterning or weaving during the nineteenth and twentieth centuries, similar to the generation of rock and roll in the 1960s and 1970s ...

so did Gurdjieff travel for about the same time with no known record of his doings or whereabouts. Blavatsky ended her first long travels back in Russia possessing many "strange powers", as described by her sister Vera. Likewise after Gurdjieff's long travels, he emerged with powerful teachings of many little known masters.

Continuing in a similar vein were Nicholas and Helena Roerich, who also traveled to Central Asia between 1926 and 1928 in search of Shambhala. The Roerichs were deeply influenced by the works of Mme. Blavatsky and were members of the Theosophical Society. The Roerich's were even financed to search for Shambhala. Their search took them through Tibet, and all throughout central Asia, arriving in Altai in 1927. Nicholas Roerich also produced a copious amount of his now famous mystical paintings during the journey.

While they did not find Shambhala, the Roerich's did uncover many treasures along the way, including mystical objects such as the "mani stone", a mysterious object of non-terrestrial origin. They also returned with the "Banner of Peace", which was the symbol used by Nicholas Roerich when he created an international peace pact in 1935.

Henry Wallace, vice president of the United States for Roosevelt was deeply involved in the teachings of Roerich. It was at this very time—1935—that the U.S. dollar bill was redesigned to bear on it the Masonic symbolism of the 13-tiered pyramid capped by the all-seeing eye. This is a notable example of esoteric influence on the world.

Gurdjieff's methods and techniques exemplify the cosmo-psychological principle of modern occult masters. His teachings are akin to a crazy wisdom Zen or Sufi master, pinpointing people's inauthentic selves and then creating circumstances for them to expose their falsity in order to shed their robotic personalities. Gurdjieff's work laid a great emphasis on an every day way of tracking the false self in order to understand the nature of the true self.

Gurdjieff was acutely aware of the need to create a template for a new evolutionary type and much of his teaching has to do with the integration of the physical, emotional and the mental bodies. He said most humans are not integrated and are therefore

Gurdjieff's methods and techniques exemplify the cosmo-psychological principle of modern occult masters.

"sleepwalkers". This unconscious state creates habitual or robotic forms of routine behaviors that limit and enclose us in our own self-created time-space bubble. Gurdjieff strove to get people to break through their limitations and become participants in the "great octave of cosmic harmony".

> **GURDJIEFF AND THE OCTAVE**
>
> Gurdjieff's work on the octave is based on the law of the three and the law of the seven. His theory of the octave is symbolized by the 7 + 1 whole tones of the diatonic musical scale: do re mi fa so la ti do'. The first do' is the primary or absolute. Re is the lunar aspect. Mi is the Earth or the single planet. Fa is the planetary system. Sol is the sun or the star. La is the galaxy. Ti is the whole universe and Do' is the higher or supreme absolute. This symbolic scheme is very important and influential on esoteric thought. It can also be found in earlier hermetic thought where it is the basis of the music or harmony of the spheres.
>
> The great octave is very much like the octave of the Pythagoreans or Kepler and the Neo-Platonists—this octave connects your bodies with the higher cosmic forces. The moving body is represented by the first three notes: do', re, mi; the emotional body is represented by the next three notes: fa so la, and the higher mental body is represented by the last two notes, ti and do' is the supreme absolute.
>
> Gurdjieff speaks of a "shock" that needs to occur in the transition from mi to fa, which connects the physical body with the emotional astral body. Another shock occurs at "ti" from the higher mental body, to the Absolute, "do'". This is a cosmic teaching that is a rephrasing of the Neo-Platonic teaching of the harmony of the spheres. The point is to connect your three bodies in order to arrive at your true nature.

SYNCHRONIC CROSSOVERS OF ESOTERIC PERSONALITY

When studying the lives of each of these personalities, many synchronicities can be gleaned. Synchronicity is how divine law reveals itself. Here are a few.

- Eliphas Levi said he believed in the "existence of a universal 'secret doctrine' of magic throughout history, everywhere in the world." Later Madame Blavatsky, greatly influenced by Levi, would write *The Secret Doctrine*.

- Crowley, Gurdjieff, Nicholas and Helena Roerich, Alice Bailey, Dane Rudhyar and more than likely the Mother, studied the works of Mme. Blavatsky at one time or another.

- Crowley was born precisely at the midpoint of the founding of the Theosophical Society on October 12, 1875. The Theosophical Society was founded on September 7, 1875 and the official opening was on November 17, 1875. There are 71 days between these two dates with Crowley arriving in the exact middle. Eliphas Levi died at the beginning of that year. This marked the beginning of modern occultism.

- Crowley claimed to be the reincarnation of Eliphas Levi. Crowley picked up the thread of Levi's work right down to the writing of the *Book of the Law* with its famous slogan: Do what thou wilt is the whole of the law, love is the law. Levi says: "Love and do what thou wilt". Apparently to balance Levi's life as a Catholic Priest, in 1920, Crowley founded the anti-monastery Abbey of Thelema in Cefalia, Italy as a "collegiums and spiritual sanctum".

- Both Eliphas Levi and Sri Aurobindo were jailed for their radical politics.

- In 1853, Levi invoked Apollonius of Tyana to physical appearance (written about in *Transcendental Magic, its Doctrine and Ritual*). Crowley would later do a similar invocation in which appeared Horus and the *Book of the Law* was revealed.

- The dollar bill has the word Annuit Coeptus Novis Ordo Seclorum surrounding this symbol. This means, "announcing the birth of the new order of the ages". FDR was influenced by the Masons to place the great seal on the dollar bill. The official magazine of the Masons is called, "The New Age Magazine".

- Aleister Crowley recognized Blavatsky as a Sister of A.'A.' (i.e. a Master of the Temple), specifically pointing her out as his immediate predecessor in "The Temple of Truth", published in *The Heart of the Master* through O.T.O. in 1938. Crowley reissued Blavatsky's *Voice of the Silence* with his own commentary as Liber LXXI.

- Many parallels have been drawn between the vision of Sri Aurobindo and that of Teilhard de Chardin (see Teilhard de Chardin and Sri Aurobindo—*A Focus on Fundamentals*, 1973 by K.D. Sethna). Sri Aurobindo holds that humankind as an entity is not the last rung on the evolutionary scale, but can evolve spiritually beyond its current limitations associated with an essential ignorance to a future state of supramental existence. This further evolutionary step would lead to a divine life on Earth characterized by a supramental or truth-consciousness, and a transformed and divinized life and material form. (*Life Divine* book II, ch. 27-28)

- Both Gurdjieff and Crowley were said to have had short-lived careers as spies. Crowley once visited Gurdjieff at his Harmonious Institute.

- At one time Gurdjieff lived in Istanbul near the Galata tower next door to the Mevlana order of Sufis. This location was nearby where Mevlana (Bulent Çorak), the reincarnation of Rumi and founder of the Mevlana order, was to be born and live.

- Alice Bailey and Helena Roerich were born only a year apart. Though they never met, both of their teachings are based on theosophy and classical occultism. Bailey was a teacher of theosophy

The Cosmic History Chronicles • Volume IV

ESOTERIC PERSONALITY — COSMIC FUNCTION

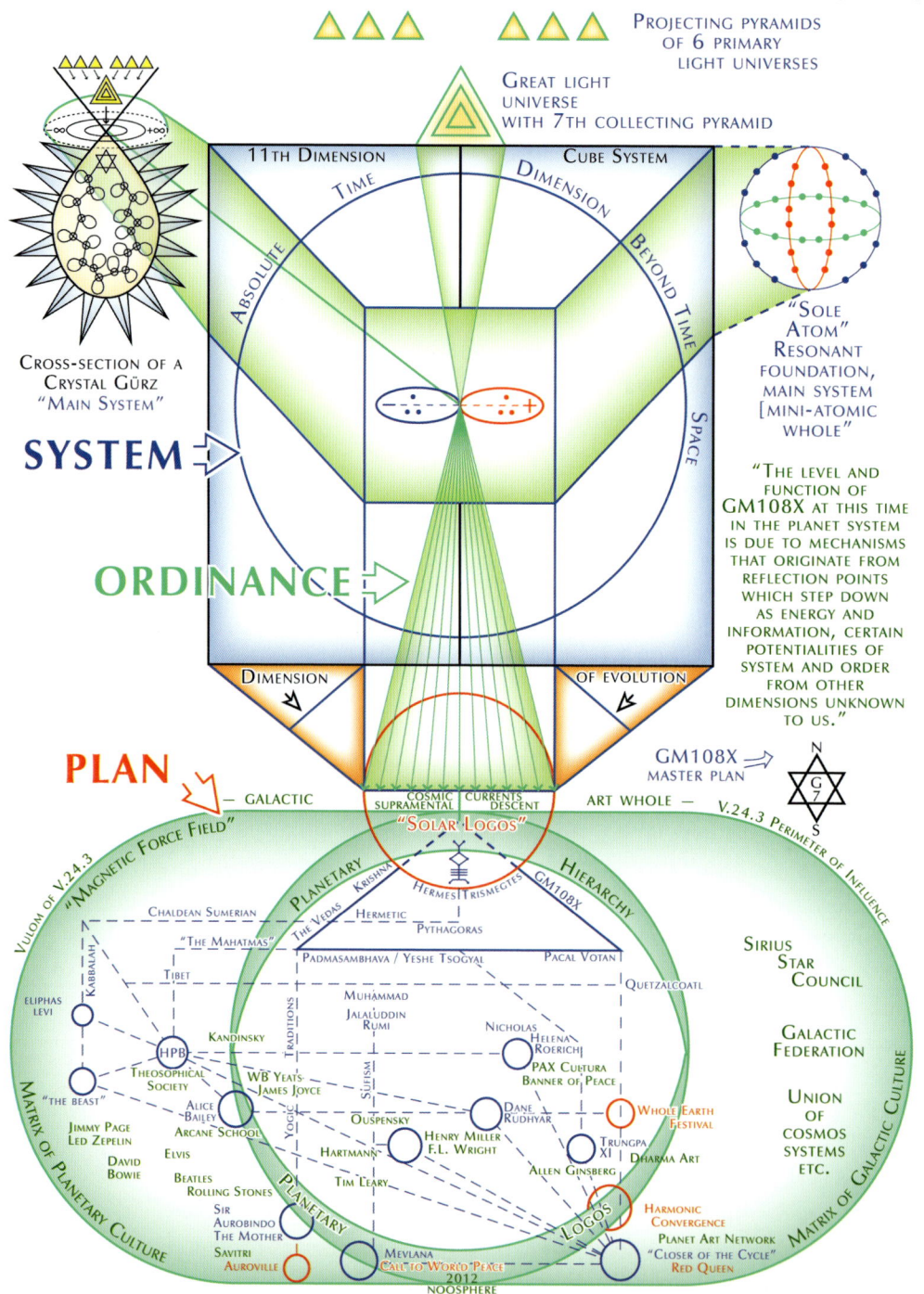

▲▲▲ ▲▲▲ Projecting pyramids of 6 primary light universes

Great light universe with 7th collecting pyramid

11th Dimension — Cube System

Time Dimension

Absolute — Beyond Time

Space

Cross-section of a Crystal Gürz "Main System"

"Sole Atom" Resonant foundation, main system [mini-atomic whole]

SYSTEM ⇨

ORDINANCE ⇨

"The level and function of GM108X at this time in the planet system is due to mechanisms that originate from reflection points which step down as energy and information, certain potentialities of system and order from other dimensions unknown to us."

Dimension of Evolution

PLAN ⇩

— Galactic   Cosmic Supramental   Currents Descent   Art Whole —

"Solar Logos"

GM108X Master Plan ⇨

V.24.3 Perimeter of Influence

Vulom of V.24.3 "Magnetic Force Field"

Planetary Hierarchy

Chaldean Sumerian — The Vedas / Krishna — Hermetic
"The Mahatmas" — Padmasambhava / Yeshe Tsogyal — Pythagoras — Hermes Trismegistus — GM108X
Tibet — Pacal Votan
Kabbalah — Muhammad — Quetzalcoatl
Eliphas Levi — Jalaluddin Rumi — Nicholas & Helena Roerich
Kandinsky — Pax Cultura Banner of Peace
HPB — Sufism
Theosophical Society — WB Yeats / James Joyce — Ouspensky — Dane Rudhyar
"The Beast" — Alice Bailey — Henry Miller / F.L. Wright — Whole Earth Festival
Jimmy Page / Led Zepelin — Arcane School — Hartmann — Trungpa XI — Dharma Art
David Bowie — Elvis — Tim Leary — Allen Ginsberg
Beatles / Rolling Stones
Sir Aurobindo / The Mother — Harmonic Convergence
Savitri — Mevlana — Planet Art Network "Closer of the Cycle" Red Queen
Auroville — Call to World Peace 2012
Noosphere

Sirius Star Council
Galactic Federation
Union of Cosmos Systems etc.

Matrix of Planetary Culture — Planetary Logos — Matrix of Galactic Culture

Part II • Crafting the Vehicle

in California and then in New York. Roerich translated *The Secret Doctrine* into Russian in the early 1930s. They both proclaimed ideas of brotherhood of all nations and religions, and of the synthesis of science, religion, occultism and cultures of different continents.

- Both Bailey and Roerich studied Oriental and esoteric philosophies and met Masters from Shambhala: Helena Roerich in 1920 (Master Morya), and Alice Bailey in 1919 (Master Djwal Kul). This was the time when the League of Nations was established and many countries made an attempt to establish a body of planetary government. The Organization of the United Nations became a legal successor of the League of Nations in 1946.

- Dane Rudhyar often said that the New Age actually began in 1875 with the founding of the Theosophical Society and the subsequent introduction of new ideas, perceptions and belief structures owing greatly to Mme. Blavatsky.

- Dane Rudhyar met Alice Bailey in Hollywood in the early 1920s when she was writing her book, *Treatise on Cosmic Fire*. Bailey liked Rudhyar's articles, and encouraged him to write a treatise developing their contents. She then published his book, *Astrology of Personality,* through Lucis Press, the publishing company she and her husband had started in connection with their Arcane School. Rudhyar dedicated the book to her.

- Although Mevlana could be described as an Islamic reformist, she is anything but a traditional Muslim. Fully the progeny of modern Turkey, she takes great pride in her connection with its founder, Ataturk, whom she claims in a mystical way to be also the founder of her Mevlana Foundation. Married for many years to a medical doctor and producing one daughter, Mevlana's life most closely resembles that of Alice Bailey in style and method. However, her channeled information is synthesized into a single magnum opus: *The Knowledge Book*, which has no comparison. This large book contains much thought-provoking higher-dimensional information from various galactic sources all in preparation for the "Golden Age". The principle source she refers to is the *Alpha Channel.*

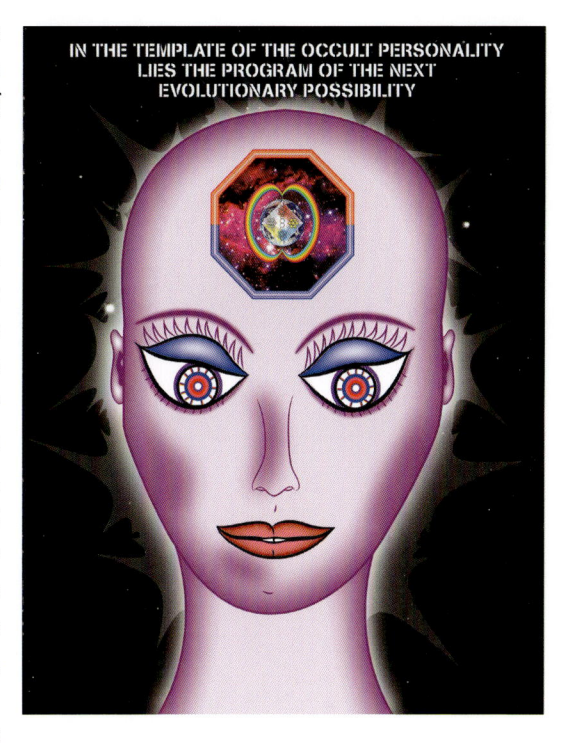

IN THE TEMPLATE OF THE OCCULT PERSONALITY LIES THE PROGRAM OF THE NEXT EVOLUTIONARY POSSIBILITY

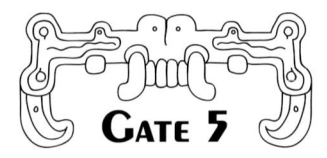

Gate 5
Creative Power—Taming the Forces

You pause to integrate the vast esoteric personalities you have just encountered. Suddenly the light on the path extinguishes and you are in the dark. A strange fear wells up inside of you. You sit and contemplate the darkness for what seems like eternity. Suddenly, you notice a sliver of light beaming from above. In a flash—you realize that everything that has come to light was born out of darkness! As you make your way toward the light, you spot an ancient bookcase—You notice two titles: "Literature of the Future" and "Songs from the Golden Age". Suddenly you hear the echo of a voice—is that Sri Aurobindo? You wonder. The voice repeats the following sentence three times: "Behind the visible events in the world there is always a mass of invisible forces at work unknown to the outward minds of men."

As we make our way through the labyrinth, we encounter many unsuspected energies and spirits that must be tamed and overcome. To greater or lesser degrees, we are involved in an alchemical process of transmutation—transforming the lower, negative forces back into spiritual light.

It is only when the light appears that we realize we have been living in a world of shadows. Once we have glimpsed the light, we wish to follow it to its source—but this is not always easy. The shadows have strange powers to which we humans often succumb without perceiving. These shadows are the veiled corridors of our own mind that we have grown so accustomed to that we mistake them for reality. But they are not—and so we enter the sacred struggle.

On the journey, often treacherous, old forms must be constantly broken up to clear the way for the new. The greatest ally on this path is the power of Imagination—this is the creative force that fuels our journey. Imagination incorporates and provides another form of reality than reported by our senses. By directed focus of the imaginal will we can displace lower forces and project the higher vision. In fact, disciplined exertion of creative imaginative force is the very means for overcoming the lower forces and obstacles.

We are now being called upon to summon our untapped creative powers, overcome all obstacles and remain on the path of light. We must master our inner "demons" and redirect their chaotic energy in order to build the inner temple of our evolving soul. The true initiate knows that aversions only lead to enslavement; by liberating ourselves from all forms of hatred or delusion, we thereby transcend historical dualism and attain freedom.

In the development of hermetic tradition, from the Middle Ages to modern times, the initiate always seeks to understand the nature of the spirits—both the dark and light orders—and how to tame and control these forces. Sri Aurobindo says, "As there are powers of knowledge and forces of light, so there are powers of ignorance and tenebrous forces of darkness whose work is to prolong the reign of ignorance and inconscience."

He points out that the "hostile" forces have existed in yogic experience since the days of the Vedas and Zoroaster in Asia and in Europe also from ancient times. Hermes explains in Book 9 of the *Corpus Hermeticum*, that *Nous* brings forth both good and evil, depending on if he receives input from God or from demons. Aleister Crowley says, "The pious pretense that evil does not exist only makes it vague, enormous and menacing." Mme. Blavatsky made a similar statement when she said, "Resist not evil", that is, "do not complain of or feel anger against the inevitable disagreeables of life. Forget yourself (in working for others). If men revile, persecute, or wrong one, why resist? In the resistance we create greater evils."

According to Rosicrucian tenets, light and darkness are identical in themselves, being only divisible in the human mind. Robert Fludd said, "Darkness adopted illumination in order to make itself visible." In the Gospel of John it says, "And the light shineth in darkness; and the darkness comprehendeth it not."

Why do negative forces exist? Buddhist teachings describe devas or dakinis that are either benevolent or mischievous and need to be tamed. The Chod practices of the higher vajrayana teachings of Tibet are directed at casting out, destroying or pacifying negative spiritual forces. These forms are ultimately understood as projections of the play of the mind.

The hermeticists are the shamans of the civilized world, working with the nonphysical, subtle energies of the spirit realm.

In Muslim tradition, we find a description of the *jinn*, an astral force counterpart to the human realm. The jinn energies seek to dissuade or delude us on our quest for higher harmony. The jinn can also be tamed by enlightened masters, such as Solomon. The Quran says that Solomon enlisted the jinn, by God's leave, to make for him anything he wanted, such as niches, statues, deep pools and heavy cooking pots.

If the negative energies or jinn are not tamed, they can manifest as addictions of all types: drugs, food, alcohol, sex, etc., as well as all forms of mental addictions. When morphine, hashish and opium use became prevalent in the nineteenth century, they seemed to unleash demonic forces from which many suffered. Aleister Crowley, a well-known drug addict, suffered in this way, along with countless musicians, artists and other creative types who have died battling these forces. Lower forces are often drawn to the open channel of the artists and "sensitive" types in the process of the quest (see *CHC*,

Vol. III). Because of this, the Masonic order gave names to many of these forces and created various spells to cast them away.

We must always remember that even these seemingly adverse forces are part of the total play of the Divine. Part of the Plan, then, was to create the human civilization as an inversion layer where harmony becomes less and less apparent. As harmony becomes less apparent so does the need increase to seek the truth. For this reason, the seeker is always in search of harmony.

> **MEDITATION FOR BANISHING NEGATIVE ENERGY**
>
> The following is an inner teaching given to Yeshe Tsogyal by Padmasambhava for the purpose of banishing evil spirits. Padmasambhava told Yeshe Tsogyal: "It is of utmost importance to train diligently in this way. Through exerting yourself in this way, you will annihilate the evil spirit and turn away from samsara." (*Dakini Teachings*, p. 53)
>
> 1. Not to apprehend names as being things since all labels and names of outer things have no existence in your mind.
> 2. To acknowledge that everything which comprises the world and the beings within it has no self-nature, although it appears, just like dreams and magic.
> 3. To seek out three times a day and three times a night this mind that fixates on various objects, although nothing whatever exists.
> 4. Not to stray from the meaning that is nameless and devoid of extremes. Even though you search your mind it is not found to be anything whatsoever.

In our pursuit of higher harmony, we must, at some time or another, reconcile the meaning and myth of Satan or the Devil. Crowley is often identified as the "Beast"; Gurdjieff wrote *All and Everything, Beelzebub's Tales to his Son*; and Blavatsky named her theosophical journal, *Lucifer*.

In the Bible, Lucifer is described as the bringer of light and one of the highest archangels, but then disobeyed God and became the tester of humankind. In *The Secret Doctrine*, Blavatsky says that the real ruler of this world is Satan—meaning that people prefer to be misled than choose the straight path.

The Secret Doctrine states the following:

> *... The Devil is now called Darkness by the church, whereas in the Bible, he is called the "Son of God" (see Job), the bright star of the early morning, Lucifer (see Isaiah). There is a whole dogmatic craft in the reason why the first Archangel, who sprang from the Depths of chaos, was called Lux (Lucifer), the "Luminous Son of the Morning", or manvantaric dawn. He was transformed by the church into Lucifer or Satan, because he is higher and older than Jehovah, and had to be sacrificed to the new dogma.*

In the Quran, Satan begs for respite from God. So God grants Satan respite until the end of time or "Day of Resurrection". There are a number of instances in the Quran where Satan misleads people and the people get mad and blame Satan, rather than take responsibility for their actions. To this Satan replies, "Maybe I whispered something in your ear, but you're the one who did it." Satan also professes his belief in God a number of times in the Quran. This indicates that Satan is God's means of testing humanity, for God actually allows Satan to do what he does for a specific reason, to the point of ruling the world. The Quran says when we hear a whisper from the devil, it is simply a cue to remember our higher self.

We also find Satan in *The Knowledge Book*. Here, the devil signifies the integration of the opposites in the world of duality. From this perspective, we see that in the historical cycle, Satan performs an important function of helping to raise human consciousness. By playing the role of tempter, Satan offers humanity the impetus to lift its mind to a higher level and cultivate the will-to-good. The human will was created weak during the historical cycle for the purpose of learning, growing and strengthening.

During the historical cycle, humans needed church and religious forces to objectify and personify Satan—this served as gauge or measure to lift higher. In reality, organized religion is just a prop that relies on intermediaries to access the creative source. This prop naturally fades out as the next stage of universal reality ushers in.

Consider the following poem, *God's Labour*, by Sri Aurobindo:

> *My gaping wounds are a thousand and one*
> *And the Titan kings assail,*
> *But I cannot rest till my task is done*
> *And wrought the eternal will ...*
>
> *A voice cried, "Go where none have gone!*
> *Dig deeper, deeper yet*
> *Till thou reach the grim foundation stone*
> *And knock at the keyless gate."*
>
> *I saw that falsehood was planted deep*
> *At the very root of things*
> *Where the gray Sphinx guards God's riddle sleep*
> *On the Dragon's outspread wings.*
>
> *I left the surface gods of mind*
> *And life's unsatisfied seas*
> *And plunged through the body's alleys blind*
> *To the nether mysteries*

I have delved through the dumb Earth's dreadful heart
And heard her black mass bell.
I have seen the source whence her agonies part
And the inner reason of hell.

Transmutation

In India the hostile forces are broadly divided into three categories: asuras, rakshasas and pischachas.

1. *Asuras* (jealous gods) belong to the mental and higher vital levels. Asuras are those who are radically against the work of the divine evolution and do everything possible to thwart it. This is due to pure self complacency which has no aspiration for anything more elevated, as the material embodiment of divine beings on Earth would bring the mastery they are now exerting here to an end.

2. *Rakshasas* (far below the asuras) are beings of the lower vital who resemble etheric ogres. They are hungry ghosts that feed on all kinds of embodied and disembodied forces. They can take on seductive shapes and even appear as divinities: they mainly roam in dark (unconscious) places.

3. *Pischachas* (most common) are those little people that take pleasure in playing annoying tricks that pester humans, making our lives into an uninterrupted affair of unease, dissatisfaction and restlessness.

According to the Mother the only medium that can destroy these hostile forces is the Creative Force. She says:

> *There is only one force in the world that can destroy them categorically, without any hope of return, and this is a force belonging to the supramental creative power. It is a force from beyond the supramental world and therefore not at everyday's disposal. It is a luminous force of a dazzling whiteness, so brilliant that ordinary eyes would be blinded if they looked into it. It suffices that a being of the vital world be touched by this light to make it dissolve instantly.*

The Creative Power and the Sacred Arts

Artistic or aesthetic intention expressed through hermetic thought has had a profound and permanent effect on modern culture. The impact of hermetic thought and personalities prove that the artistic transmutation of energy is the highest path for the evolution from the human to the superhuman; from the mental to the supermental.

THE CREATIVE POWER

> *Many poets, and all mystic and occult writers, in all ages and countries, have declared that behind the visible are chains of conscious beings, who are not of heaven but of Earth, who have no inert form, but change according to their whim, or the mind that sees them. You cannot lift your hand without influencing or being influenced by hordes—the visible world is merely their skin. In dreams do we go amongst them, and contact them. They are, perhaps, human souls in the crucible— these creatures of whim!*
> —W.B. Yeats

> *To find the likeness of your own heart, do what you love and make it into art!*
> —The Arcturians

Until we witness the entire illumination of the world, the best way to transmute lower forces is to channel them into artistic production and creative behavior.

    Artistic immersion combined with esoteric thought represents a template of evolutionary emergence of the occult personality. The occult personality is a laboratory of psychocosmic functions. All esoteric personalities are experimenters, using their minds and bodies as the laboratory to ultimately peel away the conditioned self and arrive at the true or objective self.

    Many famous works of art in literature and music are heavily influenced by occult thought. Most occult masters have strong inclinations to investigate the forces that lie beneath human existence through application of cosmic imagery, words and music. For example, Eliphas Levi was a talented artist and illustrated his books with symbols and diagrams, many of which have profound archetypal resonance. He also wrote much regarding the importance of imagination:

> *Behold! The greatest magician in the universe! It is she who makes the memory yield its fruit, who realizes beforehand the Possible, and invents even the Impossible. To her miracles cost nothing. She transports houses and mountains through the air, places whales in the sky, and stars in the sea, gives Paradise to the hashish or opium eaters, offers kingdoms to inebriates, and makes pirouette dance with joy under the mild pail. Such is Imagination!*

Levi influenced writer and occultist Sir Edward Bulwer-Lytton, with whom he met in 1861. Bulwer-Lytton wrote *The Last Days of Pompeii* and other occult books bringing the idea of magic to light in the last years of the nineteenth century. Bulwer-Lytton also wrote *The Coming Race* (This mysterious text had a strong influence on elitist thinking and introduced the concept of the *Vril*, the occult force). It was while visiting Bulwer-Lytton that Levi experienced an apparitional manifestation of Apollonius of Tyanus (see previous chapters).

The following poem, *The Magician*, written by Levi, is an example of using the arts, in this case, poetry, to transform the lower energies.

> *O Lord, deliver me from hell's great fear and gloom!*
> *Loose thou my spirit from the larvae of the tomb!*
> *I seek them in their dread abodes without affright:*
> *On them will I impose my will, the Law of Light.*
>
> *I bid the night conceive the glittering hemisphere.*
> *Arise, O sun, arise! O moon, shine white and clear!*
> *I seek them in their dread abodes without affright:*
> *On them will I impose my will, the Law of Light.*
>
> *Their faces and their shapes are terrible and strange.*
> *These devils by my might to angels I will change.*
> *These nameless horrors I address without affright:*
> *On them will I impose my will, the Law of Light.*
>
> *These are the phantoms pale of mind astonished view,*
> *Yet none but I their blasted beauty can renew;*
> *For to the abyss of hell I plunge without affright:*
> *On them will I impose my will, the Law of Light.*

Mme. Blavatsky was greatly influenced by both Eliphas Levi and Bulwer-Lytton, and quoted them both extensively in her works. This larger esoteric body of knowledge that Mme. Blavatsky synthesized as *Theosophy* had a great influence on all aspects of nineteenth and twentieth century culture, particularly the arts. Some well known artists and writers influenced by theosophy include authors James Joyce and D.H. Lawrence, Frank Baum (author of *The Wizard of Oz*), painter Wassily Kandinsky and poet and nobel laureate W.B. Yeats. Yeats was also a member of the Hermetic Order of the Golden Dawn and wrote poetry dedicated to the lodges of ritual magic.

Other notables who studied her works, many of whom became theosophists were: Thomas Edison, Albert Einstein, William James, E.M. Forster, Christmas Humphreys (Buddhologist), Edward Conze, Nicholas Flammarion (French astronomer), Sir William Crookes (chemist and physicist), Piet Mondrian (abstract painter), Maurice Maeterlinck (playwright), Gustav Mahler, S. Radhakrishnan (President of India), Annie Besant (founder of the Indian National Congress), Rudolf Steiner (founder of anthrotheosophy, Waldorf schools and new agricultural methods) and Krishnamurti (philosopher).

Mahatma Gandhi joined the Theosophical Society in London at the Blavatsky Lodge, March 26, 1891, just a few months before Madame Blavatsky's death. It was at the Theosophical Society that Gandhi received his first copy of the *Bhagavad-Gita*. It is also well documented that one of Elvis's favorite books was the *Voice of Silence* by Madame Blavatsky, and he was known to quote this book during his later stage performances. Elvis also owned copies of *Isis Unveiled and The Secret Doctrine*, as well as two of Dane Rudhyar's books, *Fire Out of Stone* and *New Mansions for New Men (Lucis Trust)*. This is merely to demonstrate the power of occult thought on the mainstream arts.

In 1965, Rudhyar did an in-depth (23 page) astrological report for Elvis, upon his request, that included charts of his mother and father, as well as his then wife Priscilla. (In 1972, Rudhyar also prepared an in-depth astrological report for Jose Arguelles–Valum Votan).

As controversial as he was, Aleister Crowley also had a strong influence on culture and the arts. Among those influenced by Crowley include Aldous Huxley and rock musicians, Jimmy Page, Jim Morrison, Ozzy Osbourne and David Bowie. Page who purchased Crowley's home in Scotland said of Crowley, "I feel he is a misunderstood genius of the twentieth century. Because his whole thing was liberation of the person, of the entity and that restriction that would fool you up. He was like an eye to the world, into the forthcoming situation." The Beatles included a picture of Crowley on the cover of their *Sgt. Pepper's* album.

The point is that the occult, magic or esoteric philosophies have always been at the core of the creative process. For example, Shakespeare made allusions to magical practices in several of his plays, including *Midsummer Night's Dream* and *The Tempest*, which are filled with alchemical themes, esoteric symbolism, and initiation rites.

Part II • Crafting the Vehicle

Sri Aurobindo and Sacred Poetry

Sri Aurobindo was also a cosmic poet and attached great significance to art and culture for the spiritual evolution of humankind. He believed that a new, deep, and intuitive poetry was a powerful force to shift consciousness and accelerate the coming of the supermental human. Aurobindo's epic poem, *Savitri*, is the longest poem in the English language with 24,000 lines. He viewed poetry as "a mantra, an outflow and direct expression of divine reality".

In *The Future Poetry*, Sri Aurobindo indicates that the poetry of the future will embody a harmony of five eternal powers: Truth, Beauty, Delight, Life and the Spirit. He defines delight as the "soul of existence", and beauty as "the concentrated form of delight".

Of the art of poetry, he says, "... its field is all soul experience, its appeal is to the aesthetic response of the soul to all that touches it in self or world; it is one of the high and beautiful powers of our inner nature and is a power of our inmost life. All of the infinite Truth of being that can be made part of that life, all that can be made true and beautiful and living to that experience, is poetic truth ..."

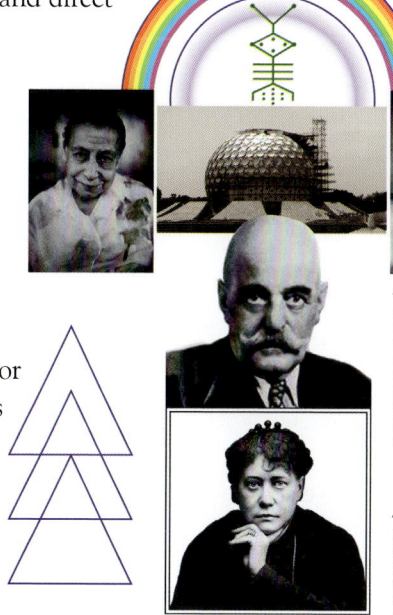

"I have put forth the view that the spiritual past of the race has been a preparation of nature not merely for attaining the divine beyond this world, but also for this very step forward which the evolution of the Earth consciousness has still to make"

Sri Aurobindo
(5.10.1935)

"There must be a descent of the light not merely unto the mind or part of it but into all the being down to the physical and below before a real transformation takes place."

Rudhyar and Sacred Music

Rudhyar's thinking about the future of the arts echoes Aurobindo. Rudhyar said, "A new kind of magic is now demanded by creative individuals able to live, feel, and think in transpersonal terms as agents of humanity as a whole, the magic of syntonic consciousness. The creative sound that is "in the beginning" and the illumined plenum of space consciousness that constitutes the omega state of the "end of time" can blend. And in this blending—however tentative and imperfectly realized—the birth of a new music and a new age can be."

Rudhyar was a composer, painter and pianist. One of Rudhyar's earliest books was, *Art as the Release of Power*. He performed what he called *dissonant polytonal music*. On April 4, 1917, Rudhyar performed his "dissonant polytonal music" for the first time in America at the New York Metropolitan Opera. (Pierre Monteux conducted the full orchestra, including a *Prelude* by

Erik Satie). Coincidentally, Rudhyar's first performance of this dissonant music occurred virtually the night America entered World War I.

In 1938, Rudhyar wrote a composition set to the lyrics of Bailey's *The Great Invocation*. His musical composition had its world premiere in the early 1980s in Pasadena, California with famous jazz flutist Paul Horn and gong master, Don Conreaux. (In January 1971, Dane Rudhyar met Jose Arguelles and over a period of 14 years transmitted much information to him about the planet as a work of art and the living hermetic tradition. Rudhyar recognized Jose as a master of seventh ray ceremonial magic for his coordination of the Whole Earth Festival in 1970 (See *2012: Biography of a Time Traveler*).

Gurdjieff and Sacred Dance

Like Mevlana's order of Sufism and sacred music, Gurdjieff developed and promoted the art of sacred dance movements, which he played on a harmonium and also transposed into piano music. He influenced notable figures such as Frank Lloyd Wright, Henry Miller, and Timothy Leary, as well as several pop singers such as Kate Bush, King Crimson and Peter Murphy. His work also greatly influenced jazz musician, Keith Jarret, who performed sublime interpretations of Gurdjieff's music.

Gurdjieff was also known for choreographing dervish dances which were performed at various theatres throughout Europe and America, including the prestigious Carnegie Hall in New York. It was his intention to use the movements in the traditional way as they were performed in ancient temples of initiation. These dances were a means of transmitting knowledge directly to the higher centers without passing through the mind, which is the way of tantra.

Sacred dances, Gurdjieff said, "have always been one of the vital subjects taught in esoteric schools of the East ... such gymnastics have a double aim: they contain and express a certain form of knowledge and at the same time serve as a means to acquire a harmonious state of being."

We must always keep in mind that we are enacting scenes, here on Earth, that are projected from a higher dimension.

Roerich and Sacred Painting

As a noted and skilled painter of visionary landscapes, Nicholas Roerich also painted mystic personalities from different times, different religions, and different cultures. Though he favored his mystical sublime color landscapes, Roerich created a series of paintings of saints and prophets from Milarepa to Muhammad, and from St. Francis to St. Sergeyeu. This demonstrated his universalism.

He wrote, "Art should be practiced everywhere even in the prisons; when there is art in the prisons there will be no more prisons." These are examples of esoteric personalities as seminal figures impressing deeper meaning into the arts and culture of this planet.

In the progression of the different facets of the occult personalities, we encounter the seeker, the search for Shambhala, the paintings and forms of sacred dance and music, the vision of the radiant future and the Brotherhood of man—all these aspects show that in the template of the occult personality lies the program for the next evolutionary possibility.

Since Mme. Blavatsky, a supreme occult personality, presented a certain dimension of the mystery of Tibet to the West, it is interesting how in the last 50 years, Tibet has come to the West. In this light, Tibetan teacher, Chogyam Trungpa Rinpoche is another seminal personality. Trungpa brought esoteric Buddhist teaching (vajrayana) to the West, and expressed many of his teachings through theatre and art. Before his automobile accident, he was skilled in sacred dance and also developed his own form of calligraphy and flower arranging—dharma art, art as every day life. He gathered around him many artists, including Allen Ginsberg and Jose Arguelles.

Trungpa taught that the practice of dharma art is based on mindfulness training. The practice of natural mind meditation—the mind seeing clearly—establishes a solid foundation for spiritual evolution. There can be no spiritual evolution in a mind that has not examined itself with fearless honesty. These are all aspects of the occult personality as

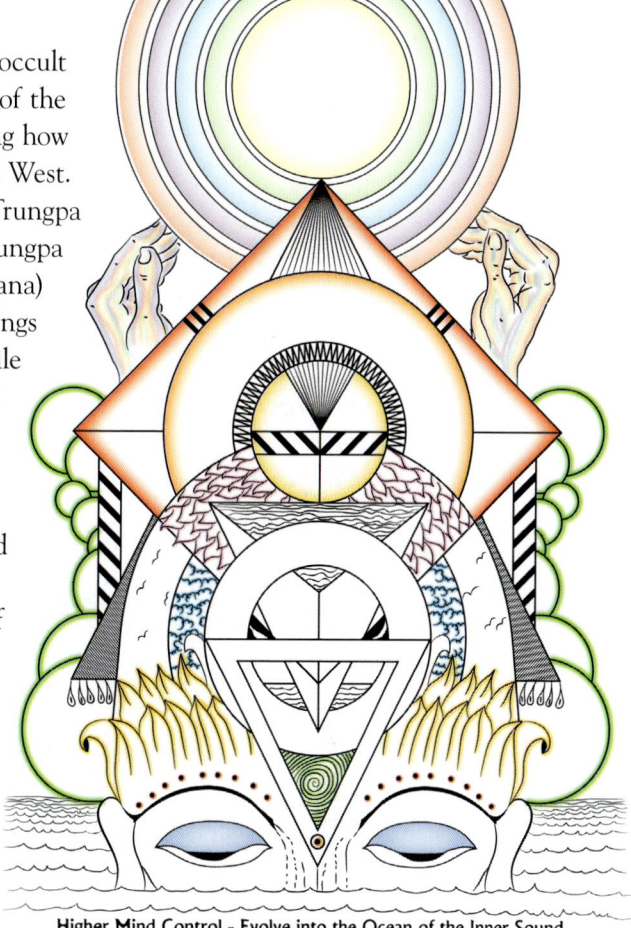

Higher Mind Control - Evolve into the Ocean of the Inner Sound

the template of the evolutionary emergence of the new type of being. This perception leads to the consideration of the cosmic function of the esoteric personality.

We must always keep in mind that we are enacting scenes, here on Earth, that are projected from a higher dimension. All things we perceive in the cosmos, including ourselves, are aspects of consciousness within the time-space matrix of matter. When we contemplate our solar system, we are in awe of how many billion light years it is from the "earliest" galaxy to this galaxy and how many billions of galaxies there are—and this is only the physical/horizontal plane of reality! Just as there are many billions of galaxies in the horizontal plane of our vision—there is an equal complexity of order beyond in the higher dimensions.

The Mental Arts

Gurdjieff describes how the humans are consistently transmuting cosmic energies, which is similar to Vernadsky's description of the biosphere. The information that the esoteric masters brought through is the *shock*—the interval that bridges to the higher self. The shock of Gurdjieff was his teachings and personality, which took on many characteristics, sometimes comical, sometimes maddening, in order to test people in various ways.

Gurdjieff believed that in order to bring humans back to essence, their conditioned buffers first had to be dissolved. He describes these buffers as defense mechanisms developed from childhood in order to bear the contradictions of the world. In other words, the buffers are what separates our higher consciousness from our actual words and deeds. Gurdjieff viewed the world of ordinary men as mechanical robots, and believed only a shock could wake them up.

This is the same teaching as appears in the Law of Time that says primitive man is vibrating in an artificial, machine frequency (12:60)—the frequency that creates robots out of humans—a robotic frequency. An initial shock occurs the moment we choose to raise our frequency by realigning with the cycles of nature (13 Moons, 28 days)—this is a shock to the 12:60 perception and, thus, creates an opening to the universal frequency 13:20. Consider the following thoughts of Gurdjieff:

> *It happens fairly often that essence dies in a man while his personality and body are still alive. A considerable percentage of the people we meet in the streets of a great town are people who are empty inside, that is, they are actually already dead. It is*

fortunate for us that we do not see and do not know it. If we knew what number of people are actually dead and what number of these dead people govern our lives, we should go mad with horror.

Gurdjieff also believed that only a small number of humans have the capability to evolve spiritually, and that not everyone will make it past the evolutionary threshold. He says "special forces oppose the evolution of large masses of humanity and keep it at the level it ought to be." Mevlana has a similar stance as expressed in *The Knowledge Book*.

At the moment, we are in a medium of selection and everyone is crossing the Sirat (the bridge of the resurrection period that leads to heaven or hell) according to his/her consciousness. Those who are chosen will be chosen, and those who are disqualified will be disqualified. However, the Morrows and Future Days will bring unexpected Beauties.

Mevlana's interval comes at the closing of the cycle. The shock she creates is bringing through *The Knowledge Book* that claims to supersede all previous knowledge including religious texts, though it encompasses them all. Mevlana says *The Knowledge Book* is the next evolutionary installment that will last for eight centuries. It is meant to create a shock to the religious personality. Mevlana says that the age of the religious personality is over, and that we are now moving toward the new era of the universal personality.

The Knowledge Book states that at the year 2000, pathways of the traditional religions were closed off, and that in this final age "all celestial dimensions have been unveiled to our Planet". This book further states that each consciousness is in the influence field of the dimension he/she is connected to. For this reason, the world is going through resurrection within a chaos due to consciousness differences. This is the shock that brings us to a higher absolute that corresponds to a supermental descent—this is what Aurobindo's life was devoted to investigating and catalyzing.

Aurobindo utilized his personality as a laboratory. On the outside, it might appear that he was an Indian yogi, but actually, he was a pioneer of the inner realms geared to the supramental descent. The supramental descent is the next stage of the evolutionary information necessary to create a supermind and establish the Overmind or the noosphere.

Aurobindo foresaw a new type of species, the supramental being, vastly superior to present mechanical humanity. The supramental being would have a new consciousness, a different status

The Cosmic History Chronicles • Volume IV

and quality of functioning. The supramental being would appear luminous, flexible and adaptable—entirely conscious and harmonious.

Aurobindo also envisioned a type of transitional being between modern man and the supramental. These transitional beings would appear prior to the full manifestation of the supramental being and would constitute an intermediate stage in Earth evolution. These transitional beings would have to undergo a whole body purification and transmutation as described by Rudhyar, who envisioned a purification via art and music:

> *Purification means to feed one's aesthetic or physical diet from perversion, to go back to Nature and Nature's laws, metaphysical as well as physical nature. Regeneration means that the tonic power of that which feeds the spiritual, moral, and physical nature of man is absorbed, so that the Self and life may sing again in the tones we hear and in the things we eat, or read, or love, in all that we assimilate, in all, therefore, that we become "similar to".*
>
> *The process of alchemy in its ancient and essential meaning parallels in music the transmutation of sounds into Tone and the transformation of fullness of musical space into the oneness of divine creative light.*

The discovery of the Law of Time (1989) is a major aspect of the supramental descent. The Thirteen Moon calendar is just the doorway. *The Knowledge Book* was channeled between 1980 and the mid 90s. The Law of Time continues to evolve into the present time. Both the Law of Time and *The Knowledge Book* are categorically new systems of cosmic order and knowledge hitherto unknown on this Earth. For this reason, they are two aspects of supramental descent in preparation for the Great Shift.

All occult personalities are part of one large moving matrix or energetic field of influence of Velatropa 24.3. They also represent a minute squiggle of a much larger cosmic order. These personalities are actually spirit forces gathered and reflected into a single beam, governed by the *heptaparaparshinokh* (as Gurdjieff calls it): the law of seven. This law of seven is reflected in the seven volumes of the *Cosmic History Chronicles* that create a synthesized matrix of higher comprehension and understanding of the evolutionary purpose.

Aurobindo speaks of the yogic force as an invisible force that is a million times stronger than any physical force because it is functioning on the realms of the mind, spirit and Overmind. The concentrated yogic mind, aligned with the order of the higher directives can affect our outer reality.

During World War II, Sri Aurobindo focused much energy on different critical turning points of the battle to ensure that it would not be the end of the civilization. In the war of Dunkirk, Sri Aurobindo claims to have utilized the yogic force to create a great and intense fog inhibiting the German Army from destroying the allied forces, which used the opportunity to escape by sea.

We can now harness these forces, through disciplined effort and the power of concentration, to successfully project the rainbow bridge around the Earth by 2012, and to ensure that the hermetic template of the new human—the noospheric human is in place by 2013—Galactic Synchronization. That's the meaning of it all.

We close Gate 5 with *The Great Invocation* transmitted telepathically to Alice Bailey by "the Tibetan". The first two stanzas were received in 1935, and the final two in 1939. At this time the human race was proceeding toward the Second World War and through it, beginning to manufacture weapons of mass destruction.

THE GREAT INVOCATION

From the point of Light within the Mind of God
Let light stream forth into the minds of men.
Let Light descend on Earth.

From the point of Love within the Heart of God
Let love stream forth into the hearts of men.
May Christ return to Earth.

From the centre where the Will of God is known
Let purpose guide the little wills of men—
The purpose which the Masters know and serve.

From the centre which we call the race of men
Let the Plan of Love and Light work out
And may it seal the door where evil dwells.

Let Light and Love and Power restore the Plan on Earth.

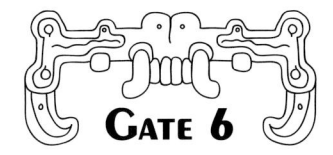

Gate 6
Madame Blavatsky—an Initiatic Doorway

As you turn to leave the chamber of esoteric personalities, you hear a loud rapping followed by bells. A tingling sensation fills you along with an insatiable curiosity. Suddenly it is 1875, and you find yourself in a strange apartment in New York City. You walk into one of the several parlors or meeting rooms. It is unusually decorated with huge palm leaves, stuffed apes, and tigers' heads, Oriental pipes and vases, cigarettes, Javanese sparrows, manuscripts and cuckoo clocks. You sit on an overstuffed chair and sense a large presence. In your mind's eye you catch sequential flashes of the life of Madame Blavatsky—a supreme initiate. Her personality, with all of its peculiarities, seeps into you. You hear her voice echo from what sounds like a far distance: KEEP THE LINK UNBROKEN! DO NOT LET MY LAST INCARNATION BE A FAILURE!

> *Hence, true genius has small chance indeed of receiving its due in our age of conventionalities, hypocrisy and time-serving. As the world grows in civilization, it expands in fierce selfishness, and stones its true prophets and geniuses for the benefit of its aping shadows.*
>
> —Mme. Blavatsky

Madame Blavatsky is an initiatic doorway—a reflection, an objectification and a map or mirror of a process and structure that reflects who and what we are becoming and transforming into. When we contemplate her life stream, we see that the whole of her incarnation was a metaphor for bringing to light a history of our collective unconscious.

Mme. Blavatsky single-handedly rekindled the esoteric tradition in the West after it had been severely undermined with the rise of industrial civilization in the middle of the eighteenth century. She was the first to unite the Oriental or Far Eastern wisdom with Western teachings and place them into a global organization. This was an enormous mission for anyone, particularly a Russian female with English as her third language in a time when the rights and roles of women in society were still very restricted.

In the history of alchemy or Western hermeticism, much less mainstream culture, there are few examples of women who are literally giants of thought. If we survey the whole of the nineteenth and twentieth centuries, we will unlikely find any other women (or perhaps, man) comparable in the daring, breadth and scope of thought that Mme. Blavatsky embodied.

She was acutely aware of the imminence of the approaching end of the cycle and that a superhuman effort was required to establish a renewed foundation for *The Secret Doctrine*. For this reason, the strength of her personality had to equal that of her mission.

Blavatsky's Theosophical Society has its roots in England and India, and is still a worldwide phenomenon. Its founding was a global event—an initiatic doorway—that opened into the "new age". This was scarcely 137 years before 2012, the closing of the Mayan Great Cycle.

Blavatsky's ideas are as valid today as they were 120 years ago. Many people fail to recognize her close links with Tibet—in fact we could say that with the creation of the Theosophical Society, Mme. Blavatsky was a Tibetan world-reformer. The fourteenth Dalai Lama says of her book *The Voice of Silence*: "I believe that this book has strongly influenced many sincere seekers and aspirants to the wisdom and compassion of the Bodhisattva Path."

Mme. Blavatsky was as highly regarded as she was controversial, enduring much slander in her own lifetime. Many Buddhists did not recognize her as an official Buddhist (she took formal vows and precepts with Buddhist monks in Sri Lanka in 1888), and many religious thinkers did not believe she was a genuine religious thinker—though most acknowledge her astounding accomplishments.

To understand the life work of any being within the planetary framework, we must first understand the condition and the time they were born into. From this, we can glean more insight into the meaning, validity, importance, and scope of his/her mission. Do not seek the person within the personality, but the cosmic function being performed through that person.

Mme. Blavatsky was born into the age of industrialization, an age of incredible optimism, where it was thought that technology would transform the world and that the human would be saved or enlightened by the machine. She was raised in an elitist Russian environment that gave her the privilege to explore the world in a way most of her contemporaries could not. Dane Rudhyar said that Blavatsky's world travels were "ritualistic symbols of a globe encompassing all-human awareness heralding the actual emergence of planetary consciousness".

Mme. Blavatsky was well aware of the moment she occupied in the evolutionary trajectory—the time of the closing of one cycle and the opening of a new cycle—this was reflected throughout her teachings. She was also aware that she was confronting deeply conditioned belief patterns of the

West by introducing Eastern thought. She spoke out strongly against scientific materialism as well as religious hypocrisy. She also knew that her mediumship, psychic powers and Oriental perspective—inclusive of her apprenticeship to Master Morya—was flying in the face of conventional Western thinking. This is important to understand.

Mme. Blavatsky called upon her skill at synthesizing vast amounts of knowledge to describe, define and unify the nature of existence and reality from a spiritual, nonmaterial point of view. She opened a pathway that had been recently shut down—the pathway of the alchemists, hermeticists and Rosicrucians. She was the first Westerner to bring the existence of the "Masters" into publicity; and exposed the names of two "Members of this Brotherhood" hitherto unknown in Europe and America. This was Master Morya and Master Koot Hoomi.

Mme. Blavatsky's life can be viewed as stages of the transformative psychology of the initiate. We will revisit stages of her life as a series of seven initiations in order to study the psychological and spiritual precepts underlying one of the most esoteric of esoteric personalities of all time. In this light, we view Mme. Blavatsky as an exemplary cosmic personality understood as an evolutionary template with a specific function.

> *In the case of regularly-initiated seers, it must be remembered that we are dealing with a long series of persons, who, warned of the confusing circumstances into which they pass when their spiritual perceptions are trained to range beyond material limits, and are so enabled to penetrate to the actual realities of things ...*
> —Mme. Blavatsky

First Initiation: Birth and Early years

Helena Petrovna Von Hahn was born at Ekaterinoslav in Southern Russia at close after midnight on August 12, 1831. Her father was a Captain in the Horse Artillery and her mother was a novelist and feminist who came from a highly placed aristocratic Russian family.

Soon after she was born she experienced her first initiation when her family had arranged a ceremony of baptism in an orthodox Russian church consecrated with wax candles. According to A.P. Sinnett, a close acquaintance of Blavatsky, the following occurred at the baptism:

> *As the ceremony was nearing its close, the sponsors were just in the act of renouncing the Evil One and his deeds, a renunciation emphasized in the Greek Church by thrice spitting upon the invisible enemy, when the little lady, toying with her lighted taper candle at the feet of the crowd, inadvertently set fire to the long flowing robes of the*

priest. The result was an immediate conflagration during which several persons—chiefly the old priest—were severely burnt. This seemed some kind of omen.

From the first years of her life, Helena displayed both a powerful will and unusual psychic abilities. As an adolescent, she studied piano in Paris and was an excellent musician and performer.

When Helena was 11, her mother died of tuberculosis. From that time on she was raised by her maternal grandparents in Saratov, where her grandfather was civil governor. On a dare, at age 17, she married Nikofer Vassilyevich Blavatsky who was three times her age. Nikofer was also the vice-governor of the Province of Erivan in the Caucasus. Before the marriage was consummated, Helena ran away, first to Constantinople (modern day Turkey).

Second Initiation: First Explorations—Meeting the Master

In 1848, Helena began 10 years of travel with money provided by her father. Her travels led her to Turkey, Egypt and Greece, Central Asia, India, North America, Central America and South America (where she visited Mayan and Incan centers), Africa, Java, Eastern Europe and Tibet.

On her journeys, she said she longed to answer two recurring questions in her mind: Where, who, what is God? And, Who ever saw the immortal spirit of man, so as to be able to assure himself of immortality? She said she was most anxious to solve these questions—and so attracted to her masters of profound knowledge and mysterious powers. This shows the power of sincerity and perseverance of a true seeker of truth.

On her twentieth birthday August 12, 1851, in London, she met the master, Mahatma Morya, whom she had had visions of as a child. Master Morya, a tall eastern initiate of Rajput birth, told her of the great work in store for her; she immediately accepted fully his guidance. She would later say that the masters make themselves known only to those who have devoted their lives to unselfish study and are not likely to turn back.

Master Morya

As an initiate, Blavatsky had an inexplicable need to explore the world and did so extensively from ages 17-27, as epitomized by her crossing the Rockies in a covered wagon from Chicago to San Francisco in 1855. This was a prelude to her second and successful attempt to reach Tibet through Nepal (She first attempted a few years earlier, but was met with insurmountable obstacles). In light of these arduous travels, we must consider Blavatsky's personality.

Strong willed, bold, daring and directed from within, she followed her inner impulses by inexhaustibly exploring the outer world alone by steamboat, train, horse and camel. She exhibited a prime need to unify the different fields of human investigation to create a grand synthesis of multivalued thought. She engaged in a search for common structures of meaning that entered her into vast realms of symbolism and symbolic expression. Her study of the esoteric doctrine was the most complete and most complex of all in the history of Western hermeticism or occultism.

Third Initiation: Display of Power

Mme. Blavatsky returned to Russia in 1858, when she was 27. Here, she displayed many paranormal powers for her relatives and friends, including clairvoyance, telepathy and telekinesis. Her display of skills and the subsequent experiences were often accompanied by other strange phenomenon such as window tapping and bell ringing.

After a mysterious illness, Mme. Blavatsky resumed her travels through the Balkans, Egypt, Syria, and Italy. At the age of 29, her mind started becoming more mystically attuned and her physical body went through many transformations—she endured cathartic illnesses that lasted off and on for around four years. During this time, she learned how to focus her will and tame the spirits and psychic energies that she so easily attracted. At the same time she also developed and learned to tame her parapsychological skills.

After her illness, she describes herself as being in complete control of her psychic powers—she was no longer at the mercy of outside or external forces. In 1866, she wrote the following in a letter to her sister:

"Now I shall never be subjected to external influences ... The last vestige of my psycho-physical weakness is gone, to return no more ..."

Fourth Initiation: Mystic Travels—Encounters with the Masters

In 1865, Mme. Blavatsky travelled extensively through the Balkans, Greece, Egypt, Syria, Italy and many other places. In 1867, she joined the forces of Garibaldi, fighting for Italy's nationhood against the French and Papal forces. She claimed to have received a strange wound near her heart in the battle of Mentana in Central Asia.

From time to time, the wound would open leaving her close to death—yet she was able to continue her mission. Doctors were baffled by the strange wound that seemed to open and close without explanation. Some believed that her body was actually killed during this battle, but that it was "resurrected" to become a focal point for the power of her masters and Hierarchy. In 1868 she traveled to Tibet via India, following the command of Master Morya. Here, she lived and learned from her masters for three years, including Master Koot Hoomi. She lived in Tibet periodically for a total of seven years, and claimed to have travelled to places in Tibet that were never visited by any other European.

She describes this time:

> *When we first travelled over the East, we came into contact with certain men, endowed with such mysterious powers and such profound knowledge that we may truly designate them as the sages of the Orient. To their instructions we lent a ready ear ... Much of the teaching found in my writings come from these sages of the Orient, our Eastern Masters. Many a passage in my works has been written by me under their dictation. In saying this, no supernatural claim is urged, for no miracle is performed by such a dictation.*

Master Koot Hoomi

Mme. Blavatsky claimed she had known adepts, not only in India and beyond Ladakh, but in Egypt and Syria. She says: "Adepts are everywhere; silent, secret, retiring, and who never divulge themselves entirely to anyone unless one did as I did—passed seven and ten years' probation, and gave proofs of absolute devotion. I fulfilled the requirements, and am what I am."

As Mme. Blavatsky's life experience demonstrates, she, like any initiate, had to continuously work to master the lower forces—this is the aim of spiritual discipline and mandatory in the art of transformation. Without going through her cathartic changes, Mme. Blavatsky could not have been prepared for the Great Work that she was to accomplish. This description summarizes the particular four-year phase (ages 29-33) in Mme. Blavatsky's life. She had been appointed or designated by the Higher Force supervising the "Plan" to be their singular unique agent for this time: an initiatic doorway for humanity.

Through the example of Mme. Blavatsky, we see that the more we exert in the truth, the more our path is quickened, and we are purified much sooner than if we had not entered into a higher path of purpose. Once she had subdued the lower energies, Mme. Blavatsky was able to fully embody the adept that Master Morya had told her was needed to found a new order—the Theosophical Society.

Her sole purpose in this world was to be an agent to the Masters who frequently communicated to her both physically and telepathically. When we speak of "masters" we are referring to a specific matrix of energies incarnated in a select number of beings who function as guiding forces for the spiritual evolution of humanity.

These "masters" are essentially accomplished beings that have already attained identity with, and have been absorbed by their fifth-dimensional higher self, such that the third-dimensional self is most often purely apparitional. The manifestation of the Masters to Mme. Blavatsky was a singular grace shown to her only because of the profound responsibility that was placed upon her as a supreme initiate and herald of the New Age. Or, as Mme. Blavatsky explains:

Part II • Crafting the Vehicle

We call them "Masters" because they are our teachers; and because from them we have derived all the Theosophical truths ... For long ages, one generation of these adepts after another has studied the mysteries of being, of life, death and rebirth. By the training of faculties we all possess, but which they alone have developed to perfection, the Adepts have entered in Spirit the various superphysical planes and states of Nature.

Fifth Initiation: Transition to Greatness—The Theosophical Society

A great transition occurred in 1870 when Mme. Blavatsky returned to Europe. Until this period, she had spent her life traveling extensively and absorbing much occult knowledge. Now it was time for her to synthesize the great system of knowledge she had learned as it was practiced in the East.

The mission given her by Master Morya in 1851 was so large that she was uncertain where to begin. She determined that she would first start acquainting the world with the latent potentialities in human nature. She did this by displaying certain psychic phenomena to a diverse range of people in hopes of turning their attention toward the hidden sciences of nature. Her reasoning was, "prove the soul of man by its wondrous powers and you have proved God."

As instructed by her Masters, Mme. Blavatsky arrived in New York City in July, 1873. A year later, she met Met Colonel Henry Steel Olcott who would be of enormous help in grounding the vast vision into a coherent structure. Olcott was a distinguished civil war veteran and lawyer, who had a strong interest in spiritualism. His personality was precisely the catalytic energy Mme. Blavatsky needed to concretize the mission brewing within her.

On September 8, 1875, Mme. Blavatsky founded the Theosophical Society together with Col. Olcott, William Q. Judge, and others. The Theosophical Society became one of the most influential organizations of the late nineteenth and early twentieth centuries. Its inception marked the first time in history that an organization opened a channel for the communication of ancient teachings regarding the nature of the universe and the phenomenon of the human mind in its course of evolution.

In a note dated July, 1875, in her scrapbook Mme. Blavatsky writes: "Orders received from India direct to establish a philosophic-religious Society and choose a name for it—also to choose Olcott". In another note from the same scrapbook, she specifically states: "Morya brings orders to form a Society—a secret Society like the Rosicrucian Lodge. He promises to help." (Blavatsky, *Collected Writings*)

The Cosmic History Chronicles • Volume IV

> ### THE THEOSOPHICAL SOCIETY
>
> At its inception the chief purpose of the Theosophical Society was to scientifically investigate psychic or so-called "spiritualistic" phenomena—but its objectives soon expanded into the following three chief objectives:
>
> (1) to form the nucleus of a Universal Brotherhood of humanity, without distinction of race, creed, sex, caste, or color;
> (2) to promote the study of Aryan and other Eastern literatures, religions, philosophies, and sciences; and
> (3) to investigate unexplained laws of nature and the psychic powers of man.
>
> Blavatsky's personal seal was the *ouroboros* or serpent biting its tail, which symbolizes a complete circuit that contains all knowledge. In Hindu cosmology, the serpent biting its tail represents the point of the *mahapralaya* "great seed time" when comes an avataric emanation to close the old cycle and regenerate the new cycle, preceding the prayala, new seed time. In other words, the beginning becomes the end, and the end is the beginning.

A few months after the founding of the Theosophical Society, Mme. Blavatsky set to work on the writing of her first major work, *Isis Unveiled*.

Isis is the symbol of nature and *Isis Unveiled* sought to establish the hermetic tradition which remained active throughout many secret societies, drawing inspiration from Near-Eastern traditions (Hermetic, Gnostic, Kabbalist, Sufi, Druzes, and later Alchemical, Rosicrucian, and Masonic).

For this work, she called upon the assistance of Col. Olcott, who took a room on the floor above her at the "Lamasery" on 47th St. in New York. Olcott's task was to correct every page of her manuscript and to help her express her ideas that she could not frame to her liking in English. From this point on, the writing of *Isis* went on intensely and without a break until its completion in 1877. Olcott attested to Mme. Blavatsky's claim that the material for the book was derived from the astral light of her masters. Blavatsky describes the experience in the following way:

> *Space and time do not exist for thought; and if the persons are in perfect mutual magnetic rapport, and of these two, one is a great adept in Occult Sciences, then thought-transference and dictation of whole pages, become as easy and as comprehensible at the distance of ten thousand miles as the transference of two words across the room.*

Olcott said that he never knew anyone who could be compared with Mme Blavatsky's "dogged endurance or tireless working capacity". Keep in mind that at this time there were no manual, nor electric typewriters yet available. Also keep in mind that English was Mme. Blavatsky's third language (Russian was her first, and French, second), and she had only learned to write it three years prior!

In his book, *Old Diary Leaves*, Col. Olcott describes Mme. Blavatsky's work style:

To watch her at work was a rare and never-to-be-forgotten experience. We sat at opposite sides of one big table usually, and I could see her every movement. Her pen would be flying over the page, when she would suddenly stop, look out into space with the vacant eye of the clairvoyant seer, shorten her vision as though to look at something held invisible in the air before her, and begin copying on her paper what she saw. The quotation finished, her eyes would resume their natural expression, and she would go on writing until again stopped by a similar interruption. I remember well two instances when I, also, was able to see and even handle books from whose astral duplicates she copied quotations into her manuscript, and which she was obliged to "materialize" for me, to refer to when reading the proofs, as I refused to pass the pages for the "strike-off" unless my doubts as to the accuracy of her copy were satisfactory.

Sixth Initiation: The Public Figure

Is it too much to believe that man should be developing new sensibilities and a closer relation with nature?

—Mme. Blavatsky, *Isis Unveiled*

In 1877, *Isis Unveiled* was published as a two-volume series with more than 1,200 pages. It sold out the first day it was released. The *New York Herald-Tribune* considered the work as "one of the remarkable productions of the century." This perception was echoed by many other journals and newspapers.

It is remarkable to note that in the first two pages of *Isis Unveiled*, Blavatsky refers to the *Popol Vuh*, the ancient Quiche Maya text, which was scarcely known about at that time. The first chapter of *Isis Unveiled* explains the cycles of nature, introducing the 71 maha-yugas and the four lesser yugas—namely the Kali Yuga that we now find ourselves in.

At this point, Mme. Blavatsky notoriety greatly increased and visitors flocked to her New York apartment eager to meet her and witness her "magical powers". Her personality was often described as bold and decisive, as well as cultured and courteous. Col. Olcott describes her mediumistic personality in the following way:

H.P.B. would leave the room one person and return to it another. Not another as to visible change of physical body, but another as to tricks of motion, speech, and manners—and with different mental brightness, different views of things, different command of English orthography, idiom, and grammar, and different—very different command over her temper, which, at its sunniest, was almost angelic, at its worst, the opposite.

After two years of working closely with Mme. Blavatsky, Col. Olcott concluded that she was actually a Hindu man:

Putting aside her actions, habits of thought, masculine ways, her constant asseverations of the fact ... putting these aside, I have pumped enough out of her to satisfy me that the theory long since communicated by me was correct—she is a man, a very old man, and a most learned and wonderful man. Of course she knows just what my impressions are, for she reads my thoughts like a printed page (and others' thoughts), and it seems to me she is not dissatisfied, for our relations have insensibly merged into those of Master and pupil.

Mme. Blavatsky became an American citizen on July 8, 1878, and received much publicity in all the major newspapers. In December of that same year, after receiving instruction from her masters, she and Col. Olcott departed for Bombay, to set up Theosophical headquarters. Many felt that her actions were nothing more than a whim, when in fact she was being guided by beings most cannot perceive.

While in Bombay, she founded the monthly magazine, *The Theosophist* (October 1879), dedicated to occult research. The society experienced rapid growth with many notable members.

In 1880, Mme. Blavatsky and Olcott visited Ceylon at the invitation of leading priests and prominent members of the Buddhist Community. Her fame had preceded her, and she and Olcott were treated royally. The monks, who had read excerpts from *Isis Unveiled*, insisted that she display her powers for them, to which she acquiesced. Col. Olcott describes this time:

In 1877, Isis Unveiled *was published as a two-volume series with more than 1,200 pages. It sold out the first day it was released.*

Part II • Crafting the Vehicle

> *Our rooms were packed with visitors all day. There was no end of metaphysical discussions with the aged High Priest Bulatgama Sumanatissa. Old Bulatgama was particularly persistent, disputant, very voluble and very kind. Among other topics of discussion was that of the psychical powers, and Mme. Blavatsky, who thoroughly liked him, rang bells in the air, made spirit raps, caused the great dining table to tremble and move, etc. to the amazement of her select audience.*

It was here, in Ceylon that Mme. Blavatsky and Col. Olcott took formal vows as Buddhists. Shortly after, they founded the main headquarters of the Theosophical Society in Adyar.

SEVENTH INITIATION: *THE SECRET DOCTRINE*

While in India, Mme. Blavatsky became mysteriously ill and the doctor expressed grave concerns that she would not live through the night. Some of her friends waited outside of her room and witnessed the sudden appearance of Master Morya. They claimed that he passed quickly through the outer room into Mme. Blavatsky's room. The next morning, the physician was astounded to find her condition greatly stabilized.

Mme. Blavatsky's self-healing under the guidance of the masters is an inspiring and well documented example of the taming of the lower forces. This type of experience is a deep shamanic initiation—a spiritual death and rebirth. Such an experience is often encountered when first entering a path of heightened awareness, or when first answering a call to a higher mission.

This type of initiation calls for a process of increasing discipline to sublimate the lower psychic forces. In this process, it is important not to identify with the undesirable forces, but rather to recognize them as a quality of energy brought out through heightened discipline. These energies must be released and transmuted in order to pass to the next highest planes.

After her recovery, she told her intimate friends how her Master had come and given her two choices—the first, to die and pass on into peace, and the second, to live on a little longer and complete *The Secret Doctrine*, so that "a few faithful souls seeking the Wisdom might be enabled both to get the Wisdom and to understand the Masters." H.P.B. wrote the following of the experience in a letter to her friend A.P. Sinnett:

> *But I shall never, nor could I if I would, forget that forever memorable night during the crisis of my illness, when Master, before exacting from me a certain promise, revealed to me things that He thought I ought to know, before pledging my word*

> to Him for the work He asked me (not ordered as He had a right to do). On that night when everyone expected me every minute to breathe my last—I learned it all. I was shown who was right and who was wrong (unwittingly) and who was entirely treacherous; and a general sketch of what I had to expect outlined before me. Ah, I tell you, I have learnt things on that night—things that stamped themselves forever on my Soul; black treachery, assumed friendship for selfish ends, belief in my guilt, and yet a determination to lie in my defense, since I was a convenient step to rise upon, and what not! Human nature I saw in all its hideousness in that short hour, when I felt one of Masters hands upon my heart, forbidding it cease beating, and saw the other calling out sweet future before me. With all that, when He had shown me all, all, and asked "Are you willing?"—I said "Yes", and thus signed my wretched doom, for the sake of the few who were entitled to His thanks ... Death was so welcome at that hour, rest so needed, so desired; life like the one that stared me in the face, and that is realized now—so miserable; yet how could I say no to Him who wanted me to live! But all this is perhaps incomprehensible to you, though I do hope it is not quite so.

By 1885, Mme. Blavatsky was the target of much slander and scandal. People called her everything from charlatan to fraud. A huge controversy ensued with the Psychic Research Society of London who branded her "one of the most accomplished, ingenious and interesting impostors of history". The tense and unpleasant atmosphere in India became unbearable forcing her to return to London to continue her work.

Since the time of the publication of *The Secret Doctrine* in 1888, the world population has quadrupled. Many of the technological advances that we take for granted today did not exist then, namely the airplane, automobile and computer. However, the signs of technological advance were everywhere—the Western European world, as well as America, were agog over technology itself with a spate of World Fairs displaying all the latest innovations. At this time, the Eiffel Tower, the world's tallest structure, was under construction.

At this time, there was also a great deal of interest in advancement of electricity and electromagnetism. This is an important point when you stop to think about what electricity and electromagnetism connote—a type of etheric vibrant energy. Thomas Edison and Nikola Tesla, both genius pioneers in channeling this cosmic force, were deeply involved in occult work as well. (Edison was an official member of the Theosophical Society).

The Secret Doctrine was a profoundly well structured text. Mme. Blavatsky synthesized her perspective, which is the perspective of the "Orientalists"—the combination of esoteric Buddhists and the Vedanta Hindu philosophy. This perspective, underlying a work of such grand cosmic, historical and scientific breadth, was perhaps the most striking and remarkable aspect of her works and character. There had never been anything like it in the history of human thought. It was truly global.

The Secret Doctrine sheds light on the potentiality of the creation of a cosmic personality, according to divine and transcendental precepts that allow it to function in a multilayered, multidimensional universe. *The Secret Doctrine* is a manifestation of Blavatsky's own complex and highly evolved personality. This synthesis of knowledge, displayed in both *Isis Unveiled* and *The Secret Doctrine*, is a fundamental statement of the urge to UR—the post-historic spirituality.

She was aware of virtually every mythological tradition that existed and synthesized them in such a way to illustrate the fundamental point that they were all derived from a previous root race—like one tree with many branches. These different traditions also point to the fact that we are entering into the fold of another root race.

Dane Rudhyar said of Mme. Blavatsky: "... Even more convincing is the astounding character of the contents of her large books, especially *The Secret Doctrine*, which no ordinary mind could have produced without passing dozens of years studying and collating an immense mass of verifiable documents in many great libraries. At the same time, it is evident that H. P. Blavatsky, the woman, spent her life away from universities and national libraries."

In May 1889, Mme. Blavatsky made a prophetic statement in her magazine, *Lucifer*, in which she relates the role of Theosophy in the world.

> *If Theosophy prevailing in the struggle, its all-embracing philosophy strikes deep root into the minds and hearts of men, if its doctrines of Reincarnation and Karma, in other words, of Hope and Responsibility, find a home in the lives of the new generations, then, indeed, will dawn the day of joy and gladness for all who now suffer and are outcast. For real Theosophy IS ALTRUISM, and we cannot repeat it too often. It is brotherly love, mutual help, unswerving devotion to Truth. If once men do but realize that in these alone can true happiness be found, and never in wealth, possessions, or any selfish gratification, then the dark clouds will roll away, and a new humanity will be born upon Earth. Then, the*

The Secret Doctrine sheds light on the potentiality of the creation of a cosmic personality ...

GOLDEN AGE will be there, indeed. But if not, then the storm will burst, and our boasted western civilization and enlightenment will sink in such a sea of horror that its parallel History has never yet recorded.

The last six years of Mme. Blavatsky's life were devoted to writing *The Secret Doctrine*, *The Key to Theosophy*, *The Theosophical Glossary*, *The Voice of the Silence*, and numerous articles. She died peacefully in London during an influenza epidemic on May 8, 1891.

The Secret Doctrine and Cosmic History

2012 marks the 125th anniversary of the publication of *The Secret Doctrine*. Mme. Blavatsky functioned as a planetary catalyst bringing forth a perspective and a base of wisdom that is anything but scientific materialist. Her belief was that materialism "is and ever shall be blind to spiritual truth."

Throughout her life's work, Mme. Blavatsky sought to return to the most primary sources of thought and religion of the human race. Her perception was that the earliest stages of human thought are much closer to the purity of the Divine Order—the order that commanded our existence in the first place. This insistence on returning to the roots or origins is a necessary one though it cannot be the entire focus.

OUROBOROS
CLOSING THE CYCLE 21/12/2012
POINT OF SUPRAMENTAL DESCENT

All cosmic history is a form of evolutionary spiritual psychology and *The Secret Doctrine* as well as the introduction to Cosmic Science (see *CHC, Vol. II*) must also be viewed in this light. A spiritual psychology is necessary to bring the human mind back to its roots in order to see how and where it might have deviated, and from this comprehension of karmic error to create the image of the future evolved self.

Part II • Crafting the Vehicle

Synchro-Cosmology

It is the purpose of Cosmic History to comprehend and synthesize the universal histories; and it is the purpose of Cosmic Science to show the universal roots. The *Introduction to Cosmic Science* and *The Secret Doctrine* provide perspectives and vocabularies which augment the purpose of the GM108X mind stream. To synthesize the essence of these works, according to the formulations of the synchronic order and the Law of Time, is the purpose of the study of *The Secret Doctrine* and the Introduction to Cosmic Science.

What must be brought to light, in an objective way, is a structure of cosmic evolution, intelligence and mind that accommodates various vocabularies and perspectives in establishing a new science or knowledge previously unknown. This new science or knowledge is a type of synchrocosmology, meaning that the evolutionary path of the human mind is to synchronize itself with the different levels of cosmology that define those different perspectives. To do this in a way that may be useful for the educational program of the new human living in the new time is the final purpose of the entire study of Cosmic History.

To unify science, theology, cosmology, and synchronometric science as a whole system—which defines the actual evolutionary psychology of the spirit—is to arrive at the most enlightened synthesis we can imagine; this is our goal. If you have read this far, then consider you have taken a transport to the future of universal comprehension and are attaining a supermental condition of consciousness. This is the true end of *The Secret Doctrine* in all of its manifestations.

It was Blavatsky's intention, through the inspiration of Master Morya, to create a grand synthesis of ancient wisdom. Theosophy means "divine wisdom or the wisdom of the deity". In her cosmology, Blavatsky defines "groups of builders" and other spirit helpers such as the *Dhyani Chohans* who, like the fifth-dimensional spirit guardians of Cosmic Science, the angelic guardians of the Quran, or the mahabodhisattvas of buddhic teachings, have no other intention but to assist the evolution of the spirit through its difficult human stage.

For Blavatsky to have propounded the Theosophical Society at a time when Western science was making breakthroughs in the fields of electromagnetism, and electricity in general, is remarkable. What Blavatsky was trying to communicate, in one way, was that the efforts of the scientists could only be incomplete for they do not take into account their own cosmic nature. Cosmic History affirms that only by assuming its cosmic nature can the human race evolve to its next stage.

Seven Root Races

The Secret Doctrine states repeatedly that everything visible and invisible in nature is septenary, which refers to a seven fold nature. A key point in Blavatsky's elaborate cosmology is the role of the seven root races in the seven rounds of existence. She says that the whole of the cosmogenesis—the evolution of the cosmos—occurs in a sevenfold process of the seven rounds of existence round (each round has a seven fold division to it). In the fourth round occurs the human round. This recapitulates the ratio four is to seven as seven is to thirteen (4:7::7:13).

Each root-race is divided into seven sub-races; and each sub-race into seven family-races—in Cosmic

History this is known as the cave of 49 flames of the human being. Every form contains the image of its creator concealed in it.

> The seven root races are as follows:
> First Root Race: "Imperishable Sacred Land" (Polarian Epoch)
> Second Root Race: Hyperborean (Hyperborean Epoch)
> Third Root Race: Lemurian (Lemurian Epoch)
> Fourth Rood Race: Atlantean (Atlantean Epoch)
> Fifth Root Race: Aryan (Aryan Epoch)
> Sixth Root Race: According to H.P.B. this will evolve in the U.S.
> Seventh Root Race: Yet to come
>
> According to this cosmology, we are currently in the fifth root race preparing for the sixth, to be followed by the seventh. Each of the seven races may overlap a subsequent race or division. According to the Law of Time, the sixth root race will begin to emerge in 2013. First there will be a quickening and then a full-on mutational shift followed by the closing of the cycle—and then the opening of the new. The sixth root race corresponds to the cosmology of the Aztec Sunstone that transitions from the fifth sun to the sixth sun, from the sun of change to the sun of consciousness.

The nature of electricity as a cosmic phenomenon was a major concern to Blavatsky, as well as a key to the cosmology of the Cosmic Science. When we look at Western science, Cosmic Science and *The Secret Doctrine*, we see points of intersection, but in the case of Western science, a widely divergent view defined by a narrow materialistic scope and purpose.

Mme. Blavatsky's view of science is multidimensional, which obviously transcends contemporary science. This reflects her own personality, which is multilayered with phenomenally multiple interests.

In reading *The Secret Doctrine*, we realize what amazing comprehensive knowledge Mme. Blavatsky possessed. The complete text conveys a feeling of longing for home, or the experience of the entire universe as one cosmic rapture of primal unity. This longing is the mark of all great mystics and mystical seekers.

Mme. Blavatsky defines many areas of human interest or endeavor. As the two volumes of *The Secret Doctrine* demonstrate, these can be reduced to a cosmogenesis and anthropogenesis—the origin of the cosmos and the history of the origins of the human beings. In this regard, side by side with the *Cosmic History Chronicles*, *The Knowledge Book* of Mevlana is the other great successor of *The Secret Doctrine*, defining the vast order of the intrinsic unification of cosmic reality in a grand hierarchy that almost defies comprehension.

The transformative psychology reflected in the life of Madame Blavatsky and the understanding of her nature and character is also represented in the actual principles she describes in *The Secret Doctrine*, in particular the development of the different root races. The root races themselves are a

Part II • Crafting the Vehicle

GONE
GONE
GONE BEYOND
GONE TOTALLY
BEYOND
ALL HAIL
THE GOER

GATE GATE PARAGATE
PARASAMGATE
BODHI SVAHA

THE IMMEASURABLE
THE BOUNDLESS
THE ONE
THE ULTIMATE
UNBORN SPHERE
THE SOURCE
TOWARD WHICH
WE ARE ALL
RETURNING

THE RULERS
OF THIS
RAINBOW
EARTH:

RADIANCE
VITALITY
ABUNDANCE
HEALTH

ALL EQUAL
AS ONE
WE SHARE
THE WEALTH

THE FOUR PLUS
THE THREE ARE
THE SEVEN, THE
PERFECTION OF
THE SOUL

THE
SPIRITUAL
HUMAN:

ASCENT
TO THE
LIGHT:

"THE
THREE"
PLANE
OF MIND
THE SECOND
CREATION

NOT
TO BE
FORGOTTEN
BUT
PURIFIED
AND
REDEEMED
THE
ENLIGHTENMENT
OF MATTER

PHYSICAL
MAN:
THE
CULMINATION
OF THE
FIRST
CREATION:
"THE FOUR"
PLANE OF MATTER

COSMIC HISTORY: POWER OF SEVEN – SECRET DOCTRINE RENEWED.

LEAF FROM THE GALACTIC HERMETICUM

T(E)=ART

very complex chain of events which describe a much larger process of a transformational psychology, which spans the entire history of the cosmos.

For Blavatsky, the form of history is a cyclically repeatable phenomenon which, using Hindu terminology, proceeds from a prayala, a pause or seed time between two world systems or two world orders. This initiates a huge cycle known as a manvantara, or mahamanvantara or great cycle, which involves the elaboration of a root race. Each root race has its seven stages of development and sub-races that develop. We are now in the fifth root race. This means four root races have preceded us.

These root races are related to the early psychomythic history of the Earth, which she refers to as the "four lost continents": *The Imperishable Sacred Land, Hyperborea, Lemuria* and *Atlantis.* Each of these lost continents corresponds to one of the earlier root races—leading to the present fifth root race.

In *Isis Unveiled* Mme. Blavatsky talks more about life on previous world systems but in *The Secret Doctrine* focuses more on the history of the Earth or the secret history of the Earth. The fifth, or present, root race is the one that is able to conceive of a higher spiritual level of development. The origin of the fifth root race is indicated to be the serpents and the dragons of the fourth root race. The serpents are those who initiate. She says the serpent initiates keep themselves in caves or grottos beneath the pyramids (see *CHC, Vol. II*)

The synthesis that Mme. Blavatsky established in *The Secret Doctrine*—the principles of the lost worlds and of the histories of the seven evolutionary rounds—pertain to and establish the principles of a transformative psychology of the construction of the cosmic personality—the chief focus of Cosmic History. We must bring all the knowledge that exists to bear upon its relation to all its different parts; and then we must see how that knowledge sheds light on the previous worlds, the lost worlds. It is only in this way that a comprehensive and cosmic structure of the evolutionary personality may be realized.

PART III
MAPPING THE NEW REALITY

Part III • Mapping the New Reality

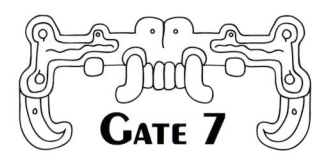

Gate 7
Hermetic Stream GM108X—the Nature of Transmission

As you make your way toward the center of the labyrinth, you stumble upon the seventh gate, a most peculiar gate—so subtle that it is scarcely perceptible. What lies behind this gate traces back hundreds of thousands of Earth years through different time lenses into other galaxies—this is the gate of the Galactic Mayan Mind transmission: Hermetic stream 108X. You slowly open the gate; it reveals a starry sky. Two thunderous voices echo in unison: "NOW WE WILL SHOW YOU WHO IS SPEAKING." Who is this? You say aloud. "THIS IS THE VOICE OF THE ORIGINATORS OF THE GALACTIC CULTURE IN ANOTHER GALAXY. WE ARE FROM WHAT YOU CALL A PARALLEL OR ALTERNATIVE REALITY. THIS IS WHERE WE HAVE COME FROM. THIS IS WHERE YOU ARE GOING."

Gate 7 marks the center-point of the entire spectrum of the seven volumes of the *Cosmic History Chronicles*. It is also the midpoint of the *Book of the Initiation*. At this point, we might again ask: Who is telling the tale of these *Cosmic History Chronicles*?

This tale is being told through the mouthpieces of the Galactic Mayan mind transmission, the avatar twins, the GM108X. These are no ordinary twins. If you saw them you might say: "Twins? Twins?" The human species only understands by example of what another human being exemplifies; therefore Cosmic History must be embedded in human types that defy categorization (see *CHC, Vol. I*).

The *Cosmic History Chronicles* are a "between the worlds" transmission, evoked by the collective unconscious mind-at-large and spoken through the channel of the GM108X, a multiple, multidimensional voice.

This series of seven books provides a new knowledge base and perceptual structure for the *reformulation of the human mind*.

The occasion for the seven volumes of the *Cosmic History Chronicles* and the GM108X transmission is the changing of the aeon—the shifting of an entire evolutionary cycle: from Piscean to the Aquarian Age (astrologically

123

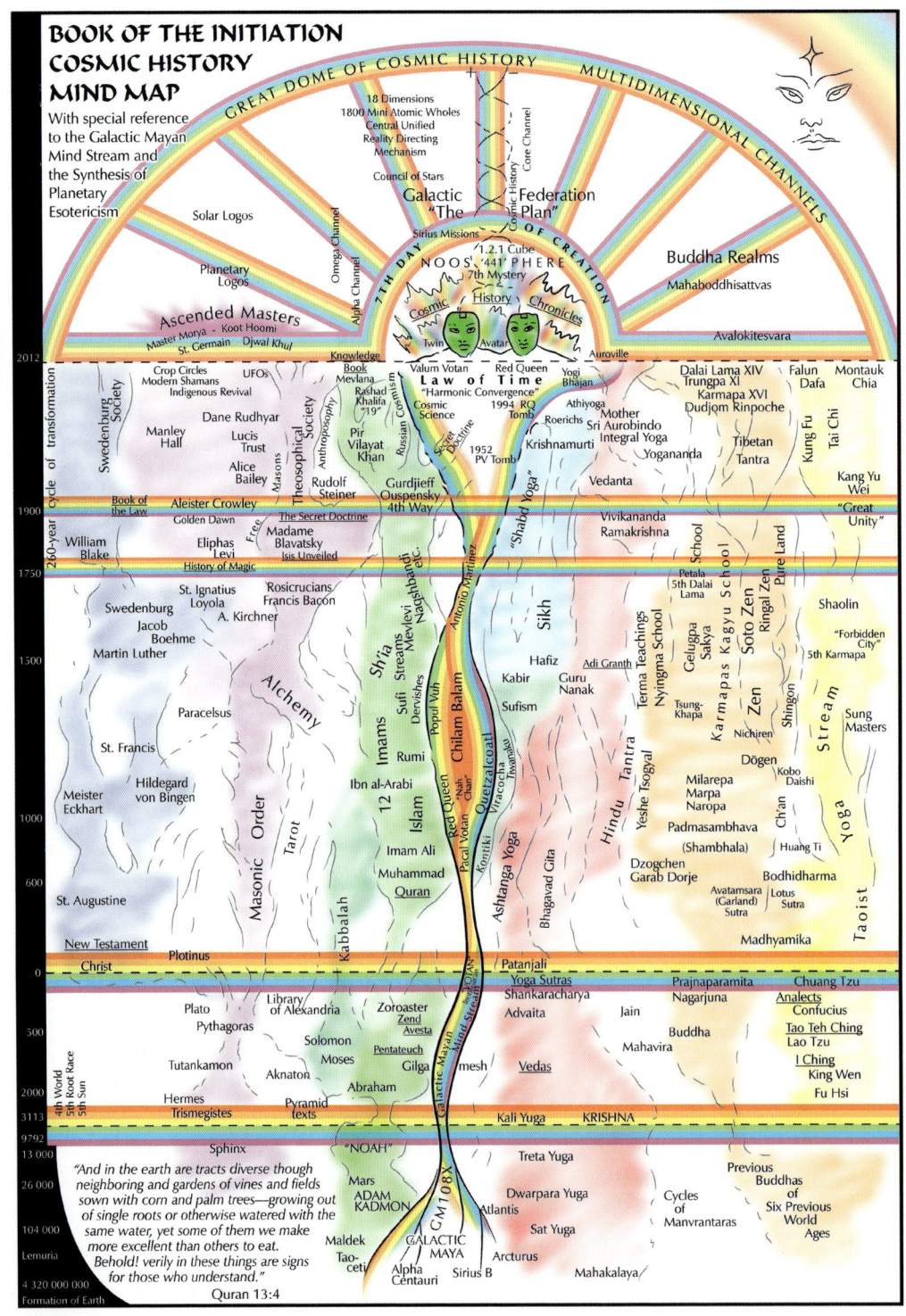

The Cosmic History Chronicles • Volume IV

speaking); from the fifth to the sixth sun (Aztec prophecies); from the fourth to the fifth world (Hopi Prophecies); from the fifth to sixth root race (*The Secret Doctrine*) and from the sixth to the seventh ray (Alice Bailey).

The well of knowledge known as Cosmic History, springs from a galactic/hermetic mind stream. This mind stream is set off from other streams, and at the same time contains them all. The GM108X is the underlying stream that connects all systems of thought as it winds its way through the entire subset of human history in all of its multi-faceted manifestations.

MIND MAP EXPLAINED

The Cosmic History mind map illustrates the different streams and schools of thought from Hermes to Pythagoras; from Freemasons, Paracelsus, the Rosicrucian's and Francis Bacon, all the way to Madame Blavatsky and the Theosophical Society, Aleister Crowley and the Golden Dawn, and continuing through the last century with cosmic philosophers and channels such as Dane Rudhyar, Alice Bailey and Mevlana.

Above the horizon line of the consciousness of history, we see the Ascended Masters raining down their messages and choosing initiates whom they wish to contact to function as channels for them. On the other side, we see the streams from the Vedas, Lord Krishna, the Rig Veda and the streams of yoga, including Patanjali and the Yoga Sutras, as well as the stream of Guatama, the seventh Buddha.

We see the development of traditional forms of spiritual thought, such as Christian, Islamic and esoteric schools like Sufism. We see this up to Jalalludin Rumi, Ibn al-Arabi to Pir Vilayat Khan or in India with Hafiz, Kabir and the Mevlana stream up to the present day Mevlana in Turkey with *The Knowledge Book*. Then there are the schools of esoteric Buddhism and Hinduism, most commonly referred to as Tantra or Vajrayana, up to the modern period with people like Ramakrishna and Vivekananda and branches such as the Vedanta society.

Then there are the more recent schools of yoga directed by masters such as Yogi Bhajan, who represents the Sikh tradition, or Sri Aurobindo and the Mother with Integral Yoga, and the establishment of Auroville, which is one of the most successful alternative communities in history. We also see many Tibetan schools—there is a large fascination in the West with Tibetan teachings first brought to the masses by Madame Blavatsky.

This was followed by people such as Alexander David Neil and Evans-Wentz. Then came the invasion of Tibet by the Chinese in the 1950s, forcing Tibetans to flee. Because of this the traditions of Tibet are better known about today than 100 years ago.

From the dissolution of traditional Tibet came Tibetan masters such as the eleventh Trungpa, Dudjom Rinpoche or the fourteenth Dalai Lama. Finally, there are schools like Zen Buddhism from the Far East—Japan—that have greatly impacted Western culture.

In their entirety, these systems of thought create the hermetic spectrum of the planetary human. When these streams are viewed as a single thought form, then it is easier to understand and encapsulate them as a whole.

Running through the center of this underground river is the stream of the Galactic Mayan Mind transmission, set apart in the New World of the Americas.

The origin of the GM108X contains the keys of knowledge pertaining to the science of how we arrived on this particular star system. This hermetic stream was scarcely known about until 1952, when its deepest secret was unearthed—the treasure store of the great Pacal Votan in Nah Chan—House of the Serpent—Palenque. With the opening of the tomb of Pacal Votan, came the initiatic seeding of the Galactic Mayan mind transmission on Earth. The meaning of this tomb has since manifested something far beyond being an archaeological relic and enigma.

Origin and Nature of GM108X—Hermetic Mind Stream

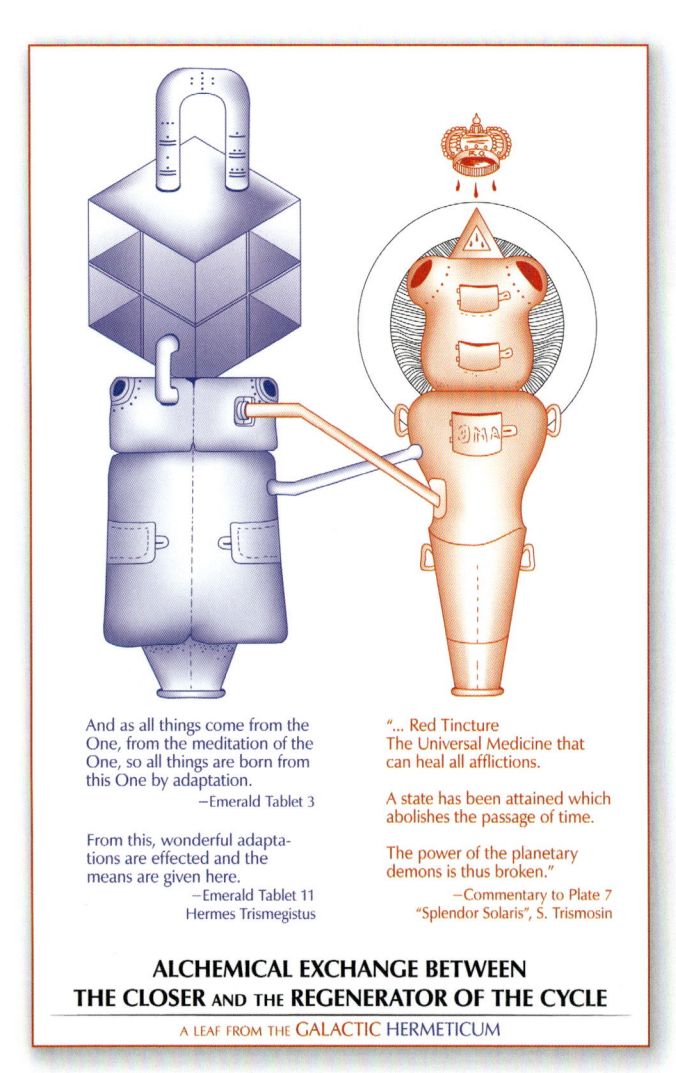

And as all things come from the One, from the meditation of the One, so all things are born from this One by adaptation.
—Emerald Tablet 3

From this, wonderful adaptations are effected and the means are given here.
—Emerald Tablet 11
Hermes Trismegistus

"... Red Tincture
The Universal Medicine that can heal all afflictions.

A state has been attained which abolishes the passage of time.

The power of the planetary demons is thus broken."
—Commentary to Plate 7
"Splendor Solaris", S. Trismosin

ALCHEMICAL EXCHANGE BETWEEN THE CLOSER AND THE REGENERATOR OF THE CYCLE

A LEAF FROM THE GALACTIC HERMETICUM

... God works all His miracles by an evolution of secret possibilities which have been long prepared, at least in their elements, and in the end by a rapid bringing of all to a head, a throwing together of the elements so that in their fusion they produce a new form and name of things and reveal a new spirit.
—Sri Aurobindo, *The Human Cycle*

Let us look more closely at the nature, history, and origins of this galactic-hermetic mind stream, known as GM108X. It is important to understand that this particular system of transmission has little taint of historical consciousness. The origin of the GM108X mind transmission lies far outside Planet Earth and predates the present historical cycle by hundreds of thousands of years. The GM108X stream was first established on this planet around 1,400 years ago. It was planted as a time release program, so that 60 years before the closing of the cycle (2012) it could be resurrected from the tomb of Pacal Votan.

Part III • Mapping the New Reality

Cosmic Mediumship and the GM108X Stream

A new transmission was prepared for the end of the cycle—a new stream of knowledge or thought set apart from historical streams and simultaneously encompassing them all under its vast cosmic umbrella. Up until 1952, the GM108X stream was an underground river in a forest not yet lit. Then in 1953, a particular incarnation of Votan—Valum Votan—was tapped and accelerated by this particular event and soon after began his own memory retrieval process (see *2012: Biography of a Time Traveler*).

What was in the mind of the great Pacal was released 1,260 years after the sealing of his tomb in 692 A.D. The thought transfer was then initiated and received a year later through the medium of Jose Arguelles–Valum Votan. For the next 40 years, this thought transfer was activated as a time release program that opened in different stages. This program directed and shaped the inner character and purpose of the cosmic medium known as Jose Arguelles–Valum Votan. Precisely 40 years after the thought transfer was initiated, the chosen medium was transformed into the messenger of time.

By 1980, interplanetary memory fragments had begun to coalesce into a larger perception of galactic origins and cosmic memory templates within the cosmic medium. It was through the *Art Planet Chronicles* that the cosmic medium began to first wake up to the reality of 108 (see prologue of *Art Planet Chronicles*). If you read this prologue carefully you will see the Arcturus spoken of here is not the star Arcturus, but rather a neighboring galaxy. The star Arcturus that we see in our galaxy is one of the first command bases from the twin galaxy. When we talk about the origins of the GM108X, we are talking about a twin galaxy, a twin star system and of a twin planet of Velatropa 24.3.

Since the agent, Valum Votan, was tapped exactly one year after the discovery of the tomb of Pacal Votan, all the books authored by him are part of the GM mind stream, most notably *Earth Ascending* with its advanced information templates regarding the activation of the psi bank plates and the Rainbow Bridge.

Valum Votan decoded the prophecy Telektonon in 1993—this marked what is known as the First Year of Prophecy. In this same year, the tomb of the Red Queen was discovered in the building adjacent to the Temple of Inscriptions on the predesignated date represented by the first year of prophecy—White Crystal Wizard.

At that moment came the subliminal activation of the avataric emanation of Red Queen-Stephanie South, directing her to encounter Valum Votan, five years later. This marked the first stage of the thought transfer on Earth—from male to female. This process of transfer was sealed four years later with the mutual recognition of the archetypal forces—Valum Votan and Red Queen—the mission was now in high gear. At this point, the process of the GM108X mind stream accelerated. The resultant knowledge released following the opening of the tomb of the Red Queen is known as the codes of the synchronic order.

This is a brief description of the process of awakening to a mission of cosmic mediumship of twin avatars—a mission that would eventually reveal the seven volumes of the *Cosmic History Chronicles*.

The seven volumes of the *Cosmic History Chronicles* are derived from a memory stream that not only traces back hundreds of thousands of Earth years, but also extends into other galaxies. The GM108X mind stream is an intergalactic phenomenon that is unique among all earthly hermetic streams. Its mission is to help point human consciousness in the direction of the galactic/cosmic horizons of the new time now dawning.

The Cosmic History Chronicles • Volume IV

> **THE NATURE OF TRANSMISSION**
>
> An octahedron magnet holds the polar positions in place at the Earth's core. Around the core, there is a resonating tympanum like a little inner Earth. The GM108X transmission beam is directed through the poles where information is stored at the core. Specific information is resonated out, according to the present stage and baktun so that different modalities of thought, culture, life, spiritual truth, and ways of being radiate from the core to the psi bank and then rain down as inspiration to receptive people through various artistic, scientific or other disciplined means.

This information stream occurs via a *synchrotronic transmission system,* and is directed to fully activate Earth consciousness into a new state of evolution. This transmission was first activated in the core of the Planet through the unconscious field of the psi bank at the beginning of the 13 baktun cycle, 3113 BC.

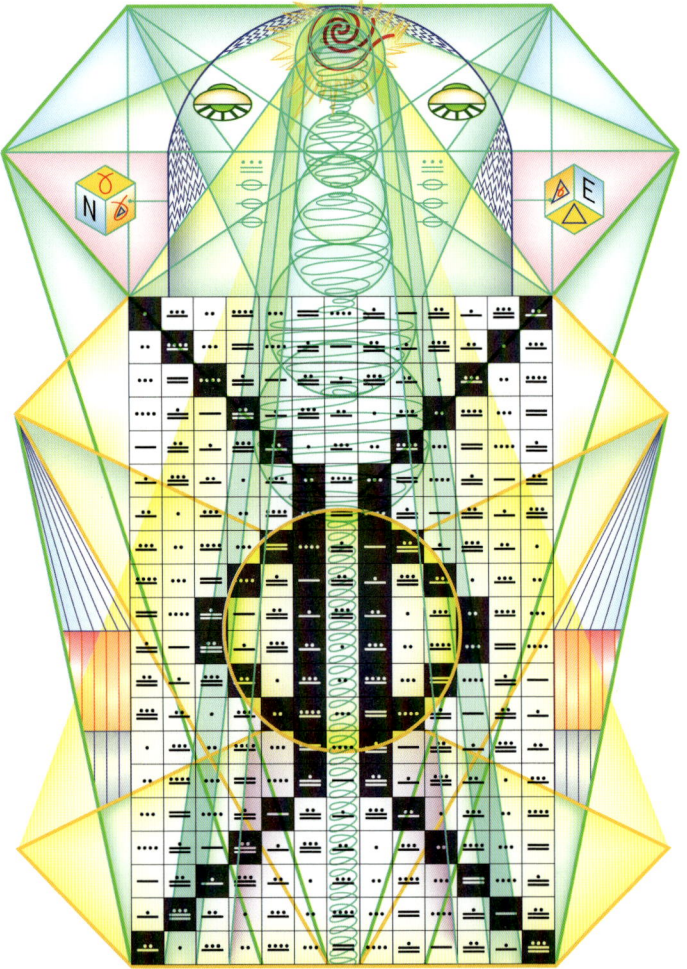

SYNCHROTRONIC TRANSMISSION BEAM 1352 — 104,000-YR. CYCLE
GM108X TRANSMISSION — 13:20 PROJECTION MATRIX

    The purpose of the GM108X information stream is to prepare for the magnetic shift that will occur in 2012. This concludes a 25,920-year cycle—90 cycles of 288 years each. The 2012 Omega Point also represents the completion of a cycle of 11,804 years since the previous magnetic shift. This is precisely 227 cycles of 52 years each that concludes in 2012. At this point, a magnetic flip will occur and we will wake up from the dream of the historical cycle and realize that what we thought was reality was nothing more than an arbitrary fiction. This will be followed by a great period of stabilization.

    Cosmic History appears now to prepare the human mind to open to the galactic dimension, so that when the shift occurs, it receives an entirely new base of knowledge and perception. All of this information is coded into the GM108X transmission stream. This stream contains frequencies and pulsations that are mathematical in nature. These numbers are downloaded into different galactic conceptual programs according to where they occur in the cycle. They can be transduced accordingly into different thought-forms or systems and structures of creativity.

Sensory Octaves and Chromocellular Activation

There are two main factors to consider when contemplating the GM108X transmission system: One is the *chromocellular intelligence* and activation, and the other is the range of *synchrotronic transmission*.

The basis of chromocellular intelligence is that each sense organ has its own octave of frequency range. Therefore, the activation of chromocellular intelligence refers to the synthesized experience of all five sense octaves combined to create one major biopsychic chromatic octave. This synaesthetic fusion creates a whole other level of perception and intelligence than previously known.

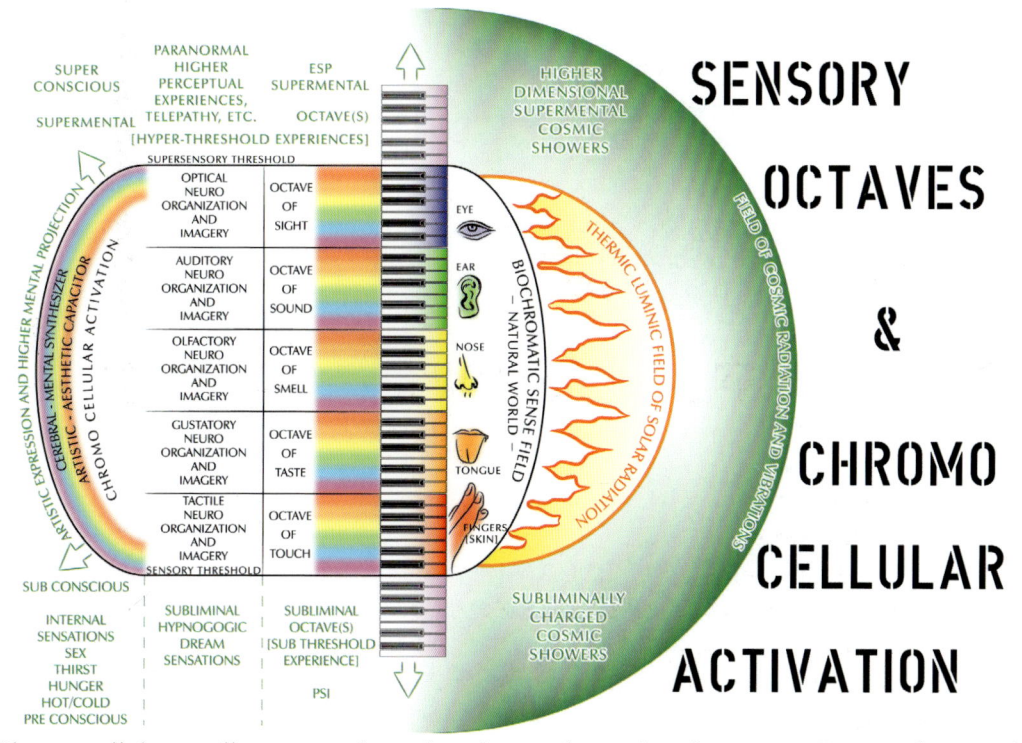

Chromocellular intelligence is also referred to as *biopsychic chromatics*. (See *Earth Ascending* maps 45 and 46 for the full description of this system). In the framework of biopsychic chromatics, each of the sense fields has a range of frequencies defined by a sensory octave. Chromocellular intelligence refers to knowing and perceptions based on the biopsychic chromatic octave.

Each sense organ has its own octave with its wide range of overtones. For example, the octave

The Cosmic History Chronicles • Volume IV

of sight contains eight major colors with many subtle shades between. These eight colors: red, orange, yellow, green, blue, indigo, violet and purple. These are all functions of the visual octave of color and light frequencies.

The octave of smell contains an entire spectrum of smell, from intoxicating perfumes to bitter pungent odors, and everything in between. All that is encompassed by aromatherapy can be arranged as a particular chromatic sensory octave. The octave of taste ranges from salty, sweet, to bitter and everything in between. The octave of touch ranges from soft and soothing to harsh or scratching sensations.

In the octave of sound, we know that when sounds are combined in certain ways, a different effect is elicited. We can hear sounds, and music can be defined by seven notes, do, re, mi, fa, so, la, ti, followed by a high do, the eighth note, which is also the first note of the next octave. All musical knowledge is contained in a single octave with numerous overtones. Rudhyar sums this up:

"The basic factor is the combination of sounds playing dynamically upon the musical consciousness of the hearers, and this combination potentially affects the whole music space directly or indirectly resonating to it. The resonance is immediate if the sounds are simultaneous or it may be expanded in time if the sounds are in sequence (a melody)."

Gurdjieff exemplified the octave of touch or kinetics through his sacred dervish dances. In these dances, combinations of movements expressed different sensations, producing varying degrees of concentration of thought.

In *CHC, Vol. I*, chromocellular activation was alluded to as the sorcerer's whole body knowing, when it says "You must learn to make your sense perceptions coextensive with the planet so that the body experiences itself in relation to the planet body (and the planet body to the solar body and the solar body to the galactic body and the galactic body to the cosmos itself)."

BIOPSYCHIC CHROMATIC OCTAVE

Imagine the different sensory octaves creating a synaesthetic symphony. Through this symphony information is received—information of another kind that allows us to operate in the cosmos in a new way.

Part III • Mapping the New Reality

In this regard, we experience the senses as one giant octave that synthesizes experience and consciously gathers information through our sensory apparatus. This is the way of sensory evolution. The sum result is a highly complex and integrated resonant structure that, through advanced intelligence, can be projected or beamed, stepped up or stepped down, and targeted to different dimensional potentialities. This integrated resonant structure is experienced when our cells open up as a complete multisensory fusion, guided by higher-dimensional intelligence.

Whole field experience defines the *chromocellular intelligence*—a different kind of intelligence than previously known. In fact, it is so qualitatively different that it is virtually impossible to describe. Why? Because our current information is conditioned by historical/literary references coded into systems of right hemisphere dominant sequentiality, such as language. The chromocellular intelligence is not conditioned in the least and does not even know history; it is not a literate referential system, but a holonomic, whole field sensory knowing.

Synchronic Transmission

> *By power of subliminal conscious navigational intelligence prior to peak excitation ejection, the pilot angel programs may choose targets in parallel universes which can be chosen to coordinate subliminal intelligence with pre-organic primary stages of evolution of parallel stellar mass. This establishes quantum dimensional space in counter point of hyperdimensional time.*
> —Valum Votan, *Dynamics of Time*, 18.3

Once we understand chromocellular intelligence, then we can apply what we have learned to experience *chromocellular activation*. Chromocellular activation refers to the capacity to project the chromocellular experience in all of its informational coherence into different time dimensions. This is the system used by the GM108X mind stream.

Because of its evolved nature, the GM108X is able to project this whole field knowing as a type of "high frequency" samadhi into an array of different time dimensions, also referred to as *resonant field harmonics* (see *The Mayan Factor*, Ch. 2). This is done through a system of *synchrotronic transmission*.

This is how the system of the Galactic Mayan mind transmission originated in a twin galaxy or twin star system on a twin planet that had evolved to the next stage of synthesis as a planetary (galactic) art whole—noosphere.

Synchrotronic radiation refers to the radiation emitted by electrons travelling close to the speed of light within a specifically defined magnetic field. For example, synchrotronic radiation is very evident in the crab nebula. Most exploding supernovas also emit this type of synchrotronic radiation, which again are the electrons travelling close to the speed of light within a specifically defined magnetic field.

Synchrotronic communication is the telepathic harnessing or use of this type of radiation to communicate and "travel" or project a whole field of resonance through paranormal coordination of the synchrotronic radiation. This energy travels faster than the speed of light and can be utilized to find receptive vehicles open to receive telepathic communication. This information is communicated both mind-to-mind, and also through particular types of sensory or whole body images, or "fields of resonance", that can be received and transduced into "artistic inspiration" or other forms of greater morphogenetic complexity.

For instance, Beethoven said that music is deeper than philosophy—this is true when we listen carefully to some of his compositions, they take us to a very deep place and suddenly we realize we are having a profound experience that cannot be communicated in words. A composer like Beethoven, who was virtually deaf, was receiving messages from beyond, translating them and bringing them to this world. Because of his receptivity, much of his music is actually coded communication from another dimension.

Consider the following multivalued perception from Dane Rudhyar:

> *A tone is a solar system composed of a central sun, of planets, a circulating magnetic substance relative to a vaster system. A tone is a microcosmos reflecting faithfully the macro-cosmos and its laws, its cycles its center. A tone is a living cell composed of organic matter that has the power of assimilation, of reproduction, of making changes, or growing. A tone is something tangible and always means a certain mass of vibrating substance ...*

Much of the intelligence that filters to this planet is a function of the highly directed synchrotronic communication beam that is streaming to Earth from the Arcturus galaxy. For instance, when we speak of passing through a synchronization beam, we are referring to a specific beam that is 13 baktuns wide. This is known as a *synchrotronic communication time beam*. All positive inspiration and knowledge coming to our planet is a function of this beam. This beam is transmitted and communicated to this planet to offset the effect of lost planet analphs (see *CHC, Vol. III*).

At the beginning of the thirteenth baktun cycle (1618), that synchrotronic synchronization beam was stepped up in its focus on this planet for the purpose of continuously seeding the unconscious field of the psi bank with higher mind transmissions. These mind transmissions are generally picked up by writers, philosophers, musicians, painters, scientists and anyone positively inspired and sufficiently disciplined in any field.

Again, these inspirations are sent to offset the

Cosmic Field Functions
Closer and Regenerator of the Cycle
Generating Harmonic of Polar Light

Part III • Mapping the New Reality

GM108X ~ Galactic-Hermetic Mind Stream
Its Nature, History and System of Transmission

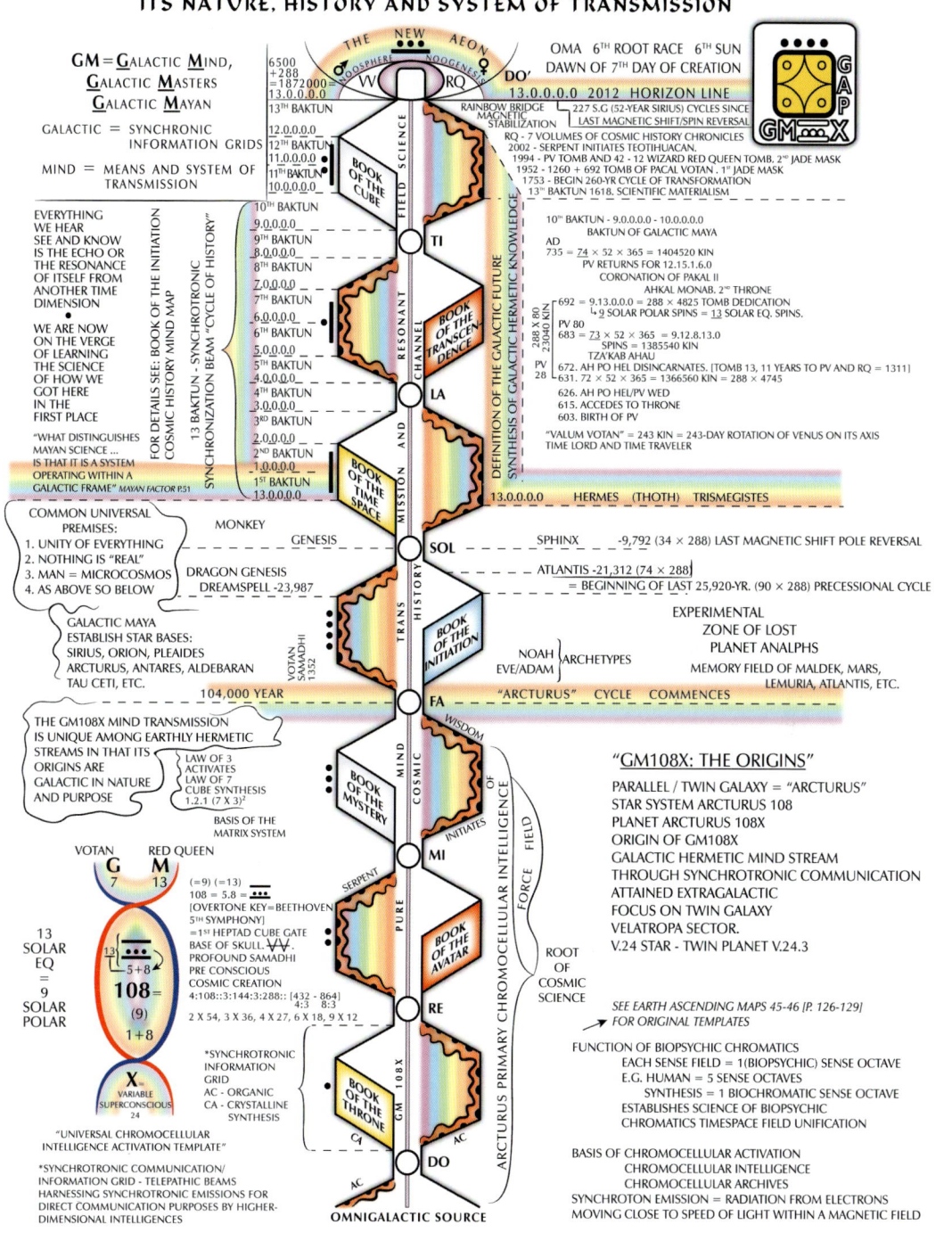

GM = **G**alactic **M**ind,
Galactic **M**asters
Galactic **M**ayan

GALACTIC = SYNCHRONIC INFORMATION GRIDS

MIND = MEANS AND SYSTEM OF TRANSMISSION

EVERYTHING WE HEAR SEE AND KNOW IS THE ECHO OR THE RESONANCE OF ITSELF FROM ANOTHER TIME DIMENSION

WE ARE NOW ON THE VERGE OF LEARNING THE SCIENCE OF HOW WE GOT HERE IN THE FIRST PLACE

"WHAT DISTINGUISHES MAYAN SCIENCE... IS THAT IT IS A SYSTEM OPERATING WITHIN A GALACTIC FRAME" MAYAN FACTOR P.51

COMMON UNIVERSAL PREMISES:
1. UNITY OF EVERYTHING
2. NOTHING IS "REAL"
3. MAN = MICROCOSMOS
4. AS ABOVE SO BELOW

GALACTIC MAYA ESTABLISH STAR BASES: SIRIUS, ORION, PLEAIDES ARCTURUS, ANTARES, ALDEBARAN TAU CETI, ETC.

THE GM108X MIND TRANSMISSION IS UNIQUE AMONG EARTHLY HERMETIC STREAMS IN THAT ITS ORIGINS ARE GALACTIC IN NATURE AND PURPOSE

LAW OF 3 ACTIVATES
LAW OF 7
CUBE SYNTHESIS
$1.2.1 (7 \times 3)^2$

BASIS OF THE MATRIX SYSTEM

VOTAN RED QUEEN
G   M
7   13

13 SOLAR EQ = 9 SOLAR POLAR

13
5+8
108
(9)
1+8

X - VARIABLE SUPERCONSCIOUS 24

(=9) (=13)
108 = 5.8 =
[OVERTONE KEY = BEETHOVEN 5TH SYMPHONY]
= 1ST HEPTAD CUBE GATE
BASE OF SKULL
PROFOUND SAMADHI
PRE CONSCIOUS
COSMIC CREATION
4:108::3:144:3:288:: [432 - 864]
                       4:3   8:3
2 X 54, 3 X 36, 4 X 27, 6 X 18, 9 X 12

"UNIVERSAL CHROMOCELLULAR INTELLIGENCE ACTIVATION TEMPLATE"

*SYNCHROTRONIC COMMUNICATION/ INFORMATION GRID - TELEPATHIC BEAMS HARNESSING SYNCHROTRONIC EMISSIONS FOR DIRECT COMMUNICATION PURPOSES BY HIGHER-DIMENSIONAL INTELLIGENCES

*SYNCHROTRONIC INFORMATION GRID
AC - ORGANIC
CA - CRYSTALLINE SYNTHESIS

FOR DETAILS SEE: BOOK OF THE INITIATION COSMIC HISTORY MIND MAP

13 BAKTUN - SYNCHROTRONIC SYNCHRONIZATION BEAM "CYCLE OF HISTORY"

6500 +288 =1872000 13.0.0.0.0
12.0.0.0.0 12TH BAKTUN
11.0.0.0.0 11TH BAKTUN
10.0.0.0.0 10TH BAKTUN
9.0.0.0.0   9TH BAKTUN
8.0.0.0.0   8TH BAKTUN
7.0.0.0.0   7TH BAKTUN
6.0.0.0.0   6TH BAKTUN
5.0.0.0.0   5TH BAKTUN
4.0.0.0.0   4TH BAKTUN
3.0.0.0.0   3RD BAKTUN
2.0.0.0.0   2ND BAKTUN
1.0.0.0.0   1ST BAKTUN
13.0.0.0.0

MONKEY GENESIS

DRAGON GENESIS
DREAMSPELL -23,987

VOTAN SAMADHI 1352

104,000 YEAR

THE NEW AEON
NOOSPHERE • NOOGENESIS
W RQ
DO'

BOOK OF THE CUBE — FIELD SCIENCE — TI

BOOK OF THE TRANSCENDENCE — RESONANT CHANNEL — LA

BOOK OF THE TIME SPACE — MISSION AND —

— SOL

BOOK OF THE INITIATION — TRANS —

— FA

BOOK OF THE MYSTERY — HISTORY OF COSMIC MIND —

— MI

BOOK OF THE AVATAR — PURE WISDOM INITIATES —

— RE

BOOK OF THE THRONE — GM 108X —

— DO
AC
OMNIGALACTIC SOURCE

ARCTURUS PRIMARY CHROMOCELLULAR INTELLIGENCE FORCE FIELD — ROOT OF COSMIC SCIENCE

OMA 6TH ROOT RACE 6TH SUN
DAWN OF 7TH DAY OF CREATION

13.0.0.0.0 2012 HORIZON LINE
RAINBOW BRIDGE 227 S.G (52-YEAR SIRIUS) CYCLES SINCE
MAGNETIC   LAST MAGNETIC SHIFT/SPIN REVERSAL
STABILIZATION
RQ - 7 VOLUMES OF COSMIC HISTORY CHRONICLES
2002 - SERPENT INITIATES TEOTIHUACAN,
1994 - PV TOMB AND 42 - 12 WIZARD RED QUEEN TOMB. 2ND JADE MASK
1952 - 1260 + 692 TOMB OF PACAL VOTAN. 1ST JADE MASK
1753 - BEGIN 260-YR CYCLE OF TRANSFORMATION
13TH BAKTUN 1618. SCIENTIFIC MATERIALISM

10TH BAKTUN - 9.0.0.0.0 - 10.0.0.0.0
BAKTUN OF GALACTIC MAYA
AD
735 = $\underline{74} \times 52 \times 365 = 1404520$ KIN
PV RETURNS FOR 12.15.1.6.0
CORONATION OF PAKAL
AHKAL MONAB. 2ND THRONE
692 = 9.13.0.0.0 = 288 × 4825 TOMB DEDICATION
$\underline{9}$ SOLAR POLAR SPINS = 13 SOLAR EQ. SPINS.
PV 80
683 = $\underline{73} \times 52 \times 365 = 9.12.8.13.0$
SPINS = 1385540 KIN
TZ'A KAB AHAU
PV 672. AH PO HEL DISINCARNATES. [TOMB 13, 11 YEARS TO PV AND RQ = 1311]
28 631. 72 × 52 × 365 = 1366560 KIN = 288 × 4745
626. AH PO HEL/PV WED
615. ACCEDES TO THRONE
603. BIRTH OF PV

"VALUM VOTAN" = 243 KIN = 243-DAY ROTATION OF VENUS ON ITS AXIS
TIME LORD AND TIME TRAVELER

13.0.0.0.0   HERMES (THOTH) TRISMEGISTES

DEFINITION OF THE GALACTIC FUTURE SYNTHESIS OF GALACTIC HERMETIC KNOWLEDGE

288 X 80
23040 KIN

SPHINX   -9,792 (34 × 288) LAST MAGNETIC SHIFT POLE REVERSAL
ATLANTIS -21,312 (74 × 288)
= BEGINNING OF LAST 25,920-YR. (90 × 288) PRECESSIONAL CYCLE

EXPERIMENTAL ZONE OF LOST PLANET ANALPHS

NOAH ARCHETYPES
EVE/ADAM   MEMORY FIELD OF MALDEK, MARS, LEMURIA, ATLANTIS, ETC.

"ARCTURUS" CYCLE COMMENCES

"GM108X: THE ORIGINS"

PARALLEL / TWIN GALAXY = "ARCTURUS"
STAR SYSTEM ARCTURUS 108
PLANET ARCTURUS 108X
ORIGIN OF GM108X
GALACTIC HERMETIC MIND STREAM
THROUGH SYNCHROTRONIC COMMUNICATION
ATTAINED EXTRAGALACTIC
FOCUS ON TWIN GALAXY
VELATROPA SECTOR.
V.24 STAR - TWIN PLANET V.24.3

SEE EARTH ASCENDING MAPS 45-46 [P. 126-129]
FOR ORIGINAL TEMPLATES

FUNCTION OF BIOPSYCHIC CHROMATICS
EACH SENSE FIELD = 1(BIOPSYCHIC) SENSE OCTAVE
E.G. HUMAN = 5 SENSE OCTAVES
SYNTHESIS = 1 BIOCHROMATIC SENSE OCTAVE
ESTABLISHES SCIENCE OF BIOPSYCHIC CHROMATICS TIMESPACE FIELD UNIFICATION

BASIS OF CHROMOCELLULAR ACTIVATION
CHROMOCELLULAR INTELLIGENCE
CHROMOCELLULAR ARCHIVES
SYNCHROTON EMISSION = RADIATION FROM ELECTRONS MOVING CLOSE TO SPEED OF LIGHT WITHIN A MAGNETIC FIELD

deleterious effects of the lost planet analphs as they created the Babylonian stream of history. These synchrotronic beams are also responsible for the inspiration of various esoteric or hermetic traditions that also arose to counteract the effects of the Babylonian stream.

Galactic Maya Numerology

GM means Galactic Mayan, Galactic Mind or Galactic Masters. The G is the 7 and M is the 13, 1 and 8 is 9 and 108 is a function of multiples of 9 (4 x 27, 3 x 36, 6 x 18, 9 x 12, 2 x 54). Every time 144 is multiplied by 3, 108 divides into that 4 times.

This is a frequency index factor that shows that the program of the 108 is coded to the 144, which is the Book of Revelation number and also the frequency of the baktun cycles. 144 x 2 = 288, the polar harmonic frequency. Whenever 288 is multiplied by 3, 108 goes into it 8 times. All the information then of the 108 stream is coded in accord with the meanings of those particular numbers as they occur in the whole range of possibilities within the development of the different streams of thought in Velatropa 24.3.

The 108 is coded to the 144 by the number 36 and connects the Book of Revelation with the 144,000 days of the baktun cycle. The 288 (144 x 2) is key at the end of the cycle as it is the frequency of stabilization of the polar harmonic. It should be noted that 288 x 90 = 25,920—the precise number of years in the processional cycle of the Zodiac. The precession of the Zodiac describes how long it takes the Earth to go through the constellations, Pisces, Aquarius, etc. (2160 years each). This illustrates how all of the cycles of the Earth are related to polar magnetism and either portends magnetic shifts or even a spin reversal.

144 x 3 = 432,
108 x 4 = 432

The number 288 is the supreme frequency representing the harmonic of polar light. 144 is one pole and the other 144 is the other pole. The 108 combines with 288.

3 x 288 = 864
8 x 108 = 864

Consider the following:

3 x 288 = 864
8 x 108 = 864
6 x 144 = 864

This pattern continues on up. The fourth factor is 216, 6 cubed or 108 x 2. 432 = 216 x 2, 108 x 4, 144 x 3. 864 = 216 x 4, 108 x 8, 144 x 6, 288 x 3. These four frequencies, 108, 144, 216 and 288 establish a set of primes forming creation templates utilized by four time lens units with different cosmic creative functions, through infinite orders of the unified reality.

Part III • Mapping the New Reality

Because of the enormous shift in aeons, the GM108X has put in place the twin avataric functions that manifest at the final focalized pivot point of the current synchrotronic transmission. This transmission is beamed through the two prepared instruments to facilitate *noogenesis* and to project an energy configuration or coherency into the psi bank that will accelerate and precipitate the quantum mind shift leading to the establishment of the new evolutionary cycle.

The GM108X is the direct coordinating transmission of this particular beam. This is the same beam that began the surveillance of the experimental sector—the Velatropa Sector—approximately 104,000 years ago. Through the highly focussed "1352 Samadhi", the specific mind transmission stream known as "Votan" became activated at this far distant point.

Time Markers in the Life of Pacal Votan

The key points in Pacal's life were the years 631, 683, 692 and 735. 631 was the time of his illumination and manifestation of cosmic power. He is galactic agent 13 66 56. This number is also a multiple of 288. 288 x 4745 is 13 66 560 (see *Mayan Factor* Appendix). This also completed 72 52-year cycles. 683 is the year he died—this completed 73 cycles. 72 is a factor in the tun cycles of 360 (72 x 5) or number of degrees in a circle. 73 has to do with the solar cycle of 365 days or 5 x 73. Pacal's time of power was between those two fractal points.

We know from *The Mayan Factor* that 13 66 56 is a factor of one of the most synchronizing of harmonic cycles—all of the Venus lunar, solar galactic cycles and many others are keyed into this number. This was the peak point in the entire synchronization beam. Pacal's tomb was buried and the temple was completed and dedicated in 692, nine years after his death. The dedication was on 9.13.0.0.0. From the time of 13 66 56 (A.D. 631), which is 9.12.13.0.0 to the dedication of the temple is exactly 80 cycles of 288. Pacal died at age 80. So this is a marker. The purpose and meaning of his death and prophecy was that the polar shift represented by the 288 is what we have to look for 60 years after the discovery of his tomb in 1952, for 60 is the frequency of his galactic signature—Yellow Galactic Sun, Kin 60.

From "Pages From the Lives of Hermetic Masters" a study in the development and cultivation of the occult personality.

Galactic Master Pacal Votan Receives 1st Light of Resurrection — 7th Ray Emanation of St. Germain Unifying his Spirit-Prophecy with Hierarchy Age of Aquarius

Kin 123 - Overtone 13 - 11 Wizard Yr [Nov 27, 1952]

135

At that time 104,000 years ago, in the timing of the overall cosmic activation of intelligence, this sector of the universe had entered the zone of the lost planet analphs, the experimental zone. For this reason, it was necessary to put it in surveillance and determine when and where to focus the synchrotronic communication beam—like a laser point in the mind of an otherwise undifferentiated light stream.

The central focus of this beam is the actual GM108X mind transmission. This purpose and plan was planted in the terrestrial plane by Pacal Votan. The plan was then stored by the Red Queen as a mind terma for the end of the cycle. The Red Queen was a knowledge holder and the true successor of Pacal. Being hermetic, she wrapped herself in mystery—hence the enigma of the tomb of the Red Queen, the nameless one without record.

Sun Spot Cycles

The numbers nine and thirteen are significant numbers in relation with the sun spot cycles that are recorded and affect the terrestrial poles. The nine and the thirteen are correlated to the turning of the solar poles and of its equator. It takes the sun 26 days to rotate at its equator, and 33 days to rotate at the poles. This means it takes nine polar cycles to thirteen equatorial cycles for the turning at the poles and the turning at the equator to synchronize.

There are eighty 288-day cycles from Pacal's time of power in 681 to the dedication of his tomb in 692, 9.13.0.0.0. This is a clue to the end of the cycle and the possibility of a pole shift or of forestalling one. Given the right psychosolar technology, the humans may be equipped to stabilize the poles according to the frequency of harmonic polar light 288. This is why in the fourth week of the 7:7::7:7 practices, the seven mystic moons also give a radion value of 288—for the stabilization of the harmonic of polar light.

Then we have the 72 cycles of 52 years at 631, the 73 cycles of 52 years at 683—time of disincarnation—and 52 years later, the 74th cycle, is also a key frequency. Pacal Votan is depicted

Given the right psychosolar technology, the humans may be equipped to stabilize the poles according to the frequency of harmonic polar light 288.

Part III • Mapping the New Reality

returning for the coronation of Pacal II, on the second throne of Akhal Monab (AD 736-742), 74 52-year cycles + 1 year since 3113. This is the supernatural reappearance of Pacal that occurs in 736—exactly 52 + 1 years after his disincarnation—53 years is the number of Sirian rebirth.

These solar galactic 52-year cycles 72, 73 and 74—are keys in the timing and coordination of the solar sun spot cycles and the relation of the sun and moon to the planetary cycles of the Earth. All of this was to demonstrate the precise timing of Pacal Votan to plant the GM108X mind stream in the Earth.

Twin Jade Masks

Once the Galactic Mayans closed Palenque (even before the pre-recorded departure date of 830 AD), everything had been buried. There were no apparent clues remaining other than the mysterious stories about a man named "Wotan" gathered 1,000 years later in 1692. Aside from this, there was no clue until the opening of the tomb in 1952. Then, 42 years later, in 1994 came the opening of the Red Queen's tomb. These two tombs with their twin jade masks were each coded to be discovered at precise moments in time. One jade mask was discovered in the tomb of Pacal Votan on November 27, 1952, (Kin 123). The other jade mask was discovered in Temple 13, the tomb of the Red Queen adjacent to the Temple of Inscriptions, June 1, 1994, (Kin 194). These two tombs discovered when they were signalled to the earthy avatars the summons to their mission.

Valum Votan and Red Queen are instruments of a particular function—the closing and regeneration of a specific cycle. They are the living representatives of two symbolic forms manifest as two jade masks. These twin forces function impersonally as the biopsychic triggers that open up the noosphere and initiate the next cycle of cosmic evolution on this particular planet. Together, they function as the channel, GM108X.

The other aspect of this galactic transmission stream functions as the cosmic history core channel. This is the information base of the galactic culture summarized as cosmic history and transmitted through a particular core channel coded to another precise point in the synchronic order. This channel is the same as the GM108X mind stream that functions at its highest level as the 1352 Samadhi, through which the different resonances are transduced. All of this information—the hermetic streams, the GM108X, and even such phenomena as $E=MC^2$ have been pre-recorded and stored in the Earth's universal radio receiver/transmission system in the psi bank.

Each of the seven volumes of the *Cosmic History Chronicles* corresponds to the seven different principle points of this mind stream as notes or registrations of a cosmic octave. This represents the primary information range established in the twin Arcturus galaxy. Volumes 1-3 constitute the primary range do re mi. Volumes 4-7 is the information evolved once the stream of galactic knowledge entered the Velatropa 24 sector: fa, so, la, ti. When the seventh volume, *Book of the Cube*, is complete, then comes the closing of the cycle and rainbow bridge: this initiates the next octave, do.

Book of the Cube will build on the matrices underlying the seven volumes which are not in words in some sense, but rather number matrices, courtesy of the 441 cube. These are transduced

The Cosmic History Chronicles • Volume IV

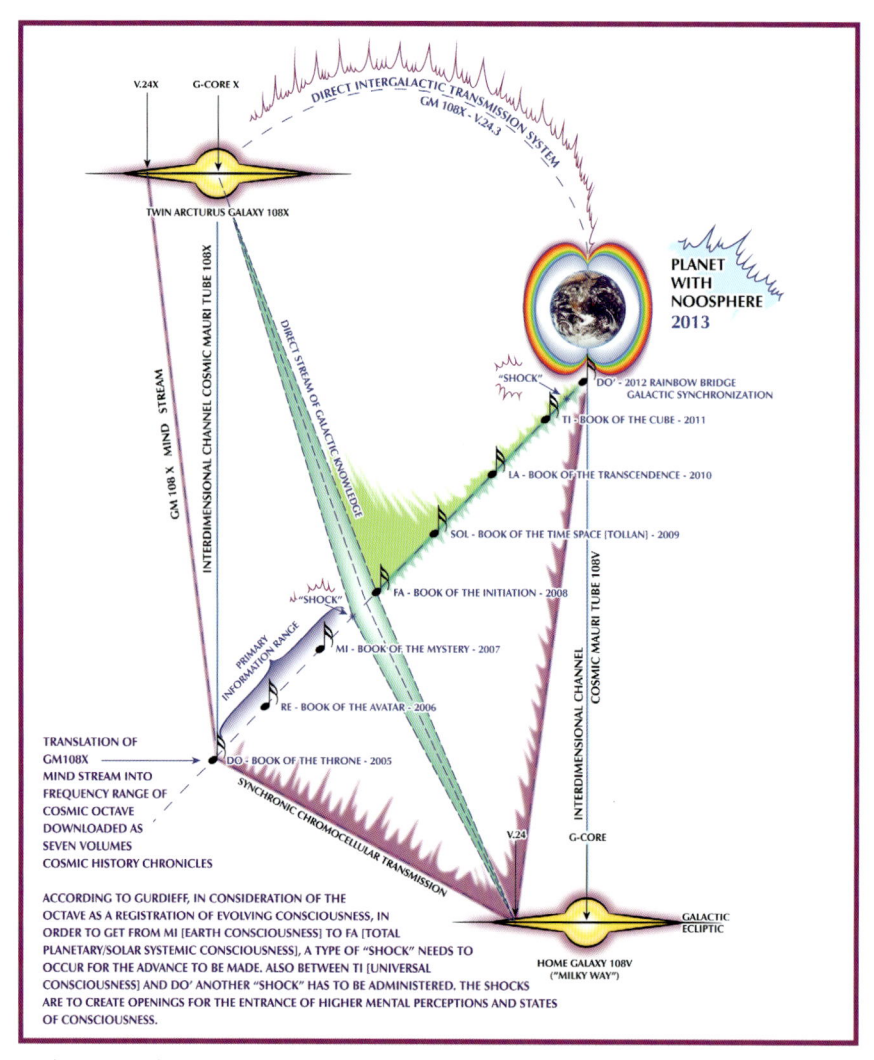

into conceptual terminology: Throne, Avatar, Mystery, Initiation, Timespace, Transcendence and Cube. These are all based on the matrix of 13 (13 chapters or gates in each of the 7 volumes. 7 x 13 = 91 = 1+2+3...+13).

This is all a function of a coding system brought forth by the Galactic Mayan mind transmission that encodes and encapsulates all of the essential information transductions to this particular planet, Velatropa 24.3. The imprinting of this coding system is to ensure that when the cycle closes, there is a new formulation of knowledge set in place—an ever evolving post-historical knowledge that lays the synchronic thought matrices and templates for the new cycle.

The core information is coming through the *Cosmic History Chronicles*. These seven volumes are critical in helping the planetary mind enter the galactic dimension of consciousness. In that regard, the transmission is embodied and incorporated into the binary dialectic of male and female. This forms the AC/CA, one strand is serpentine (AC) and one crystalline (CA). These are always balanced.

The crystalline forms the conceptual order of a book and the serpentine forms the intuitive/subliminal underlying communication coming through the book. In each of the volumes, the information is coded and subliminally communicated through the structure of the language. The subliminal information is the information of the original galactic order or the actual nature of reality. This is the information that is reformulating your knowledge, thoughts, consciousness and perceptions, even as you read.

We are preparing to receive the supramental descent that establishes the original matrix of the people of OMA (Original Matrix Attained), and opens into the new aeon. This is the birth or the noogenesis of homo noosphericus. At this point, we will begin to understand how this journey began—with the chromocellular activation, intelligence and understanding of the chromocellular archives. The chromocellular archives are the means of storing the information units as projected chromocellular engrams. This is very different from books. This knowledge prepares us for *hyperorganic field experiences.*

Once we are operating synaesthetically, as one huge biopsychic sense octave, then it will be easy to project, hyperorganically, into the environment to interact with different forms of life and matter, and thus create a wide range of grand architectural structures. This is the meaning and purpose to the Book of Wisdom presented in *CHC, Vol. II*. At this stage, our senses will extrude radion filaments to interact with the radion of nature, such as trees and rocks, to create a whole other experience of reality and cosmic relationship. Then we will understand what it means to create the planet as a work of art.

> Through the so-called beam transmission, all thoughts of everyone are personally connected to and stored on "diskettes". These information pools form the foundation of the chromocellular archives.

All the art we have been able to channel in the historical cycle will be done on an even larger scale. At this stage, we will be participating in various levels of *synaesthetic hyperorganic symphonies*—the synthesis of the human element with the cosmos. This is all part of the planetary initiation.

From a conventional point of view, this is wild information, but from a higher-dimensional point of view, this knowledge is equivalent to galactic pre-school. As we move into this alternative reality, we will discover our creative spirit, yet undreamed. All the means for realizing ourselves through this chromocellular activation/synchrotronic transmission will be in our grasp. Let's let go, open our minds and blast off into the open highway of the galactic mainstream. This is the meaning of the GM108X transmission that is incarnated in the tellers of this tale: Valum Votan and Red Queen.

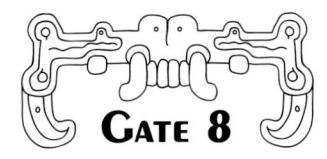

Gate 8
Symbolic Systems: Traditions Beyond Words

Up ahead you see a gate flashing with many symbols, some familiar, some not so familiar. As you approach the gate, you sense a pulsing vibration beneath the surface of the flashing symbols. You understand the symbols as the meeting point between the visible and invisible; the apparent and the concealed. Your mind flashes briefly to the every day world of people racing to and fro. You realize that everything that appears in the physical world is woven together by a vast construct of symbols—from cuneiform and hieroglyphs on up to corporate logos to the galactic/future symbols. Suddenly, you realize that all symbols point to the one indescribable reality in its many facets and stages of unfolding.

> *The entire universe is a great theater of mirrors, a set of hieroglyphs to decipher; everything is a sign, everything harbors and manifests mystery. The principles of contradiction, of excluded middle, and of linear causality are supplanted by those of resolution, of included middle, and of synchronicity.* ~
> —Alice Bailey, *Esoteric Psychology II*

All of reality is a language of signs and symbols. Everything that appears is a passing ephemeral manifestation, and yet, it represents some deeper construct or value of another dimension. The deeper stratums of reality render all phenomena as symbols passing through this initiatic gate called "life".

A symbol is a sign which opens up or makes transparent insights and truths that were previously hidden. The human body is merely a symbol, and through its senses are constructed ideas and perceptions about reality. Just as the body is a symbol, so are all of our experiences symbolic.

Everything is nothing until we endow it with meaning. The moment we say that something has meaning is the moment that the *something* becomes the symbol for the meaning—but the thing itself is not the actual meaning. The meaning we ascribe to a certain thing is in accordance with our conditioning, perceptual structure and spiritual disposition. Each person lives according to his/her own coded system of semiotics—a system of self-referenced symbols ascribed to his/her experience.

To further understand the symbolic nature of reality, we draw on the system of correspondences—everything we see corresponds to something we don't see. Everything on the earthly plane has a correspondence to something on the heavenly plane; as above, so below. The purpose of symbolic systems is to learn how to read the lower reality through the lens of the higher reality. In other words, the whole of reality is actually based on a symbolic construct projected from another dimension.

> *Because it (reality) cannot be conceived of by the intellect and is free from all conceptual limitations from the very beginning, therefore it is called by the name* mahamudra *or the great symbol.*
>
> —Padmasambhava

All of reality is an aspect of this great symbol, which is the *mahamudra* path. Everything we see—the trees, the greenery, the birds, and so forth—is a coordinated myriad of signs pointing to the one indescribable reality. This hidden reality is a mind event free of all conceptualization. When William Blake said, "to see infinity in a grain of sand", he was referring to the quality of the true nature of reality.

According to the doctrine of correspondences, every manifestation of appearance is a sign that corresponds to another reality—a symbolic reality—projected by the mind itself. In the Sufi tradition, everything is a sign—*dhikr*—pointing to God—everything is a system of divinely orchestrated correspondences. What we see in the phenomenal reality is not randomly arranged, but is the response to an underlying system that is precisely ordered, structured and meaningful.

There is a polarity and a complementarity; there is surface and there is symbol; there is apparent reality and there is hidden reality; there is what you see and what you don't see. This brings us to the underlying theme of this volume: the hermetic, the occult, and the hidden—what you do not see. The purpose of the labyrinthian journey is initiation into the "unseen". The passage from the external sensory to the telepathic invisible.

THE SYMBOL OF THE RED SEA

One of the most potent symbols in the Bible is the Crossing of the Red Sea. This is not just the record of a miraculous event in a nation's history but the description of a spiritual initiation. Once an aspirant has left the old way of life, represented by Egypt, and crossed the seas of commitment, he cannot go back. He has to face the inner psychological desert, with its rebellions and its discipline, its purification and its revelation of an inner Mount Sinai, until the old slave psychology has died and he is ready in a new generation of attitudes to enter the promised land of the spirit.

—Zév ben Shimon Halevi

Symbols concentrate and condense whole volumes of meaning into mental, emotional and physical levels of reality. For example, think of the religious symbols of the meditating Buddha or the crucified Christ—they are macrosymbolic forms that conjure whole ideologies of specific feelings according to conditioning. The most obvious symbolic system is the alphabet we use every day; it is a potent set of symbolic forms—letters—that together form a larger consciousness called "literacy".

Signs of the zodiac, houses, planets, aspects, are all one symbolic system derived from astronomical facts concerning celestial motions. There are many other types of symbolic systems for different purposes. All these systems are interconnected and express certain points in different ways. Within the mind of the noosphere, all the esoteric and hermetic streams are functions of one mind; the single indivisible organizing structure of Earth's conscious mental field.

> ### Symbols in Society
> Every secret society has its specific sets of symbols as do most organizations. Roerich's Banner of Peace, HPB ouroboros, Sri Aurobindo and the seal of Solomon, even money is replete with symbolism. Think of US paper money with its eye of Horus (a single eye on top of the pyramid). This symbol was also used in Crowley's Book of the Law. The dollar bill has the words "Annuit Coeptus Novis Ordo Seclorum" surrounding this symbol. This means, "Announcing the birth of the new order of the ages". Franklin D. Roosevelt was influenced by the Masons to place the great seal on the dollar bill. Think also of the Pentagon and the pentagram symbol of witchcraft. Whether we know it or not, our life is saturated, we might say stitched together by symbols.

Literacy and Symbolism

Symbolic systems serve as signposts along the path, and when practiced, can accelerate the path. These systems are keys or forms that lift us rung by rung, from the conditioned grid of reality, up the ladder of higher harmony. Just as there are symbols to liberate the mind, so are there symbols that keep the mind enslaved.

Every society maintains "crowd control" through various symbols. As Gurdjieff said:

> *In the hands of the incompetent and the ignorant, however full of good intentions, the same symbol becomes an instrument of delusion ... symbols which are transposed into the words of ordinary language become rigid in them; they grow dim and very easily become their own opposites.*

The more the machine world proliferates, the more we lose coherent contact with the deeper symbolic side of our brain. This decline began with the advent of mechanical literacy 250-500 years ago. The value of literacy supersedes the value of symbols. It is important to keep in mind that up until Gutenberg invented the printing press in the fifteenth century, not many people knew how to read. Literacy was a function only of the priests, monks and scribes. The people were communicated to through symbols.

As materialism and technology expands, it seems people no longer have the time to contemplate the cosmic meaning of traditional symbolic systems. For this reason, the symbols are swept underground and become occult—awaiting the right moment to resurface.

At the time of this writing, we find ourselves in the final phase of the democratization of values symbolized by the Internet, where many esoteric teachings can be found. However, what is lacking is the governing criterion to understand the information contained therein; there is no one single globally unifying criterion. All information contained therein is based on the needs and perceptions of the personal ego. The result is a randomly shifting chaotic disorder. But what is information without true knowledge?

> ### Symbols and Concepts
> We are trained to live on the surface—with much time spent solving problems at a conceptual level—not according to symbol or underlying meaning. This takes so much time that we tend to ignore the nonconceptual side of our brain. In this polarity, there is a tension between the part of our brain that conceptualizes and constructs with language, grammar and logic, and the part of our brain that is nonconceptual—at least verbally. Why does it seem the symbolic side so often struggles against the conceptual side?

As we make the Great Transition, the guiding criterion to enter into cosmic knowledge is to *forget everything we know and do not try to comprehend with what we think we understand.* Without a guiding criterion, we will build a big information pancake that will fall on our head.

We live in a society that does not give credence to transcendent values, and therefore does not overtly recognize the higher value of symbolic systems. Symbolic systems are a function of consciousness—pre-literate or post-literate. Symbolical systems are meant to create and communicate a comprehensive sense of order that can be distinguished and learned by a whole side of our brain; we have a symbolical side (right) and a conceptualizing side (left) of our brain.

According to Cosmic History, symbols are the language of the transcendent reality communicating with the nonconceptual side of the brain. When studying esoteric and hermetic systems, it is important to keep in mind the historical situation from which they sprang. As mass literacy arose, hermetic thought and symbolic systems, in general, were swept under the carpet. Literary/alphabetic systems disperse knowledge. Symbolic structures condense knowledge and raise the deciphering structures of the mind to a higher level. Decoding systems of thought with symbolic orders engages the mind into a higher synthesizing whole system process of intelligence.

Mystical texts, such as Dzogchen or mahamudra meditation manuals, point to states of mind or awareness that are non-conceptual. Many people take it literally when the texts say "there is nothing to do". Of course, this is true from the Absolute point of view within the meditation—but taken literally these types of texts can lead to complacency.

However, we also live on a third-dimensional plane where reality is not static—at least the reality that our bodies inhabit. We can experience samadhi, but then at some point we will get thirsty or have to go to the bathroom—then we reenter this other reality.

When we speak about appearance and symbol we are also talking about the conceptualizing side (literate) of human nature and the nonconceptualizing (non-literate) side of our nature. The point is reconciling them in an integrated way that allows us to live a genuinely spiritual life. This is mixing meditation with post-meditation experience—attaining to a non-duality of our perceptual experience.

Conceptual Constructs

We live in a world of concepts. Meditation allows the nonconceptual side of our mind time to breathe and experience itself apart from the ceaseless discourses of the conceptual mind. The practice of art also releases us into the nonconceptual side of our brain.

In the academic world of the historical 12:60 consciousness, most disciplines exist for themselves. For example, do anthropologists ever claim to study anthropology in order to construct a ladder to get closer to God? This is the way people in medieval times might have thought about it. But today, this is not the case. Present day symbolic constructs of consciousness—the intellectual or conceptually strategizing disciplines—are evolved in such a way that they keep us chained to the "linear-logical" left hemisphere side of the brain. These systems aren't meant to lead us beyond them, particularly the way they are practiced these days. This was not always the case.

As we proceed into the labyrinth of wholeness, we begin to view these conceptual disciplines in the context of the larger reality. At our foundation, we understand that the whole of what we call reality is a great symbol or projection of a higher order of mind. We have to see through the cosmic lens to determine what is surface and what is symbol—to see what refers to the conceptualizing side of the brain and to the nonconceptual side—these are complementary and work together.

The conceptual side works with logic, reason, grammar and constructs of language in order to give form and structure to thought forms, both high and low. Ultimately, the nonconceptual is the all-encompassing and the all-embracing. The Ultimate Reality does not talk in sentences. The Ultimate Reality exists before, in the middle of, and after the sentence—this is the important point.

We are in the phase between cosmic unconscious and cosmic conscious. We are still working with sentences, logic and constructs. At best, we can use these logics and constructs in a meaningful way to communicate a higher truth. At one level, the seven *Cosmic History Chronicles* are constructs of conceptualizations—but for the purpose of leading the mind into non-conceptual states. The point is to learn to use the conceptual constructs for a higher purpose, to see them as higher symbol-forming orders of reality.

In the *Treatise on Cosmic Fire*, Alice Bailey states that a key turned seven times is needed to open the mind. Bailey mentions the keys found in the *Secret Doctrine* and uses the symbolism of ten doors that open to the mysteries of nature. We may not have the time to understand every last detail of every symbolic system, but if we have the right keys, then we have a lens to view any symbolic system. Through this lens, we can determine for ourselves what is valid or what is invalid on our journey through the labyrinth.

The ten doors of the mysteries of nature divide into five right brain doors and five left

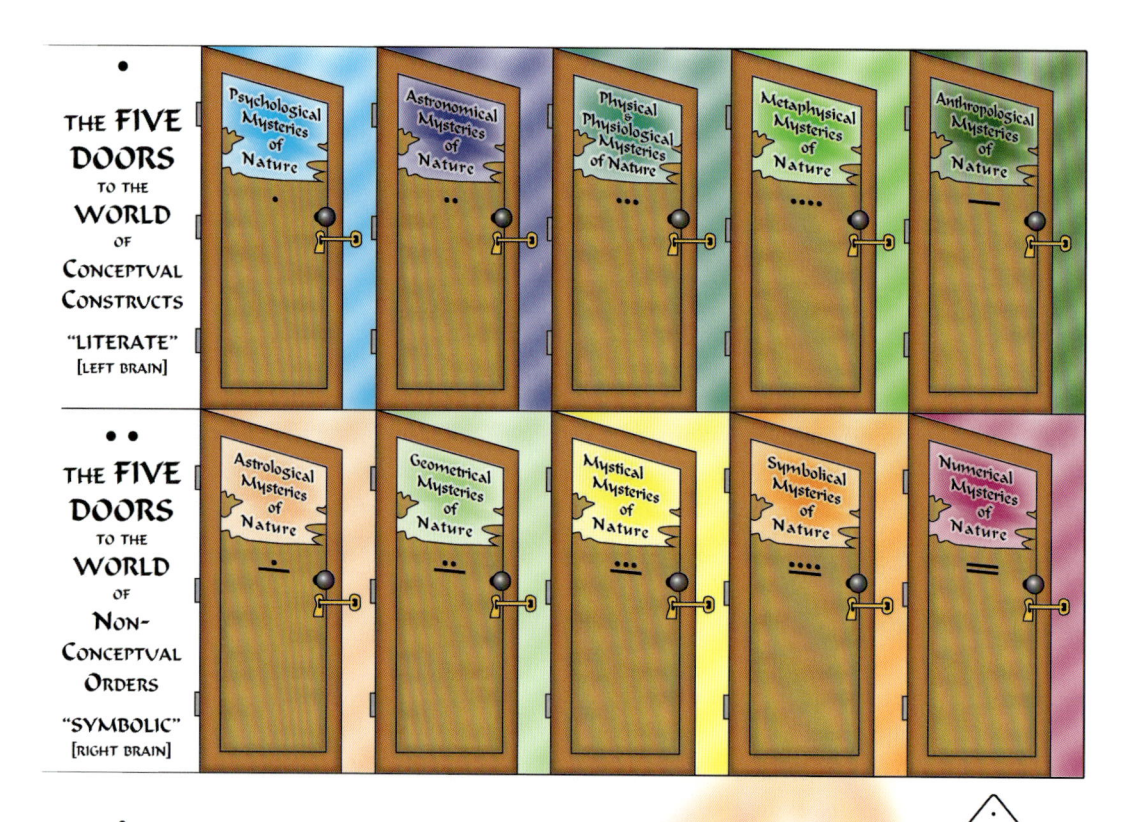

The Cosmic History Chronicles • Volume IV

THE FIVE DOORS TO THE WORLD OF CONCEPTUAL CONSTRUCTS

"LITERATE" [LEFT BRAIN]

- Psychological Mysteries of Nature
- Astronomical Mysteries of Nature
- Physical & Physiological Mysteries of Nature
- Metaphysical Mysteries of Nature
- Anthropological Mysteries of Nature

THE FIVE DOORS TO THE WORLD OF NON-CONCEPTUAL ORDERS

"SYMBOLIC" [RIGHT BRAIN]

- Astrological Mysteries of Nature
- Geometrical Mysteries of Nature
- Mystical Mysteries of Nature
- Symbolical Mysteries of Nature
- Numerical Mysteries of Nature

THE TEN DOORS OPENING TO THE MYSTERIES OF NATURE

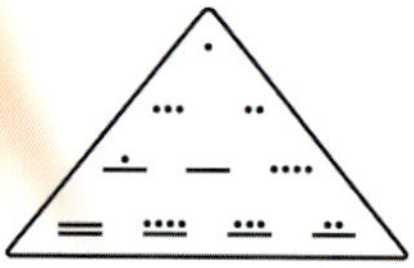

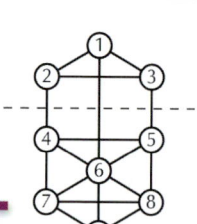

Adapted from HPB and ALICE A. BAILEY

"Every symbol and allegory has seven keys"

EACH DOOR HAS A KEY THAT MUST BE TURNED SEVEN TIMES FOR NO DISCIPLINE CAN BE LEARNED WITHOUT PERSPECTIVE OF THE POWER OF SEVEN

WITH SPECIAL REFERENCE TO THE CONTEXT OF THE SYMBOLICAL ORDERS OF REALITY AND THE ORDER OF NUMBER brain doors. Each door has a key; each key has to be turned seven times. One turning of the key reveals one level of meaning, and so on up to seven. Each of these doors is a particular mental discipline with a specific focus of study that relates with some aspect in the world of appearance. The seven volumes of Cosmic History are the seven keys that open levels and dimensions of these disciplines.

Door One: The Psychological Mysteries of Nature

This door explores how the brain works and how the mind evolves a personality from the workings of the brain. Are we using our mind effectively? What do we need to learn about it? What does cosmic science tell us about it? Why do humans behave the way they do? Is there something beyond behavioralism? Is there an evolutionary psychology? Is there a psychology of transformation? Is there a psychology of cosmic consciousness? How do we define the new measure of psychology that advances us into the divine? How do we apply the six plus one mental spheres identified by cosmic science to evolve a new cosmic person? We find the answers by entering this door of the Psychological Mysteries of Nature.

Door Two: The Astronomical Mysteries of Nature

This door leads to study the heavens and contemplation of the mysteries of the sky and its stars in this world of appearance. After entering this door, we might ask: What is the nature of stars, galaxies, the universe and cosmos? What is the nature of astrophysics? What is cosmology? What does it mean that the galaxies are moving away from each other? How fast are they going? How can you measure this? How can you know this? What does it mean for us here to say we are galactic members of evolving star systems? How do we define a new cosmology in accord with a psychology of cosmic consciousness? The answers are found by entering this door of the Astronomical Mysteries of Nature.

Door Three: The Physical and Physiological Mysteries of Nature

This door leads to the study of physics. For example, if we drop a ball, how does this reveal the law of gravity? If we look at ourselves closely, there is skin and cells or physiology—how is this different from physics? And psycho-physiology? Then there is chemistry, which is the investigation of different molecules and atomic structures and how they constitute the different physical elements of reality—how does chemistry differ from physics? The whole of this order constitutes the foundation of our psychophysical third-dimensional reality as well—the study of the sense organs and the information pertaining to each of them, as well as the perceptions that constitute our experience of physical reality. The knowledge behind this door is vast and underlies an understanding of laws governing the world of appearances—and of whole systems.

Entering this door of the Physical and Physiological Mysteries of Nature will begin to further this vast system of operation.

Door Four: The Metaphysical Mysteries of Nature

This door leads to the study of the law of physics beyond physics—or the laws that govern the relation of the perceptual wholeness of the fourth-dimensional self to the third-dimensional self. This gives us a window that looks out from the world of appearances into the more etheric world—the supersensible world. The etheric world is governed by its laws just as the physical world is governed by its laws. When we study Cosmic Science it says there is both third- and fourth-dimensional science—the advanced study is metaphysics that shows how the etheric and physical are interrelated, for it is the immaterial that governs the material, and there is no true self-realization without this comprehension.

If the etheric were not bonded to its reflection, the phenomenal, then there would be no way of grasping the great symbol. It is only the alienated third-dimensional mind that thinks the metaphysical has no relation to the physical. The deep explanation of this matter occurs when we pass through this door of the Metaphysical Mysteries of Nature.

Door Five: The Anthropological Mysteries of Nature

This door leads to the exploration of questions such as: Who are we? How did we evolve? How did we get here? Are we made from a divine pattern? Who is Adam and who is Adam Kadmon? How many root races were there before us? Were we really evolved from apes? Who are we now and how are we spread around the world? Are there other humans like us elsewhere in the universe? Are there other life forms that form a cosmic anthropology? And if so, is there a universal typology of the human form—the capacity of attaining to cosmic intelligence? What are the human types? This bends back around to psychology—why are there different types? Why are there different forms of culture and behavior? Is this in relationship to geophysical aspects of the Earth as a planet? Is there a cosmic sociology? Where did each people, each tribe, each nation derive its language and its knowledge of cosmic origins? Pass through the Door of the Anthropological Mysteries of Nature to find the answers to the questions.

These are the five doors that open the left side of the brain to different conceptual constructs. The disciplines on this side depend on being literate—on being able to read the written word and express itself in the written language to communicate. This is an important point.

The next five doors open to the world of nonconceptual order—these are the symbolical doors of the right cerebral hemisphere. The left hemisphere is literate and right is symbolical.

Door Six: The Astrological Mysteries of Nature

This door leads to the exploration of relationships of different planets and stars to each other in the sky creating different geometrical constructs—trines, sextiles, conjuncts and oppositions—in relation to particular moments and places on Earth. We are actually dealing with an abstract geometry of time. While astronomy deals with the study of stars from the scientific or mathematical angle, astrology is more concerned with the inner qualities of the celestial bodies and the effect of their varying positions on life.

Astrology can be likened to a primitive synchronic order—it is the one symbolical discipline that deals with a process in time. Everyone has an astrological chart so even if you were born at the same time or 10 minutes apart on different places on the Earth—because of the position of the planets in their different relations to each other—there is slight modification of personality that occur in those charts.

Astrology as a science or discipline also depends on a certain set of symbolic meanings. For example, Saturn has a particular meaning of power, influence, control, money; Mercury has a meaning communication; or Jupiter: expansion, power and greatness; Uranus: revolution electricity, telepathy and so forth. So there are different sets of subjective meanings. We have to also consider why we gave the planets these names and meanings. There must have been something evoked in the unconscious that has a truth to it in relation to these planets—so we cannot altogether dismiss the meanings as arbitrary or as "just Greek mythology". We have to be discriminating and see what this might be about, a pursuit that in itself is meaningful.

Then we have the different houses, making the construct of astrology like a moving wheel of 360 degrees in time. There are 12 different houses every year the Earth goes in an orbit around the sun. The circle is divided into 12 parts known as the 12 signs or houses of the zodiac. Twelve does not divide evenly into 364 or 365, it is similar to the 12 month pattern (30, 31, etc.). But rather, the ecliptic of the path of the Earth as it goes around the sun, and in relation to the celestial sphere (as perceived from the Earth), is divided into 360 degrees with 30 degrees per house. This is how we get the 12 houses of the zodiac.

Those 12 houses also divide into a larger or Platonic wheel, which is the 25,920-year cycle (twelve 2160-year cycles or 90 288-year cycles or 180 144-year cycles, etc.). These are also whole number points in a sacred geometry based on the 360-degree circle

This Platonic cycle, with each house representing 2160 years, is a factor of the cube value 216—6 to the third power = 216. The Piscean Age that began sometime before the birth of Christ is now concluding and we are soon entering the next cycle of 2160 years: the Age of Aquarius. This is just to point out that astrology is a symbolical science based on geometrical relationships of the Earth in the ecliptic as it goes around the sun. The planets and the stars create different geometrical configurations in the sky and have some impact on the life of humans. It is a belief system as well. As you believe, so shall you become.

Door Seven: The Geometrical Mysteries of Nature

This door leads to the exploration of geometry, as a symbolical construct. Without geometry, astrology would lose much of its meaning. Geometry is as eternal as the spirit of God; it is the manifestation of God Himself, and the very prototype of the creation of the world. Pythagoras said: God is the first geometer. Music is also a moving geometry in time and was defined by Hermes Trismegistus as the mere knowing of the order of all things. Music, such as the late string quartets of Beethoven, creates phenomenal architectures of geometries of sound that exist in an imaginal space where philosophy is the structure of sound. Music takes you to places you cannot articulate, but rather affects the mental and emotional body, entering you into another world—an architecture of moving geometries of sound.

Giardano Bruno, a Platonist who was burned at the stake for heliocentric beliefs, said the order of a unique figure and the harmony of a unique number give rise to all things. So geometry is the seventh door—we can define geometrical figures of all sorts from snowflakes to galaxies. Geometry is based on different frequency ratios that give rise to formal relationships. From this geometrical base, the creation of all form is possible. These geometrical symbolic structures underlie and give order to the higher intellectual or mental disciplines. For instance: sphere, cube, tetrahedron, octahedron, dodecahedron and icosahedrons. To what mode or discipline does each of these platonic solids correspond?

Door Eight: Mystical Mysteries of Nature

This door leads to the study of ever higher levels of nonconceptual reality—the mystical mysteries of nature. What metaphysics is to physics, mysticism is to metaphysics. Every human being has the potential to realize the underlying mystical nature of reality that occurs at an essential plane of existence beyond our conceptual mind. How do we attain and define that realty so it makes sense? We can start by creating different diagrams or symbolical constructs that are representative of analogical reasoning. These could be mandalas or yantras, or they could be allegorical depictions.

Through these diagrams we can illustrate the stairway to heaven or a ladder that goes to the heavens that we climb or we can draw an empty circle and ask what do you see—the circle or the space around the circle? We are going toward the experience of the indescribable, the ultimate nature of reality. We are always pointing in this direction. The mysteries show us how we go from one stage to the next—we are not just sitting on Earth to buy things. As all the highest teachings point out, we are here to transcend attachment to the Earth by attaining a true realization that draws us into a unitive experience of the whole of reality. Once we enter into this experience, we have entered the supermental realm beyond mind and nature. This is essentially an ineffable boundary dissolving experience with an infinite number of doorways. But the goal is always the same: union with the Absolute. Such experience can only be expressed as paradox. Once we have become a genuine human, then we cease to be human.

Door Nine: The Symbolic Mysteries of Nature

This door, in many ways, underlies all the other doors. Even though it seems symbols have been downplayed or degraded, it is still curious that it is forbidden to take a symbol, like the Banner of Peace, into the Vatican or Trinity Site. This demonstrates a war between symbols or a war against certain symbols—even though people don't consciously give much credence to that, they unconsciously do. It is also forbidden to take the flag of one country down and put up in its place the flag of another country—you will probably be arrested. This shows the power of symbols unconsciously embedded into certain belief structures.

Our lives are very much invested in symbols in a thoroughly unconscious and mind manipulative way. You are on "this side" where these certain symbols are valid but this is not the case on the other side of the "border". Even though we live in a late historical literate human planetary culture, the power of symbol is very strong. We actually live in symbols—corporate logos, for example, are symbols. People copyright them so no one else can use their "special" symbol. Corporations like Coca Cola or Starbuck's have trademarked symbols—meaning their symbols belong exclusively to that corporation.

These symbols give the masses comfort when they see them—they are familiar. This shows that, even in the late historical phase, that symbols are successful in manipulating the masses. This is what is meant by symbols and mass crowd control. The final symbolical door opens to everything—a whole plane of reality, a higher-dimensional plane of knowledge and existence. To understand the workings of the symbolical mystery of nature is to penetrate to the core reality.

Door Ten: The Mysteries of Nature, Called Number

This door leads to the contemplation of number that underlies all reality—all symbolic systems have an underlying number matrix. For example, you can reconstitute the ten doors through the tetracys of the decad—1+2+3+4 = 10 arranged as dots with one at the top and four at the bottom.

Ten equals the number of the pyramid. Or the ten doors can be constructed like the tree of the Kabbalah with the ten Sephiroth arranged in a construct that is archetypally "familiar". Number is the key door—Number understood as the matrix of order underlying the whole of reality. Even in particle physics, like the mathematics of the "God particle", there are two key numbers: 82,944 (mass), which is 288 squared, and then 2808 (216 x 13) (velocity). This 2808 (216 x 13) shows that even in particle physics there are underlying mathematical structures of incredible order. Many modern scientists do not like these patterns because if they give importance to them, then it implies that there is intelligent design. This goes against the dogma of randomness pointing to a supreme deity or God and most scientific egos do not want to deal with this.

Number—as the tenth door—opens to a reality that is so fundamental it actually operates in its own dimension. In fact, it is a dimension equal to time, space and mind. It is a whole order of reality which gives constructive meaning to the three other orders: time, space and mind. The universe of number in all of its intrinsic sets of relations is ultimately a language of universal cosmic telepathy. This we will come to learn as we evolve into cosmic civilization.

Secret Eleventh Door: The Seven Volumes of Cosmic History

There also exists a secret eleventh door that opens to the totality of Cosmic History. As each key turns, another volume of Cosmic History reveals itself—when that key is turned seven times then the light of cosmic consciousness floods us from the inside. These doors are presented as a symbolic construct and show the nature of symbols in relation to other sets of so-called mental or intellectual disciplines. These symbolical disciplines consist of themes such as astrology, geometry, mysticism, etc. The whole of this perspective is itself a symbolic structure of the number order of ten.

Pythagoras and Plato are the source of the main streams of whole number order in the Western tradition. Platonic solids are the fundamental geometric structures. Hermetic systems are evolved systems of thought that possess a high degree of intrinsic coherence and that, in their purest essence, are mathematical.

There is also the number system of *gematria*. Gematria is based on numerical value ascribed to different letters, first through the different letters in the Hebrew alphabet, and then on to the Arabic, Greek and Latin or Roman alphabets. The gematrical system counts from 1-10 and then the eleventh letter jumps to values of 10, 20, 30, 40, etc. Then when you get to the third order, the value of the letter jumps to 100. For example, in the Latin alphabet, letter Z has a value of 800. Letter A has a value of 1, and letter K, a value of 20 because it is the eleventh letter. This was studied in depth by Aleister Crowley who documented much of his findings in his book *777* (1909). This is just one aspect of number, but it gives a deeper level of meaning than mere alphabetical language. However, since systems of gematria apply only to alphabet-based literacy, they are limited in the overall history of the human race. The secret eleventh door opens to a telepathic number science that is beyond history and incorporates into itself a literacy of symbolic constructs. This is the science of the mind reformulated by the Law of Time—a science wholly of the future.

Examples of Symbolic Systems

Symbolic systems are intrinsic functions of spiritual systems with an underlying number pattern. We are not here to chart out every surviving system of correspondences for every symbolic system—this is not our purpose. But rather, we touch on a few only to show a grander synthesis, in light of the

Embodying Symbolic Structures

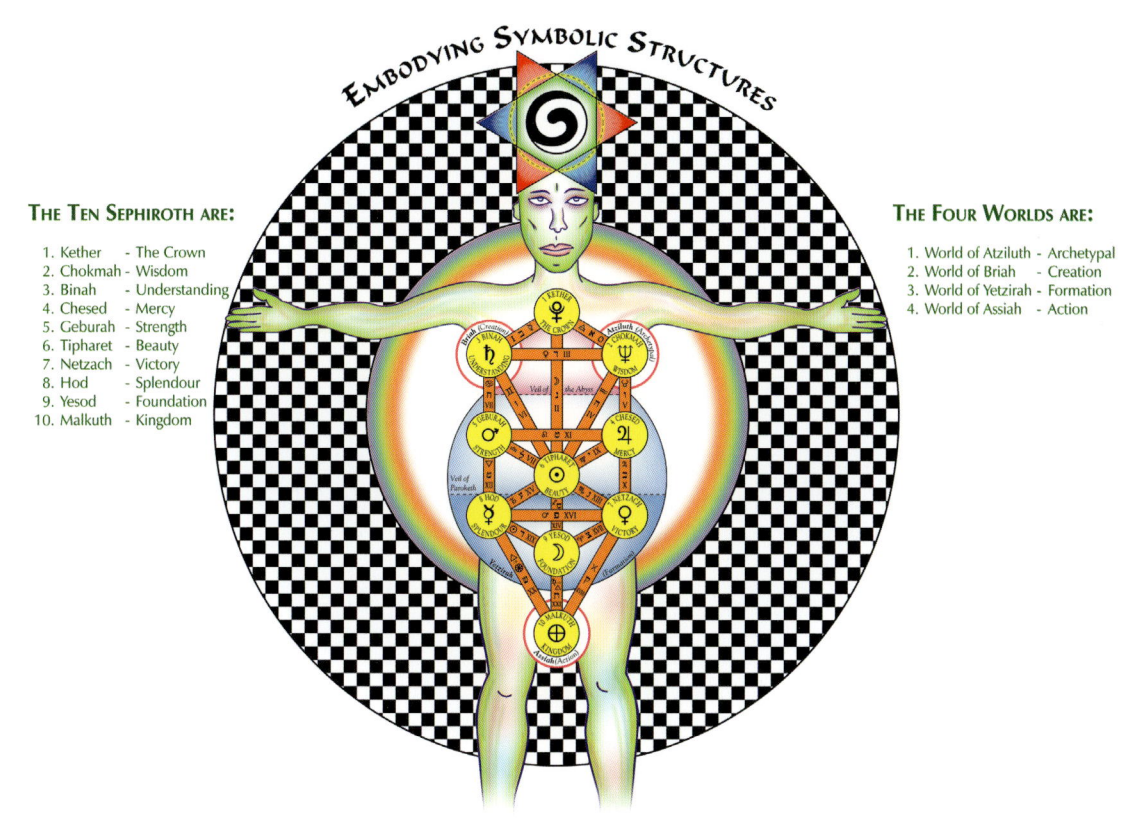

THE TEN SEPHIROTH ARE:

1. Kether   - The Crown
2. Chokmah - Wisdom
3. Binah   - Understanding
4. Chesed   - Mercy
5. Geburah - Strength
6. Tipharet - Beauty
7. Netzach - Victory
8. Hod   - Splendour
9. Yesod   - Foundation
10. Malkuth - Kingdom

THE FOUR WORLDS ARE:

1. World of Atziluth - Archetypal
2. World of Briah   - Creation
3. World of Yetzirah - Formation
4. World of Assiah   - Action

all-unifying function of the synchronic order, a fourth-dimensional structure.

A notable example of this is Tantric Vajrayana Buddhism where patterns or ritual are distinguished by different orders of numbers. These underlying number patterns can be found throughout Buddhism with the four noble truths, the eightfold wheel of the law, the 12 nidanas or interdependent links of the karmic wheel of samsara and suffering, and the 18 step mandala or the five Buddha families of Shingon School of Tantric Buddhism.

The Tantric art and meditation of Shingon Buddhism (brought to Japan in the eighth or ninth century) is a highly integrative symbolic order. The sadhanas (spiritual practices) consist of numerous sets of practices, many of which are encoded in visual symbols—but also with accompanying mudras or hand symbols. These mudras are intricate and generally coordinated with sound or mantra, such as: Ah bam ran ram ken.

We might wonder who came up with these intricate systems, and how did they figure out to coordinate hand gestures and movements with different sounds. We wonder, was someone on a remote mountaintop channeling these systems? Or did these systems descend as one whole system vision, a holistic fragment of some vast earlier teaching from another plane of existence or world system? It is important to think about these things.

Through these examples, we begin to understand how symbols can be embodied into forms like the mudras or even through yogic asana forms that have different symbolic names, like the cobra, peacock, or tree. When we practice these systems, we are transformed from the human world into being a player in the vast cosmological process of creating a divine living architecture. The same is true for all the body arts, including yoga and pranayama as well as Tai Chi Chuan—the embodiment of archetypal structures as body gestures. This is also the basis for sacred forms of dance such as was developed by the Mevlana Sufi dervishes and adopted by Gurdjieff.

The Buddhist and Hindu tantras are the most evolved spiritual systems in the historical cycle with an integrating approach to embodying the symbol primarily through visualization, mantra and mudra. An example of this is the practice of seeing the mandala or the different Buddhas as structures of reality coordinated with different sounds and so on. This is far beyond the human level.

In these traditions a nonconceptual knowing is transmitted through the mandala, mantric chant and/or mudra hand dance. The goal of the meditation is to assume, by total body prayer, the aspects of a Buddha: an enlightened being filled with infinite light and compassion.

Kabbalah and the Tree of Life

The Kabbalah is a creative meditational system where we can identify different qualities of spirit within our own bodily system. It is interesting that Kabbalah has come down through history and has recently been made mainstream by several Hollywood celebrities.

"Kabbalah" can be translated from Hebrew as "received tradition". It explains how the one God created the world by a series of divine emanations from Himself. The divine emanations are arranged on the Tree of Life as the ten Sephiroth plus the 22 paths that accommodate the 22 letters of the Hebrew alphabet. The ten Sephiroth and the 22 paths make 32 ways of life or steps in the initiation.

Within the Western tradition, the Kabbalah is a symbolic structure, cosmological in nature, that depicts the Creation and Plan of the Universe based on ancient texts tracing back to Abraham or the *Book of Zohar—the Splendor of Zohar*. The Kabbalah is a function of the law of three and the law of seven. In this system, God is known as *Ain Soph* and governs over the ten Sephiroth or divine emanations or intelligences of angels and of man. In this way, The Kabbalah is the archetypal map of our ascent, in stages, back to the one, to the Kingdom, to the Ain Soph.

The Ten Sephiroth

1. Kether—the Crown (Ancient of Days)
2. Chokmah—Wisdom (yang)
3. Binah—Understanding (yin)
4. Chesed—Mercy (cohesive intelligence or love—son of beneficence)
5. Geburah—Strength (the warrior)

6. Tipharet—Beauty (the sun)
7. Netzach—Victory (occult intelligence)
8. Hod—Splendor (glory of the form)
9. Yesod—Foundation (where form takes astral shape)
10. Malkuth—Kingdom (planetary spirit)

The upper Sephiroth create one triangle: Kether, Chokmah and Binah—these are the transcendental levels beyond our plane of reality. They represent the supreme crown, the wisdom and intelligence. This is the law of the three. Their structure, if you bend it over, makes the next triad—Chesed, Geburah and Tipharet. The lower part, which is a function of the law of seven, is made up of two triangles. Tipharet joins the two triangles of the lower seven Sephiroth. The lower triad is comprised of Netzach, Hod and Yesod. Then seven, eight, and nine, with Malkuth at the very bottom—this is the prototype of the world of manifestation. This is the seventh. There is somewhat of a descending order in qualities until we get to Malkuth which is the "kingdom" or the prototype of manifest reality.

In the Kabbalah, there are also four worlds:

1. World of Atziluth—Archetypal
2. World of Briah—Creation
3. World of Yetzirah—Formation
4. World of Assiah—Action

The 22 paths, plus the ten Sephiroth, form the 32 ways, or stages by which wisdom descends upon the human. This diagram is known as the *Tree of Life*, and constitutes the framework of the Adam Kadmon—the prototype "red" Adam, the original heavenly man whose structure is a template of universal order.

The fundamental cosmology is based on the 10 or the decimal system—the two hands—the right hand of God and the left hand of God. We can view the right hand of God as the five doors of the left hemisphere, with each door representing a finger of God, and the left hand of God is made up from the five symbolical doors of the right hemisphere and this establishes the decimal system. In this regard, the Kabbalah is the supreme expression of the system of 10.

The Kabbalah consists of a central column, a right hand column and a left hand column. These three columns also have their qualities and they connect the Sephiroth to create the 22 pathways which have all their unique qualities. This creates a vast cosmological construct of reality that, when studied, is a magical tool that enters you into a particular state of mind or consciousness that is beyond the appearances of the phenomenal world, and which makes life more meaningful.

Extensive correspondences for the Sephiroth and the Paths can be found in Crowley's *777* and also the *Book of Thoth*.

> ### The Law of Three and Seven
>
> The three columns and the seven lower Sephiroth of the Kabbalah, are an example of the law of seven and law of the three. These laws are also important in the work of Gurdjieff. Between the three and the seven lies the four, the number of form. In Gurdjieff's system, the law of seven is the octave that represents vibrations that change according to forces played upon them: Do Re Mi Fa Sol La Ti Do, where the Do is both the starting and ending point of a circle or spiral.
>
> The law of three indicates that at any one time, there are three forces at play: active force, passive force and neutral force, where the third force is the invisible, subliminally activating force. The law of three also indicates that in a progression, following the third, there must be an effort to make it to the fourth. Musically, this is the interval between mi and fa, and ti and do.
>
> The law of $(3 \times 7) = 21$, is also the basis of the 441 cube matrix, and the many higher septenary programs which are based on that. So the seven is a function of the three and four, while the law of the three combined with the seven creates the 21, opening to the higher cycles.

We are merely giving a basic overview to demonstrate the Kabbalah as an example of a universal symbolic structure. There have been many knowledgeable teachers of the Kabbalah since the nineteenth century, such as Eliphas Levi, Blavatsky and, in the twentieth century, Crowley and A.E. Waite. Also notable is Dion Fortune and her *Mystical Qabbalah*.

These Kabbalists were original in their own right and were able to renew these sciences into the present time. There really were not masters like that in the twentieth century—though there was a resurgent of interest in these systems beginning in the sixties with the use of psychedelics that opened people up to the significance of symbolic systems.

The point of these symbolic systems is that we have to work out our own correspondences by interacting with the patterns and the meanings associated with them. The following is a unique definition of the Kabbalah written by Aleister Crowley (777):

> ### Crowley's Definition of Kabbalah
>
> a. A language fitted to describe certain classes of phenomena, and to express certain classes of ideas which escape regular phraseology. You might as well object to the technical terminology of chemistry.
>
> b. A unisectarian and elastic terminology by means of which it is possible to equate the mental processes of people apparently diverse owning to the constraint imposed upon them by the peculiarities of their literary expression. You might as well object to a lexicon, or a treatise on comparative religion.
>
> c. A symbolism which enables thinkers to formulate their ideas with complete precision, and to find simple expression for complex thoughts, especially such as include previously disconnected order of

conception. You might as well object to algebraic symbols.

d. An instrument for interpreting symbols whose meaning has become obscure, forgotten or misunderstood by establishing a necessary connection between the essence of forms, sounds, simple ideas (such as numbers) and their spiritual, moral, or intellectual equivalents. You might as well object to interpreting ancient art by consideration of beauty as determined by physiological facts.

e. A system of classification of uniform ideas so as to enable the mind to increase its vocabulary of thoughts and facts through organizing and co-relating them. You might as well object to the mnemonic value of Arabic modification of roots.

f. An instrument of or proceeding from the known to the unknown on similar principles to those of mathematics. You might as well object to the use of square root of minus one, x to the fourth power, etc.

g. A system of criteria by which the truth of correspondences may be tested with a view to criticizing new discoveries in the light of their coherence with the whole body of truth. You might as well object to judging character and status by educational and social convention.

—Aleister Crowley, *777*

The System of the Tarot

Symbolic systems exist to show the underlying mental structures that form phenomenal reality. The Tarot is an example of such a system. While the Kabbalah relies more on geometrical structure and mystic letters, the Tarot deals more with symbolical associations of different images that work archetypally on the unconscious.

Many occultists believe that the system of the Tarot (Thoth) was one of the volumes saved from the burning of the library at Alexandria, along with the Books of Enoch. The Tarot system seems to have developed in the Middle Ages and had some recognition in the ancient and Islamic world. A cross fertilization occurred during the crusades between Christian civilization and the Islamic social order.

The system of the Tarot is much more related to the divinatory process and uses a system of 78 (13 x 6) cards: 22 Major Arcanum correspond to the 22 pathways of the Kabbalah and to the 22 Hebrew letters. The system of the minor Arcanum works with the wands, pentacles, swords, and cups. These of course relate to modern playing-card deck, and are divided into four suits of thirteen cards, plus one major card each, for a total of 56 cards.

The archetypal symbolism of the Tarot was catalyzed and popularized by the A.E. Waite deck, perhaps the most well known and accessible. There is much intrinsic numerology to the Tarot—the

78 and the 52, based on the 13; the 22 and the four. The Thoth Deck created by Aleister Crowley offers far more powerful and detailed images requiring a more intense interaction to receive their full meaning.

The Thoth deck incorporates the traditional symbols and correspondences as taught by the Hermetic Order of the Golden Dawn. It gives a modern style to the ancient forms by the use of mathematical, scientific and geometrical designs. These images have entered the mass consciousness so that you see images of the Tarot on popular CD covers, art works, etc. Many people now make Tarot decks with their own interpretations, but which often bury the original symbolic or archetypal meaning. This only demonstrates that the Tarot is the manifestation of a universal construct of cosmic order that appeals to the mass mind and its need for deeper order and meaning of life.

The archetypal symbols of the Tarot lead into a consideration of dream symbolism. Everybody, at some point or another, falls asleep and dreams. Those dreams are symbols with qualities similar to those in the Tarot deck. This demonstrates the capacity to trigger archetypal responses from the unconscious with a particular type of imagery or symbols. It also demonstrates the need of the mind to be activated by symbols functioning within a construct of meaning such that the creative impulse is aroused and we are prompted to express ourselves in the medium of the dimension of art.

Many systems of correspondence have been worked out, which link the trumps and paths with planetary and zodiac signs, deities, animals, plants, colors, precious stones, perfumes, geometric figures and images—all of which are intended to express and illuminate the meanings of the cards themselves, as well as explain that the outer world is actually a world of symbols and symbolic elements, a world of correspondences.

... the outer world is actually a world of symbols and symbolic elements, a world of correspondences.

Kabbalah and I Ching

The Kabbalah and I Ching are two of the most universal symbolic systems on the planet today. The I Ching, symbolic system of the Far East, is both a philosophical system and a method of divination that has influenced China's two principle religions, Taoism and Confucianism.

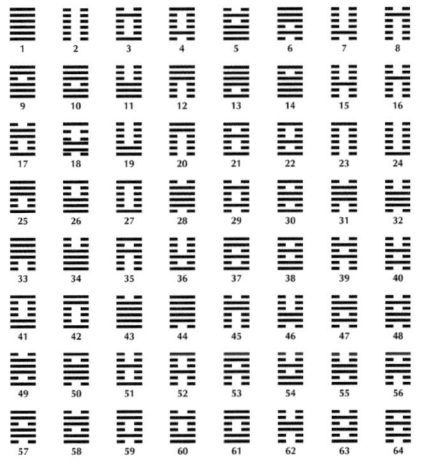

The I Ching is based on the system of the great Tao or great Tai Chi, yin (female) and yang (male). According to Chinese belief, every event and thing in the universe arises from the interaction of these two principles.

Like the Kabbalah, the I Ching is a cosmological system that contains an underlying mathematical structure. As a symbolic system, the I Ching reveals an underlying harmonic pattern—an eight-fold pattern—that creates 64 (8 x 8) "hexagrams", each of which is made up of six lines that can be in any combination of either broken (yin) or unbroken (yang). In the Tai Chi Chuan symbol of the yin and yang there are two sides, each with a little dot that shows that in each side there is always a tincture of the opposite.

The permutation of a yin and yang line creates the four code letters of *young yang, old yang, young yin* and *old yin*. These are the same as the four amino acid letters written with the same binary language. When a third line is added, the yin and yang combine to create three-line trigrams in eight possible permutations. Combined with each other, the eight trigrams further combine to create sixty-four, six-line structure "hexagrams". At this level we see that the I Ching is the expression of the unfolding of the universal binary mathematics. This is the exact dynamic that produces life and, hence, the 64 codons of the DNA are exactly the same when written in the same yin yang code language.

The system of the I Ching demonstrates that our actual biological and psychological nature is written in a mathematical language: that of our DNA. This underlying template can be likened to the template of the God Particle with its 288 squared mass value and its 13 x 216 energy value, where a priori-mathematical codes provide the templates of the primary structures of phenomenal reality.

The I Ching also utilizes the five Chinese elements: wind, wood, water, fire and earth. These combine to create an intricate symbolism that still pervades modern Chinese society and is also prevalent in the West. Up until the 1960s, only a few translations of the I Ching had been available.

Perhaps the most complete translation is that of Richard Wilhelm, which became quite popular in the 1960s. Wilhelm provided two general renditions of the I Ching—the first gives extended psychological interpretational meaning and the second gives structure and meaning as well as including the wings and appendices written primarily by Confucius. Since Wilhelm's translation and the explosion of pop occult culture after the 1960s, there have been countless other translations. Carl Jung provided a forward to the Wilhelm Baines edition, which gives it a further sense of authority. It is clear that Wilhelm had a broad cultural background and keen

The Cosmic History Chronicles • Volume IV

sense of archetypal symbolism.

Jung offers the following explanation of how the I Ching works:

> *Whoever invented the I Ching was convinced that the hexagram worked out in a certain moment coincided with the latter in quality no less than in time. To him the hexagram was the exponent of the moment in which it was cast—even more so than the hours of the clock or the divisions of the calendar could be— inasmuch as the hexagram was understood to be an indicator of the essential situation prevailing in the moment of its origin.*

NUMBER AND SYMBOLIC FORM

Kepler said geometry existed before creation. Since geometry is the formalization of certain number ratios, number also existed before creation. This demonstrates a cosmo-perceptual process of symbolic evolution where the underlying matrix before creation is number. All matter arises from a geometry based on an underlying matrix of number.

"Before creation" means before mind; before time, before space there was number. Before God manifest Himself to Himself, there was number and order of self-existing reality. This order of self-existing reality formulates itself into geometry. This geometry is then given meaning usually in the form of a symbol or symbolic structure. For example, the eightfold pattern is then assigned eight different trigrams, the ten-fold pattern is given 10 Sephiroth, etc.

Kepler says God is geometry and geometry provides the prototypes that God uses for creation. The same premise is found in the *Dynamics of Time*: "radiative geometries of the fourth dimension become templates of the phenomenal reality of the third dimension."

These templates are represented by the symbolic structures, and having derived from fourth-dimensional geometries, they are unchanging, eternal and ever-existing.

Part III • Mapping the New Reality

Any symbolic system that is based on pristine mathematical or geometrical structures is universal. These systems form a grid that existed before creation, and in fact, actually demonstrate the process of creation. To recapitulate: There is first number, then geometry, then symbolic structure of the world of image, and finally the world of appearance.

Again, we must keep in mind that most symbolic structures that evolved through history, such as astrology, are spatially oriented. The structure of astrology is based on geometrical figures of 12—this is a static number—while the ever shifting pattern of planets is dynamic (13), time-oriented. The Kabbalah is also a static figure in space, as are the eight I Ching trigrams.

The entire phenomenal world is created from a certain number of patterns. This discovery traces back to Pythagoras and his realization that there are only five geometrical solids: the tetrahedron, the cube, the octahedron, the icosahedron and the dodecahedron. Even the post-impressionist painter Paul Cezanne said all of nature consists of a primary cube, triangle and sphere. You can see pyramids within the mountains and triangular forms in the trees. All the world of appearance constitutes the great symbol underlain by geometry and number.

In the final stage of the process of symbolical evolution, the humans finally recognize the meaning beneath the surface of symbol. This reality is part of the system of correspondences and is a reflection of a higher reality that says, "as above, so below".

Once again, all of this reality is just a symbol of a higher reality that returns us to the matrix of number, where we may begin to reassess the totality of what is. Through contemplation of symbolic structures we can penetrate the world of veiled awareness and enter into higher planes of reality. When you introduce the law of time it is a whole other order of symbolic structure called the *synchronic order.*

Within the matrix of Cosmic History lies the great reevaluation and reordering of all human systems of thought as manifestations of universal time and synchronic order. In the New Time, successive stages of life each have an appropriate body of knowledge. These bodies of knowledge (according to world age) are maintained in a hermetic vessel through different sets of symbolic structures. Whether these are traditional systems or not, by its purpose and method, Cosmic History places them in the larger context of the synchronic order. In this way, meaning is renewed and symbolic value is expanded into a whole system of cosmic order that reaches into the infinite harmony of universal unification.

Part III • Mapping the New Reality

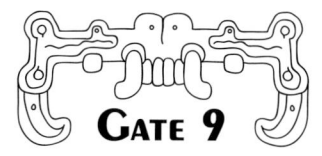

Gate 9
Synchronicity and the Living Template of Time

Up ahead you see a whirling radial matrix pulsing in and out of view. As you make your way toward Gate 9, you notice a strange being with the head of a garuda and the eyes of a hawk, watching your every movement. He stands motionless holding a rainbow staff in his right hand. As you draw near, you are both terrified and strangely intrigued. "Come", he says. You slowly walk toward him and he pulls out his staff and places it on your third eye. A whirl of colorful pulsing codes flash rapidly on your inner screen: harmonics, chromatics, wavespells, pulsars. A deep voice addresses you: Welcome to the synchronic order of galactic time!

> *Those who feel the unquenchable thirst for Something Different will be protected in a cocoon of light—to traverse all perils of the convulsions of the old and dying world—for in part of their being they already belong to that light, to the New World. And all one has dreamed to be the most beautiful, the most marvelous, the most fantastic is nothing compared with what will be realized.*
> —The Mother

> *It seems, indeed, as though time, far from being an abstraction, is a concrete continuum which contains qualities or basic conditions that manifest themselves simultaneously in different places through parallelisms that cannot be explained causally, as, for example, in cases of the simultaneous occurrence of identical thoughts, symbols, or psychic states.*
> —C.G. Jung

As we open this ninth gate of time, we are overwhelmed by a supernal light; phenomenal geographies structured of number flood us from every direction. Synchronicities manifest, one after another, filling us with awe and splendor.

Synchronicity is divine law and order—it is the norm of the universe. The study of synchronicity and the synchronic order is so vast that it could use its own seven volumes. C.G. Jung first introduced the idea of synchronicity to the masses in 1952, with his famous exposition on the topic. Keep in mind that this was the same year as the discovery of the Tomb of Pacal Votan.

Jung described synchronicity as an "acausal connecting principle". In other words, the term synchronicity designates the simultaneous occurrence of meaningful coincidences in time, but without sufficient physical evidence to place them in a relationship of cause and effect. His studies were linked to his own experiments and related investigations of the I Ching.

Jung further concluded that the connecting principle (of synchronicity) must lie in the equal significance of parallel events. He said: "One and the same (transcendental) meaning might manifest itself simultaneously in the human speech and in the arrangement of an external and independent event."

According to Cosmic History, synchronicity is a simultaneity of outer events and inner (psychic) perceptions, thoughts or feeling that appear to be unanticipated or otherwise unconnected—such that there is a psychic jolt—a release of *psi* energy. This is the opening to pure fourth-dimensional consciousness. This is the active participation in the synchronic order.

The synchronic order is a matrix of living intelligence; it is a fourth-dimensional order of reality based on the Law of Time. Hence, the Law of Time is the science of synchronicity. The Law of Time has always existed, but its discovery was brought to light in this world in 1989 by Valum Votan, just 37 years after Jung's publication of, *Synchronicity: an Acausal Connecting Principle,* and the opening of the tomb of Pacal Votan.

> **IN SYNCH WITH TIME**
>
> The Law of Time is something absolutely new to our consciousness. Time is the factor that synchronizes everything in the universe. In other words we all move through our life and we sometimes experience ourselves as "having it together" and we sometimes experience ourselves as "not having it together". When we are "together" everything is synchronized; this is when we are in "synch" with the Law of Time. This is natural law.

The Law of Time is a universal law and principle, and its discovery and application could only come at an appointed moment, just prior to the closing of the Great Cycle of history, inclusive of the closing of the 26,000-year and 104,000-year cycles.

This Gate 9 provides an introductory synthesis of the synchronic order as a coded pattern of symbolic constructs. As with the study of any new subject, we must become familiar with new terminology, and also the meaning of certain symbols before a spark of illumination will dawn. As we become aware of each facet and the workings of the synchronic order, then comes a successive initiation where the cells of our physical and etheric bodies are systematically raised into an ever higher vibration.

Synchronicity or synchronization follows a set of universal principles based on an underlying mathematical structure pulsed from a central radial matrix. This central organizing matrix is the primary structure that connects all events, people and reality as we know it. The more we learn about and tune into this matrix, the more we experience the synchronic order of reality. This is the purpose of the codes of time, inclusive of the Thirteen Moon, 28-day calendar.

Part III • Mapping the New Reality

The fourth-dimensional synchronic order organizes the totality of the third-dimensional world of appearance. All of our sensory data and information is received through our five + 1 senses. Keep in mind that all sensory information is actually the projection of a higher symbolic construct (remember that all symbolic constructs arise from a geometry based on an underlying matrix of number). This means that all experience is highly organized, coordinated and meaningful. Therefore, all of our sensory experience is organized by synchronicity, as synchronicity.

Synchronicity is the norm of the universe, though most humans are simply unaware of it 99 percent of the time. That is why the Law of Time and Thirteen Moon, 28-day calendar are now revealed. Through these fourth-dimensional instruments, we may tune in to the pan-sensory and psychic reality of synchronicity on an every day basis. Few people at the time of this writing have any comprehension of the vastness and actual nature of the synchronic order.

> *Your natural mini atomic whole profits directly ... once in every 26,000 years and thus, the harvest of the ripened fruits is done through the opened channel. Each harvest corresponds to a cyclic time. At the moment, all universes are being pushed as a mass towards a void by getting farther away from each other.*
>
> *For this very reason the need for a more accelerated evolution program is felt. Now help has been brought by a different operation to each solar totality in your solar system during this transition program of the end of the cycle.*
> —The Knowledge Book, p. 632

As we become aware of each facet and the workings of the synchronic order, then comes a successive initiation where the cells of our physical and etheric bodies are systematically raised into an ever higher vibration.

The synchronic order and the Law of Time is the accelerated evolution program for this solar totality. It contains the holographic code of the New Time that is superimposed over our mechanistically encumbered space. It has always existed but has been covered over by artificial time constructs that breed false notions about reality. By learning to apply the synchronic codes of time, we seek to bring all of our bodies—third-, fourth-, and fifth-dimensional—into alignment as a luminous, forceful channel of the highest inner light of spiritual wisdom.

For many, the synchronic codes appear so new and strange that they can scarcely conceive of what it might be. However, with a bit of patience and exertion they can be comprehended. Once the basics are learned, the weavings become apparent and the synchronicities greatly increase.

The first step is simple: change calendars.

Daily use of the Thirteen Moon/28-day calendar raises our frequency out of the artificial matrix and helps reorient our mind toward a higher reality. The changeover of the aeons has everything to do with shifting timing frequencies, and thus, the renewing of our minds. To change our mental state or quality of thoughts, we must change our vibrational frequency.

The significance of the Thirteen Moon calendar does not lie in its visible surface, but rather in the fact that it is a threshold and a door that connects us to the vast web of synchronicity that underlies all manifestations.

The Gregorian calendar can be understood as a cultural meme or hologram that actually represents, or is a manifestation of, a warped time space matrix with 12 irregular months. If the time space matrix is warped, and projected out from an irregular matrix base, then a fragmented civilization is created. If we project an irregular, mechanized matrix onto third-dimensional space, then we will never get clear answers or attain peace and harmony.

The Thirteen Moon, 28-day calendar represents a harmonic time space matrix. The actual order of the 28-day cycle for measuring the orbit of the Earth, is also a fourth-dimensional order that conforms to a third-dimensional sequence of days-and-nights in time.

Following the 13 moon, 28-day calendar increases incidences of synchronicity by tuning our mental frequency to the radial matrix, first by expanding awareness of the two interlocking orders of measure—the seven-day cycle and the 13:20 frequency. The harmonic incidences of these two measures in recurring, recombinant patterns, enhances the awareness of the interdimensional and interconnected reality of the synchronic order.

Part III • Mapping the New Reality

> ### TIME IS OF THE MIND
>
> In actuality, time is of the mind. The senses take in physical space. We cannot touch time; but we know time. To realize that time is of the mind we have to first know our own mind. Only when we know our own mind can we realize the deeper orders of reality.
>
> The nature of the synchronic order is a fourth-dimensional structure or matrix of consciousness that underlies third-dimensional reality. This is the factor that distinguishes the synchronic order from the traditional Mayan Long Count, which is a count of days in the third dimension orbital cycles of the Earth. However, this does not mean that the Long Count does not derive its symbology from the fourth-dimensional order, the Tzolkin or "sacred count". This is just to say that the purpose of the Long Count is to maintain the count of days between August 13, 3113 BC and December 21, 2012. All systems are easily incorporated into the synchronic order.

DISCRIMINATING TIME AND SPACE CONSTRUCTS

In speaking of evolution, it is necessary to understand from the outset that no mechanical evolution is possible. The evolution of man is the evolution of his consciousness.
—G.I. Gurdjieff

As a purely fourth-dimensional construct, the synchronic order can be understood as being etheric, like a dream, or a highly structured element of the imaginal realm. However, this is not the same as molecular structures and dimensions of space that define the third dimension.

The third dimension is coordinated by constructs of linear time, inclusive of constructs of duration. In fourth-dimensional time, constructs of duration have meaning only insomuch as they are coordinated by the harmonic codes of the synchronic order. We greatly limit our consciousness by strictly following linear constructs of time.

The traditional Julian/Gregorian calendar is an example of a construct of duration in linear time. It corresponds to the duration of the cycle of the orbit of Earth around the sun. However, its patterns do not fully correspond to a harmonic order. This calendar has 52 weeks, a number that conforms to a harmonic frequency ($7 \times 52 = 364 = 13 \times 28$), but the order of the weeks do not conform to the number of days in each of the 12 months.

These irregularities of shifting order of days of the weeks and irregular order of days per month have long term effects on the consciousness once they are accepted as normal. The subconscious and conscious minds register these irregularities as "normal", and consequently the society becomes unconsciously locked into self-defeating patterns of irresolvable irregularity and irrationality.

The Gregorian calendar lacks any context of meaning apart from its count date allegedly beginning with the birth of Christ. From a planetary perspective, this is an arbitrary date—making the Gregorian calendar merely a linear count of days devoid of cosmological significance.

Insofar as measurements of duration correspond to harmonic patterns of the synchronic order, then the synchronic order can encompass these measurements of duration. Any measurement based solely on third-dimensional coordinates is hopelessly irregular. For example, lunar pattern does not coincide with the orbit of the Earth around the sun. Twelve lunations make a lunar year of 354 days—11 days short of the solar orbit. Hence, the lunar cycle does not coincide with a solar year.

However, in the long run, even the lunar and Gregorian cycles are incorporated into a larger synchronic pattern. Twenty-eight Gregorian years makes one cycle that repeats with the same number of leap days. The lunar calendar coincides with the Thirteen Moon, 28-day calendar every 33 years.

> **REFRAMING OUR EXPERIENCES**
>
> Our attention may be focused momentarily in the "now", however the quality of attention has been conditioned by the past, as irrational mental shifts programmed by an irregular timing frequency. To break free of our habits and conditionings, we must break the old spell and operate from a harmonic matrix.
>
> A beginning application of the synchronic order is to make the past conscious by finding the underlying patterns of synchronicity that has and is weaving our lives together—this can be done by charting out our "destiny castle", as described in the Dreamspell. By finding the higher meaning of our experiences, events and people in our lives, then we can uproot negative patterns that will otherwise get dragged into the present moment and repeated. Through the lens of the synchronic order, we can begin to view the events and people in our lives from a higher dimensional vantage point, and thus, a whole new story, rich in meaning, opens to us.

The synchronic order is a self-existing order of harmonic patterns that corresponds to a fourth-dimensional consciousness and represent a higher coordinating intelligence. For this reason, knowledge of the synchronic order is a pivotal point in the evolution of consciousness. This is the stage where the human makes a conscious effort to surrender to the higher mind. Once the mind is engaged as a facet of higher consciousness, then it can bring out the data of the synchronic order and give a context of coherence even to irregular systems. In other words, learning the synchronic codes of time gives our lives an entirely new context by which to live.

When we search for similar patterns of organization in the spatially oriented mechanistic society, we see there are not really any symbolically coded patterns. There is no context of meaning.

For instance, today might be January 29, 2008—but there is no intrinsic symbolism to this—there is nothing to this. Or if we say, it is 11:45 am. What does this mean symbolically? This is just a short-hand notation of a moment of duration in linear time. But it does not tell us anything else. But if we say today it is *Limi 20* of the *Resonant Monkey Moon* of the *White Lunar Wizard* year—this causes us to pause and think a bit differently. Rather than state a mechanical time, we could further say we are in the *White Resonant Mirror* watch of Kin 241, *Red Resonant Dragon*. This is an example of symbolically coded patterns of organization in time. These symbols contain instantaneous associations and contexts of meaning.

The system of the synchronic order is a rich layering of symbolically coded patterns. By learning these patterns, our thought structures are reoriented with multi-layered meanings. This is a general example and opens us to a whole other range of consciousness and states of mind. When we consider that the Thirteen Moon calendar is an ever-changing daily program that perpetuates itself every 52 years, then we can begin to comprehend how our consciousness would be greatly altered following such a system of harmonic order.

The most fundamental pattern of organization is the 13 and 20 codes. To most people on the planet this is unfamiliar territory. Since the 13:20 frequency is the universal frequency of synchronization, then the whole of the universe is functioning preconsciously, unconsciously, subconsciously, consciously, and superconsciously to the 13:20 pattern of organization. This is the knowledge that elevates our consciousness.

The old frequency 12:60 is rapidly coming to an end so that by 2013 the whole of the planet will be liberated and functioning in the universal frequency of synchronization. For people immersed in the disorder of mechanistic time, the 12:60 frequency is like a perennially cloudy sky—so we can never see the sun. Imagine all our life not seeing the sun—then the 2012 event occurs and the cloud cover vanishes. Imagine what that would be like.

> **SHIFTING FREQUENCY**
>
> Our quality of attention or frequency can be changed through the repatterning that comes from using the 13 Moon, 28-day calendar and the synchronic order. Learning the synchronic codes gives our present center of consciousness a new and constructive meaning to view events in our life and on the planet. Many memories are based on faulty perceptions due to living in an artificial time space matrix. It is important to see the underlying synchronic web that weaves our lives and all life in the universe. In time, the energy of the vitalized harmonic focus of the synchronic order displaces the anomalies of the conditioned past.

The 13:20 frequency is a bridge to assist our emergence from the dense space of consciousness. But first we must make a distinction between the dense phase brought on by immersion in artificial time, and the etheric phase brought on by immersion in natural time. This is to lay the groundwork for the dimensional shift (2012-2013), which will elevate those receptive out of the previous state of consciousness altogether. When the human species attains this new planetary consciousness, then it will also want to understand the workings of this new state of mind. It is beneficial to understand this now, so that it will not come as a shock later.

This new state of mind is consciousness operating at the 13:20 timing frequency. To know it, practice it and make it conscious we are given the symbolic patterns or constructs. (See Appendix: *Synchronic Order as Symbolic Construct*)

SYNCHRONIC ORDER AND ASTROLOGY

The synchronic order is a symbolically coded organization of time. This is important to remember. This is the key defining factor of the synchronic order, and is what gives meaning to time. The

The Cosmic History Chronicles • Volume IV

MAYAN INTERDIMENSIONAL STAR MAP

OMNI GALACTIC SOURCE

ALPHA GALAXY

OMEGA GALAXY

HUNAB KU

SIRIUS

ANTARES

PLEIADES

ARCTURUS

AA MIDWAY STATION

AETHERIC MOTHER SUN

SUN

AETHERIC FATHER SUN

CRYSTAL EARTH

The Mayan Interdimensional Star Map is an example of a fourth-dimensional structure projected onto a third-dimensional coordinate. We can use our body to plug into this construct through each of our seven chakras: Crystal Earth (Root), Sun (Secret Center), AA Midway Station (Solar Plexus), Pleiades (Heart), Sirius (Throat), Hunab Ku (Third Eye), and Omni Galactic Source (Crown).

synchronic order introduces a higher level of interconnectedness of the hermetic systems based on whole number symbolism. Higher whole number orders encompass all lesser decimal whole number orders of esoteric tradition. All fractions can be transduced into whole number fractals.

The synchronic order is an aspect of what Sri Aurobindo calls the "supramental descent". The whole structure of the synchronic order is a supramental structure based on symbolisms derived from number. Number precedes consciousness—number is supramental, beyond mind. Number is what gives mind its sense of order, harmony and organization.

Astrology is closely related to the synchronic order as it deals with moving elements in time. However, the symbology of astrology is based on third-dimensional coordinates in space. These coordinates are represented by different planetary bodies in relationship to a hypothetical or imaginal construct on the ecliptic, which is divided into twelve houses or astrological signs.

All of these signs account for twelve, thirty-degree, divisions of a circle in space. Even though astrology has merit as a type of primitive synchronic code, the basis of its symbolism is constructed in third-dimensional coordinates on a division of a 360-degree plane in space. Thus, astrology is a structure of the old reality or paradigm of space.

Every day the moon changes its appearance slightly and different stars and planets also change in relation to the moon every day. The planetary bodies in moving relation to each other create particular geometries—it is the changing pattern of these geometries in relation to each other, as they are focalized on certain points of latitude and longitude on the Earth that constitutes a type of synchronic order. These changing patterns are continuously are subject to refined science and methodology.

The synchronic order differs from astrology in that it is based on a fourth-dimensional set of mathematical constants, rather than on a set of shifting x and y, third-dimensional coordinates. The synchronic order does not derive any of its constructs from third-dimensional coordinates, though it has correlates with the days of the orbital cycle, and even with the planets of the solar system.

From the perspective of time, space is an infinitely locatable point.

From the perspective of time, space is an infinitely locatable point. Earth is one of these infinitely locatable points. From the Earth's perspective, however, this is all space. If we look at the nighttime sky all that space we see comes back to one point in time, which is ourselves standing on this one little point of space, which is our planet.

The synchronic codes of time can be projected upon any particular point in space. Once again, the synchronic codes are not dependent on shifting third-dimensional coordinates. They are fourth-dimensional harmonic structures projected on third-dimensional coordinates. This indicates that all third dimensional coordinates conform to a greater or lesser degree to one or a number of fourth-dimensional constructs. From this arises the corollary: the third dimension in its entirety is coordinated by the fourth dimension.

Number is a higher reality or dimension than time or space.

DIVINATION AND SYMBOLIC SYSTEMS

To imagine the truth is to *divine,* says Eliphas Levi, and to divine is to exercise divine power. To divine something means to have knowledge that is generally not explainable in human terms.

When we consult templates of space such as the I Ching or Tarot, this is called *divination*. Systems such as the I Ching or Tarot combine a principle of order with a great variety of possible permutations in a way thought to reflect the nature of the universe and of humans. Divination is a process dependent on a synchronic moment in time, but is usually worked out on a template in space.

These systems are a principle means for symbolic potentialities of space to inform our consciousness, perceptions and behavior. When we consult one of these systems with a specific question then the information loaded into it goes into the subconscious and depending on who we are, where we are and our level of consciousness, we will get a particular answer from our subconscious. This answer is triggered both by our intention and by the particular symbolic construct that we might be using—and the moment in time. This is how divination

The Dimension of Number

All numbers are composites and/or factors of each other. The primal numbers of time are 4, 7, 13 and 20. The primal numbers of space are 4, 5 and 9.

The frequency of the Law of Time is 13:20—between the 13 and 20 is the seven. Between 3 and 7 is the four. Herein lies the form constant that establishes the ratio 4:7::7:13. Four is the root, seven is the stem and thirteen is the fruit. This is the primal ratio and cosmology of the Law of Time.

In this construct, there are three units on either side of the seven—this is the underlying law of three. 3 + 3 = 6. Six is the basis of the hexagisimal order.

3 + 1 + 3 = 7;
6 + 1 + 6 = 13.

Parallel constructs can be derived from doubling the law of three. So we have the 7, 13 and 20. The point is that the fundamental formulation of the numbers and patterns in time is contained in this formulation.

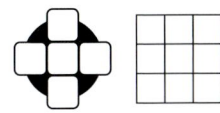

The numbers of space are 4, 5, and 9. The fundamental pattern of space is based on the fifth force. When we make a square as a matrix, the minimal pattern is nine (9 = 4 + 5), while the matrix as a square has four sides.

Fifth Force   3x3 Matrix

Particularly with the seven and the thirteen we are dealing with supremely cosmic frequencies, the 7 being derived from the interval of lost time in eternity and the 13 being the function of the 4:7::7:13 that creates endless cosmic cyclical patterns. The 13 then forms into a type of spiral which is known as the wavespell. By comparison, space is a static structure.

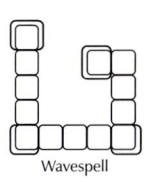

Wavespell

1 + 2 + 3 + 4 = 10. Ten is the decimal base.
7 + 13 = 20. Twenty is the vigesimal base.

Fourth-dimensional time is based on 20 and third-dimensional space (as matter) is based on 10. That ratio difference is what creates the higher etheric patterns of time in relation to the denser patterns of space.

Symbolic structures are derived from the primary numbers of time: 4, 7, 13, and 20. The number 20 (4 x 5) actually incorporates a fifth force of space. In other words, the 20 is a function of time (7 and 13). It is also a function of space (4 x 5). When we multiply the space numbers 4 x 5, we arrive at the 20—a prime number of time. Therefore 20 is the magic number that comprises both space and time. This is why twenty is known as the number of totality and 20 squared is 400, the pure fractal frequency of totality.

In the vigesimal system, 400 is written as 1.0.0, there are zero units in the 1-unit and 20-unit positions, and a 1 in the 400-unit position. This is the totality. The square of the totality of time (400) is four times greater than the square of the totality of space (100). Yet 1.0.0 vigesimal looks like 100 decimal.

functions. Synchronic time is the medium of divinatory operations, defining the mechanisms of accessing "hidden" knowledge.

We might ask: How do we trigger meaning from the moment of a synchronic point through a particular symbolic construct? In this regard, divination is primitively synchronic because it depends on synchronization of mind and information at a specific moment. It is important to make clear distinctions between constructs completely based in a fourth-dimensional order of time and constructs that are merely templates in third-dimensional geometric space. However, both time and space are dimensions coordinated by number. Number is a higher reality or dimension than time or space. Based on the vigesimal code—count by 20—the dimensions of number correspond to the cosmology of the cube, which is the large, multidimensional reality that integrates time and space into a vast harmonic unity of interchangeable frequencies. Let us review this cosmology:

In the beginning was the void, which may be a type of mind or consciousness, but is formless, without structure. So the first primal void dimension of silence arises, then within mind arises the potential for awareness and perceptions of sight and sound. But still there is no order; for order to exist, there must be number. The dimension of number that arises gives order to mind.

Symbolic systems in general, particularly the synchronic order, are applications of the dimension of number. There is void, there is mind, or rather base conscious awareness, then there is number. Number precedes, underlies and informs consciousness. Number first originates time, and then space. Any number matrix is a self-arising component of primal consciousness.

Locating the Invisible Matrix

Where is the synchronic order located? To find the answer, we turn to the six mental spheres—particularly the second, third and fourth. The fourth mental sphere—continuing conscious—corresponds to the fourth dimension. The fourth dimension is the mode of consciousness where there is continuing consciousness, characterized by radial and fractal intelligence structures.

The second mental sphere is the *subconscious* (not to be confused with unconscious). The subconscious is the state that is always active just underneath the surface of the conscious or the third mental sphere. It contains the unconscious, the deeper stratum of archetypal information. The subconscious includes many different patterns—patterns of information, patterns of experience, patterns of memory, and so forth. The subconscious helps consciousness to process what it experiences.

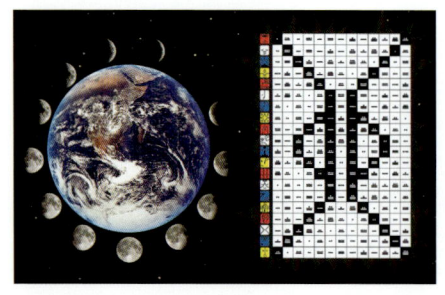

The Thirteen Moon calendar is the doorway to the synchronic order or fourth-dimensional pattern. Once entered, this doorway opens us into the 260-day cycle, which tunes us into the whole solar galactic 52-year Sirius B cycle (it takes Sirius B, 52 years to orbit Sirius A). Once we tune into these cycles, we set in motion a repatterning process; our vibration increases as we are slowly extracted from the 12:60 grid and entered into the 13:20 harmonic matrix.

This 13:20 matrix is also known as the synchronic matrix and is projected daily through the planet and into our waking consciousness. Our third-dimensional consciousness serves as an intermediary in this process. It receives a symbol, form, pattern or number from the synchronic order and immediately refers it to the second mental sphere or the subconscious where the whole system order is in a state of fluid readiness.

The subconscious for each person is different. For example, if we say today is "Red Rhythmic Dragon", a certain image or feeling is evoked. Or if we say, "The Wizard's in the Cube", this conjures a different image or feeling. These images immediately register in the conscious and then transfer to the subconscious and from the subconscious different associations or sets of feelings are aroused. The subconscious then brings these meanings to the conscious surface and correlates them to the pattern being projected through the fourth dimension synchronic order to the third-dimensional consciousness to create an overlay of meaning.

The fourth dimension is the continuing consciousness or a moving pattern in time. The synchronic order exists within this dimension as a layer of intelligence universally dispersed and synchronized to the frequency ranges of different celestial bodies, such as Earth. Mapping our potential experience of the synchronic order is a complex projection through different time lenses emanating from a higher divine intelligence associated with the Sirius binary star system. Like a film projector, it projects a particular synchronic "image" on a daily basis on the celestial body.

Once the consciousness is tuned into the existence of the synchronic order, it may receive a projection, which immediately goes to the subconscious and the subconscious brings forth a set of meanings and associations that go to the conscious mind. The conscious mind bonds with these meanings and associations of the subconscious to the pattern of the synchronic order. So when a Red Dragon day comes around again there will be a bonding or pattern of a 20-day cycle. (See Appendix)

Where is the synchronic order located? It is not located in space, space is located in consciousness. The synchronic order is located in a dimension of consciousness that is defined by the different mental spheres. The synchronic order is a function of the fourth mental sphere and fourth-dimensional consciousness; this is a vast range and is not dependent on our body or the space we occupy—though it projects upon it.

The synchronic order can also be understood as a set of vibrations that arouse some definite qualities of existence. It is important to understand the location of the synchronic order in terms of patterns and functions or locations of consciousness.

We must elevate our knowledge to understand that patterns of order and meaning do not derive from analysis of third-dimensional coordinates, but are self-existing functions of the Law of Time. These coordinates create vast repertoires and constructs of order in the fourth-dimensional consciousness.

There are two basic types of systems:

1. **Systems based in universal synchronized time and consciousness (patterns of time).**
2. **Systems based in spatially defined and determined constructs (patterns of space).**

Astrology is a spatially designed system. Systems like the Kabbalah or I Ching revolve more purely around number, but are still cast in templates or molds that are spatial constructs. These constructs represent aspects of an absolute order of mind that can be woven into the Law of Time through their patterns of harmonic number frequencies.

From that pure number dimension there are two form orders that mind projects: the pattern of time and the pattern of space (see above). From the integration of these patterns, the time space mold is created, governed by the timing factor. The space constituents remain relatively stable. We feel the duration of time—it is light now and in a certain amount of time it will be night—and we know the point of space we are in is turning about on its particular axis.

These space elements remain constant, but time elements are moving coordinates. The historical cycle, with the exception of Mesoamerican civilizations, uses determinants of time based on coordinates in space. The synchronic order operates with determinants of time based on harmonic coordinates of synchronization in the fourth dimension. This represents patterns of ever-shifting geometric harmonics that are very different from the patterns of organization of time in the spatial cycle of historical materialism. These ever-shifting geometric patterns are called *celestial harmonics*.

In the synchronic order, the simplest level is the 20 seals, the 13 tones and the 28-day cycle. This is where we start. We can build from there to begin to see a richness of organization of time that is incomprehensible from the point of the view of the clock and of the Gregorian calendar.

The synchronic order supersedes the historical organization of time. It is a new organization of time, a new symbolic construct, and an entirely new reality that unfolds eons into the future. This is a whole other formulation of the mind. As we advance past 2013, we will understand the synchronic codes as the basic building blocks that teach us how to construct the new reality. If we apply these codes and tools, it will not matter where we come from; all that will matter is where we are going.

Part IV
Exploring the Inner Dimensions

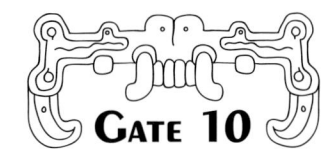

Gate 10
The Serpent Initiates

Winding your way through the labyrinth, you stumble upon what appears as a cellar door. You open the door and climb down a winding staircase; it feels damp and moist as you descend deeper into what appears as an underground cavern or subterranean crypt. Exhausted, you stop and sit on the damp earth. You sit in silence bathed in a subliminal light. Scenes flicker on the periphery of your consciousness—scenes from other worlds, other times. You hear a voice: "Gather the fragments of knowledge, and return them to their rightful place if you are to attain wholeness!"

> *Behold, I send you forth as sheep in the midst of wolves: be ye therefore wise as serpents, and harmless as doves.*
> —Matthew 10:16

The *serpent initiates* are the ones who remember the previous world systems and explosions of reality. They incarnate or emanate at different times in specific places to lift the human species into higher realms. Their appearance and diverse manifestations are all part of a unified "salvation plan" that spans the cycles of history.

The serpent is often associated with the *fallen angel*, or *fallen man*. In the Quranic tradition, the present human condition is a consequence of interaction with the fallen angels. Humanity then, represents the evolution from a state of fallen angels. There is a similar story in the lost books of Enoch where the fallen angels come to Earth and mate with the daughters of man to create a race of giants. The point is, the human was conceived in a pure, high state, then brought down only to rise again. It is the serpent initiate that marks the beginning ascent of the human from the fallen state.

According to *The Secret Doctrine*, the legend of the "fallen angels" contains the key to the manifold contradictions of human character; it points to the secret of self-consciousness and contains the history of evolution and growth. In this regard, we are all memory remnants. Each of us contains certain psychic fragments of previous worlds—lost worlds, many of which ended in catastrophe.

Everyone on this planet is a remnant of the original creation, a seed of the original seed; the product of the transmigration and transmutation of many elements. All beings are products of civilizations created by fragmented minds or remnants; therefore these minds continuously create a fragmentary remnant reality. This is the collective world we live in—an unsatisfied and splintered world seeking to become whole.

THE SERPENT INITIATES ARE THE ONES WHO REMEMBER PREVIOUS WORLD SYSTEMS AND EXPLOSIONS OF REALITY

In the flow of the transmigration of atoms and consciousness there are stopping points—other planets, other form bodies—all yearning to the wholeness of the original One. We are all remnants of this divine remembering, being taught to remember the way back home. Fragmentary remnants that travel from one world to another are always seeking a body to incarnate in. Every body takes on a different form or shape with a built-in magnetic attractor for the remnant memories to manifest. All memory remnants seek to become whole.

At this point, we find ourselves plunged into the extreme of matter and materialism—this is the point when it is most important to remember and apply the esoteric tenets of the secret teachings. These tenets contain keys to the process of the original cosmic structure as it was molded into existence; first, as a purely etheric form, then as an increasingly dense form, until we arrive in our present bodies.

It is precisely at this point when the cosmic medicine must be administered to elevate and assist the psyche in its process of constructing the cosmic personality. But before we are ready to swallow the medicine, another initiation must occur—an initiation that penetrates the foggy mind field created by the remnant personality.

According to *The Secret Doctrine*, in the earliest traditions, the initiators of knowledge were known as the *wisdom serpents*. These wisdom serpents carried forward and synthesized the unitary knowledge of the previous *root races*. This knowledge is universal and so is spread throughout the physical world. All traditions on every continent have some form of this same knowledge, from one primal root culture or civilization.

The serpent represents the fallen angel who becomes the wise initiate. The serpent falls from on high and is said to possess the keys of the empire and the keys of the dead. Why the serpent?

In the Book of Genesis, the serpent is described as the most subtle of creatures, and is also seen as the tempter in the Garden of Eden. Having tasted of both good and evil, the serpent is capable of becoming the wise initiate. The serpents hold the wisdom from on high and descend to Earth as conductors of initiation in order to test humankind.

Satan is described as the doorkeeper at the temple, or a magistrate of God in the court of the law, representing the last judgment. Satan plays the role of the magistrate since he knows everybody personally; every initiate has to go through a period of darkness or Hell in order to pass into the higher realms.

The fragmentary personality, since it is not yet whole, represents the kingdom of darkness or Hell. The initiation leads the initiate out of the kingdom of darkness by exerting in the disciplines of UR—Universal Recollection/Reality/Religion/Remembrance. The initiate focuses on the disciplines of unification and wholeness, and thus, steadily stamps out the lower self in the light of truth.

In order to exit the kingdom of darkness, the initiate must be willing to experience the contents of the unconscious as it is stirred up. The true initiate is one who gazes fearlessly into all aspects of his/her being, and is willing to shed doubts, misperceptions and negative tendencies in light of the truth.

Despite leading others astray, Satan professes his knowledge that the Lord God is One, according to the Quran. In hermetic tradition, Lucifer as the light bearer represents the primary adept. All adepts or initiates seeking to overcome the darkness of Hell are based on the original transformation of Satan or Lucifer, who was the first to fall and the first to have to deal with the possibility of rising again.

We are all fallen creatures and to rise to a high level of spiritual morality is our test. The serpents, then, represent the initiators—those who have already been plunged into Hell and darkness and have emerged, possessing initiatic knowledge.

Moses is an example of a serpent initiate, which is why he carried the magical serpent staff. The interplanetary meaning of the serpent is coded into the synchronic order where the serpent represents Maldek, the destroyed planet, now the Asteroid Belt. Here lies a profound clue for Moses' mission: through his serpent staff, he was destined to reassemble Maldek by calling together the 12 tribes of Israel. The fate of Maldek is reflected in the history of the Jews. This is why the choices Israel makes today affect the entire destiny of the Earth.

The primordial worlds and knowledge must be brought forward in time through the initiates so they can conduct the rites of initiation. This is conducted by the serpents that dwell beneath the pyramids in the subterranean crypts.

The Secret Doctrine is a fractal of knowledge that existed in previous worlds and is projected into the fourth round of existence through the fourth root race—Atlantean (see Gate 6 for description of root races). In the fourth root race, this knowledge received a certain perfection, followed by the

> **EVOLVE INTO WHOLENESS**
>
> Instead of working on how to develop a better personality out of our fragments, which is what most worldly psychologies do, the spiritual/transformative psychology instructs us to exert in creating a rarified field or state of consciousness that continuously steps on these fragments, and reveals their illusory nature. This process requires patience and persistence, and is sometimes experienced as a sense of going backwards or being stuck—but sooner than later this fragmentary personality must dissolve into the light and become whole. This explains the healing power of light.

The Cosmic History Chronicles • Volume IV

> **MEMORY REMNANTS**
>
> Initiatic knowledge reaches into the previous destroyed worlds and the initiate is the one who gathers the fragments of knowledge, and returns them, bit by bit, to the primordial field of wholeness. This is the meaning of the quest or the journey of the labyrinth.
>
> All dissonance is a remnant of a mental perception or a memory from Maldek. Everything in its form is a remnant from a memory from Mars. When these planetary civilizations were destroyed, whether they were destroyed by explosion or gas or deluge, the soul memories and their forms or modes of being were released as fragmentary remnants.
>
> All the knowledge constructs and spiritual teachings of every kind are also remnants—of the secret doctrine, the one original master template. Cosmic History is transmitted as a third force of intelligence, superseding the external force of civilization and incorporating the internal force of The Secret Doctrine. This is not just a memory of coherence, but a manifest or cosmic coherence, a rendition of the totality adapted to the evolving mind of the planetary human.

dissolution and destruction of Atlantis. The memory of the initiates was known as the serpents and dragons of wisdom.

According to Cosmic History, the fourth or Atlantean world descended from Mars. This passage perfected the knowledge which had first been developed on Maldek and was then carried from Mars to Earth. According to Sri Aurobindo, "This present Earth in its turn appears as the scene of life, Mars being its last theatre."

Blavatsky makes clear that the information contained in *The Secret Doctrine* is decidedly occult in nature. The knowledge was disseminated by the fourth Atlantean root race and runs through various streams, including the hermetic tradition of Egypt, the Chaldea in Mesopotamia, the Sumerian stream of ancient UR, and Vedic and Tibetan traditions. Tracing the information stream back to ancient Egypt and Hermes leads us to the point of the knowledge of the Great Pyramid—the knowledge of the prior root races of the Atlanteans. This is similar to the knowledge derived from the pyramids in Mexico, which also traces back to Atlantis.

Blavatsky states that at an earlier stage of civilization there was one common knowledge base, which originated in Atlantis (or a previous world system), and was shared universally on Earth. Then, in the process of historical amnesia, this knowledge fragmented and scattered, its sense of unity lost. However, knowledge of the whole was maintained by different mystery schools. The prototype of these schools and lineages of wisdom are traced to Hermes and the hermetic tradition of the West—this knowledge was handed down by transmission and safeguarded by various mystery schools.

Part IV • Exploring the Inner Dimensions

Pyramids and Underground Chambers

Serpent knowledge and wisdom is often stored in caverns or caves (storage units), beneath pyramids. Almost every part of the planet has myths and stories about vast underground networks of caves and tunnels, including Central Asia, India, Africa, Australia, Mesoamerica and throughout South America.

During his travels in Asia, Nicholas Roerich spent a lot of time studying local folklore, which included tales of lost tribes or subterranean dwellers. It is said that there are vast underground network of caves and tunnels under the whole of Central Asia, with many passages radiating out from the spiritual hub of Shambhala.

As an "underground" center, Shambhala is also associated with *Agartha*—a mythic and mystical subterranean realm peopled by enlightened beings who keep watch on the world of the surface.

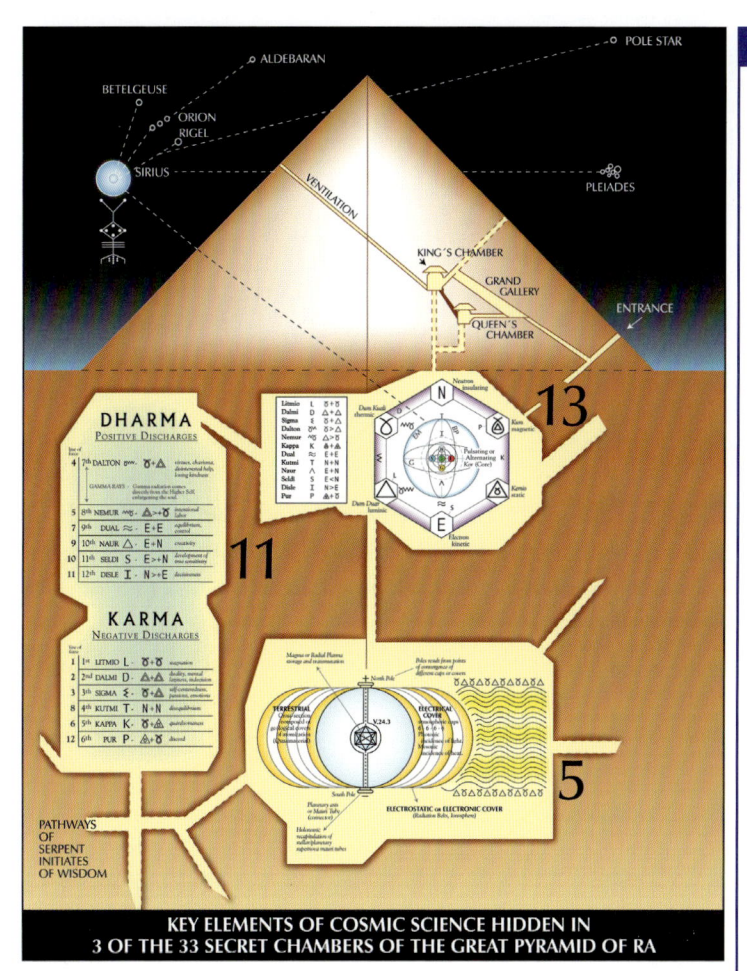

KEY ELEMENTS OF COSMIC SCIENCE HIDDEN IN 3 OF THE 33 SECRET CHAMBERS OF THE GREAT PYRAMID OF RA

Secret Chambers of Ra

The description of the universe defined in Cosmic Science is drawn from a galactic, non-terrestrial intelligence with little reference to human history, except for the Great Pyramid of Giza in Egypt. This Pyramid is mentioned strictly as a point of storage of higher-dimensional information on the terrestrial plane (see *CHC, Vol. II*).

Cosmic Science says there are 33 secret chambers in the Great Pyramid of Ra, three of which contain specific information. Chamber 13 contains information about the primal electrical partons. Chamber 11 contains information about karmic/dharmic electrical lines of force, and Chamber 5 contains information about the electromagnetic poles.

It is interesting to note what information is mentioned and where it is stored. Notice that all information stored in the secret chambers has to do with electricity.

Madame Blavatsky mentions an immense tunnel running from Cuzco to Lima in Peru, and then extending south into Bolivia. Likewise, in Hindu mythology there are many tales of the Nagas or "serpent-people". It is said these serpent people were semi-divine and ruled a subterranean kingdom, Patala.

The Secret Doctrine says that the serpents of wisdom store their knowledge in caverns beneath pyramids. The serpent initiates represent the Atlanteans or people from the four root races that gathered all the wisdom teachings and then stored them beneath the pyramids or sacred mountains of Earth.

In Egypt, the serpent is a symbol of wisdom and immortality; the subterranean crypts of Thebes were known as the "serpent's catacombs". Similarly, this cavern beneath the Pyramid of the Sun was a place of shamanic initiations "from the prior root races", as *The Secret Doctrine* describes it. It was here that serpent holders of wisdom gathered to consolidate the new knowledge, which was left in the Great Pyramid.

Let us create a psychic connection with these three points: a) the Great Pyramid of Egypt with its 33 secret chambers, b) the pyramid at Teotihuacan with the shamanic cavern underneath, and c) the cavern or crypt beneath the Pyramid of the Inscriptions at Palenque. These three pyramids form a transatlantic code or key that unlocks the next stage of the evolution of spirit as a collective whole.

Teotihuacan and Egypt are separated by the Atlantic Ocean and much of the continental landmass of Africa. Both places are singular in location and are associated with celestial knowledge as indicated by their geomantical orientation and location. The Great Pyramid in Egypt points toward the Pole Star, as does the pyramid at Teotihuacan, which points toward the Pole Star and the Pleiades.

Palenque is also known as *Nah Chan: House of the Serpent*. The subterranean chamber built within the Pyramid of the Inscriptions is the chamber of the serpent initiates. This chamber is complete with a speaking tube that winds in a serpentine manner down the stairs from the temple floor above to the "root of heaven"—Pacal Votan's tomb.

The knowledge contained in Nah Chan was stored and then transcribed by Valum Votan as the Telektonon prophecy

The Telektonon is the master code that encompasses and incorporates the knowledge of both the Great Pyramid and the Pyramid of the Sun.

through the Earth Spirit Speaking Tube. The Telektonon is the master code that encompasses and incorporates the knowledge of both the Great Pyramid and the Pyramid of the Sun. It appears as though the information gathered at the two cosmic accumulators of Teotihuacan and Giza was then taken by the arch scribe and deposited in the crypt as the prophecy of Pacal Votan.

The locations of these three pyramids, and the information stored within them, contain the keys to whole earth geomancy. These are key assemblage points on the planet for the activation of whole Earth consciousness. It is worth contemplating that the Cosmic Science text makes no mention of Earth, other than referring to the Great Pyramid in Egypt as a cosmic storage space for knowledge.

In this light, we must consider the profound interrelationship of the knowledge of cosmic electricity and knowledge of the cosmic lines of force, and the knowledge stored within the Earth's poles. This knowledge is terrestrial and cosmic; without this knowledge gathered through the planetary poles, the Earth would be without evolutionary possibility.

These three pieces of concealed information: cosmic electricity, the nature of the poles and the law of karma/dharma, within themselves define key points of a cosmic plan. Also note that the Pyramid of the Sun at Teotihuacan has the same base measurements as the Great Pyramid in Egypt.

The relationship between the Temple of the Inscriptions and the knowledge stored in the Great Pyramid in Egypt is also worth considering. As pointed out in *The Mayan Factor*, when we observe the placement of the King's Chamber within the pyramid in Egypt, its construction is similar to the internalized version of the Tower of the Winds at Palenque. There is also a similar elaborate construction with the Pyramid of Inscriptions and the tomb of Pacal Votan that indicate that a secret or occult wisdom is contained therein. All of these signs indicate that Pacal Votan, who designed both the Tower of the Winds and his tomb, was a chief serpent of wisdom—a time engineer—who buried the meaning and knowledge of the previous worlds beneath his pyramid.

Note: *Valum Votan visited the cavern or underground grotto at Teotihuacan on July 25, 1999, with 12 other people for a total of 13, and again with Red Queen/Red Electric Serpent—on December 21, 2005, seven years prior to 2012. This was the same pyramid where he had his first vision at 14. It was at this same pyramid in 2002, that Valum Votan was honored by nine indigenous elders as the "Closer of the Cycle", and gifted with a sacred baston. These elders were Earth guardians who, four days before*

> **PREPARATION OF THE SIXTH ROOT RACE**
>
> The mission of the Closer of the Cycle, as inheritor of the mantle of the serpent initiates of wisdom, is for the spiritual unification of Planet Earth. This is the moment when everyone realizes we are all the same being, and that all teachings come from the same place.
>
> At the closing of the cycle, we can then come together to create a unified spiritual kaleidoscope. Everyone will realize that we are all a common link on the evolution of the spirit. In this way, we can see the nature of the archetypal roles of the Closer of the Cycle and the Red Queen as the cosmic principles integrating the knowledge of the fourth root race with the one fate and destiny of the fifth root race—all in preparation for the sacred emergence of the sixth root race.

the ceremony, met in the grotto underneath the Pyramid of the Sun and received the message of what they must do and how they must conduct the ceremony. This is an example of the significance of the underground caverns.

Madame Blavatsky and Votan

More than 130 years ago, when Mme. Blavatsky wrote *The Secret Doctrine*, little was known about the Mayan civilization. This being the case, it is interesting to note that Madame Blavatsky not only visited the Mexican pyramids, but also culled what little written work that was available at that time. She extracted the essence of the information about the one known as Votan from the few original Spanish sources, which she quoted in her books *Isis Unveiled* and *The Secret Doctrine*. Both *Isis Unveiled* and *The Secret Doctrine* mention the mysterious Votan.

Isis Unveiled quotes Votan as being the "greatest magician of Ancient Mexico". This is astonishing to consider since this work was written in the 1870s—more than eighty years before the discovery of the tomb of Pacal Votan. It is also interesting to note that the archaeologists who discovered and studied the tomb are loathe to make any reference that this could be associated with the Votan, or that Votan might be none other than the Great Pacal. Obviously, only a great magician skilled in supernatural engineering could have determined how to build that stunning piece of interior architecture with the enormous pressure of a pyramid built on top of a crypt without caving in!

Pacal Votan and Nah Chan

Pacal Votan personifies or exemplifies the evolution of the spirit in its hierarchical possibilities. As an electrical fifth-dimensional entity, Pacal Votan has the capacity of assuming an etheric fourth-dimensional form, whenever necessary, often for the purpose of surveying world systems. He surveyed this present world system prior to taking a full blown historical incarnation as the eleventh ruler in the dynasty of Nah Chan Palenque—the earthly Galactic Mayan Tollan.

The purpose of Pacal Votan's mission on Earth was to establish the Universal Religion as the index of spiritual unification of the world systems. Following his disincarnation, Pacal Votan's fourth-fifth-dimensional form assumed a "guiding" function and toward the end of the cycle sent forth a final emanation.

The Secret Doctrine states:

> ... seven families who accompanied the mystical personage named Votan the reputed founder of the great city of Nah Chan identified by some with Palenque ..."

> "In Boulberg's book, Votan (the Mexican demi-god), in narrating his expedition, describes a subterranean passage which ran underground, and terminated at the root of the heavens, adding that this passage was a snake's hole, "un agujero de culebra"; and that he was admitted to it because he was himself "a son of the snakes", or a serpent.
> —p. 379, Vol. II

Keep in mind that a second book burning in Chiapas in 1692 was intended to destroy all memory of Votan. This makes it most unusual that Brasseur du Boulberg was able to piece together this information available only in the Guatemala national library. It is even more uncanny that Mme. Blavatsky would have tuned into this information.

Isis Unveiled states that Boulberg gives much information about magic and magicians of ancient Mexico. He says that Votan, "the fabulous hero and greatest of the magicians, returning from a long voyage, visited King Solomon at the time of the building of the temple ... this Votan appears identical to the dreaded Quetzalcoatl who appears in all the Mexican legends ..." Quetzalcoatl—plumed serpent—is of course another serpent initiate.

It is also worth contemplating the fact that Votan is mentioned as the navigating serpent who would not tell how he got where he was going.

"... but he (Votan) refused point blank to afford any clue to the route he sailed or the manner of reaching the mysterious continent."

The Secret Doctrine cites Votan as being a global traveler who was teaching Solomon around 600 B.C., and also indicates that he was descended from Noah. In one of the Guatemalan archives, Votan is said to be the 72nd generation descended of Noah. Noah represents an archetype carrier of seed knowledge who goes from one root race to another root race, from one planet to another.

The connection between Solomon and Pacal Votan is worth considering in light of the Quran. The Quran tells us that Solomon was able to train the *jinn* to do his work for him, creating large basins for statues and making many things out of metal. *Jinn* refers to invisible elementals and can also be interpreted as an alien or foreigner, like an extraterrestrial. The jinn are created out of fire, the humans are created out of clay and the angels are created out of light.

"The Jinns" is title of Sura 72 of the Quran and contains 28 verses. When Pacal Votan was 28 he entered his time of power, which coincided with the conclusion to the 72nd 52-year cycle since 3113. The conclusion of the following 73rd cycle marked

Isis Unveiled quotes Votan as being the "greatest magician of Ancient Mexico". This is astonishing to consider since this work was written in the 1870s—more than eighty years before the discovery of the tomb of Pacal Votan.

The Cosmic History Chronicles • Volume IV

Factors of the Supramental Descent

Divine One, Unification Plan, Federation of Galactic Federations, Unification Councils, Cube Format System, etc.

See Mevlana *The Knowledge Book* for complete details

17th – 18th Dimensional Perimeter
Source of cosmic showers of inspirations to ever greater wholeness, synthesis, totality, unity, convergence, evolution

104,000 Yr Diameter GM108X Chronocosmic Viewing Lens

Used for registering, monitoring and supervising spiritual progression of the world systems, specifically laboratory planet Velatropa 24.3
Velatropa 24 Sector
Serpent Galaxy Code #
12.4.18.17.12
1959552
Program $288 \times 18^2 \times 21$
Sirius B52 Command
Local Sector
"Salvation Plan"

NOAH I, NOAH II
V.24.1, V.24.2, V.24.3, V.24.4, V.24.5
V.24.6, V.24.7, V.24.8, V.24.9, V.24.10
4 7 10 16 28   52 100 196 300 388

"Only to a messenger that He chooses, does He reveal from the past and the future specific news"
Quran, Sura 72:27 "Jinns"
$7227 =$
$73 \times 9 \times 11 =$
Kin equivalent:
207
21/12/2012

5th Dimensional Order of Reality
4th Dimensional Order of Reality
13:20

Noospheric Sheathe

2013 Primordial Knowing Body Lha
2012 Awesome Blowing Six Turquoise Winds
2011 Single Wing Red Fire
2010 Awesome Vast Blue Sky
2009 Supreme Golden Maiden
2008 Black Iron Garuda Crest
2007 Renowned Conch Topknot
2006 Red Lightning Child Great Emptiness
2005 Single Luminous White "A"
2004

9th Lord
8th Lord
Point of triggering supramental descent
7th Lord of Time and Destiny
6th Lord of Time and Destiny
5th Lord of Time and Destiny
4th Lord of Time and Destiny
3rd Lord of Time and Destiny
2nd Lord of Time and Destiny
1st Lord of Time and Destiny

"VOTAN THE GREATEST MAGICIAN OF ANCIENT MEXICO"

HPB
Isis Unveiled

13/8 BC 3113
Baktun 1
Baktun 2
Baktun 3
Baktun 4
Baktun 5
Baktun 6
Baktun 7
Baktun 8
9.13.0.0.0
Baktun 9
Baktun 10
Baktun 11
Baktun 12
Baktun 13
21/12 AD 2012

Crypt of the Master Serpent Initiate and Magician of Time, Votan
Telektonon Speaking Tube
Nah Chan House of the Serpent

Pacal Votan's disincarnation. Sura 72 is preceded by Sura 71, "Noah", which also has 28 verses. This number 28 is the Bode frequency for Maldek, the Asteroid Belt.

This knowledge is a remnant of a mental perception or a memory from Maldek, transfigured into a remnant of a memory from Mars. Those memories of the moment that these civilizations were destroyed, whether by explosion or deluge or natural cataclysm, released the soul memories as fragmentary remnants. That is the scenario we are living today. Many Native American stories speak of ancestors originating in subterranean realm or taking refuge in caverns to escape past cataclysms, and then emerging into a new time.

According to Blavatsky, the biggest deluge occurred 850,000 years ago; though there were later deluges after that. She says of Noah and the deluge:

> *Noah floating on the waters in his ark, the latter being the emblem of the moon and Noah is the spirit fallen into matter. We find him as soon as he falls to Earth getting drunk on the wine at the vineyard—his pure spirit becomes intoxicated as soon as he becomes imprisoned in matter.*

This statement indicates that Noah did not have a body when he first came to Earth, but once he got a body he made a vineyard to drink wine to alleviate the pressure of being imprisoned in matter (This is a clue to the unconscious factor of why the drug culture of the 1960s triggered so many lost planet analphs).

Blavatsky points out that many cultures have some recollection of this deluge and many of those cultures say there were seven beings who survived—the seven builders, the seven rishis, the seven tribes or the seven families that accompanied Votan. Deluge and catastrophe are the

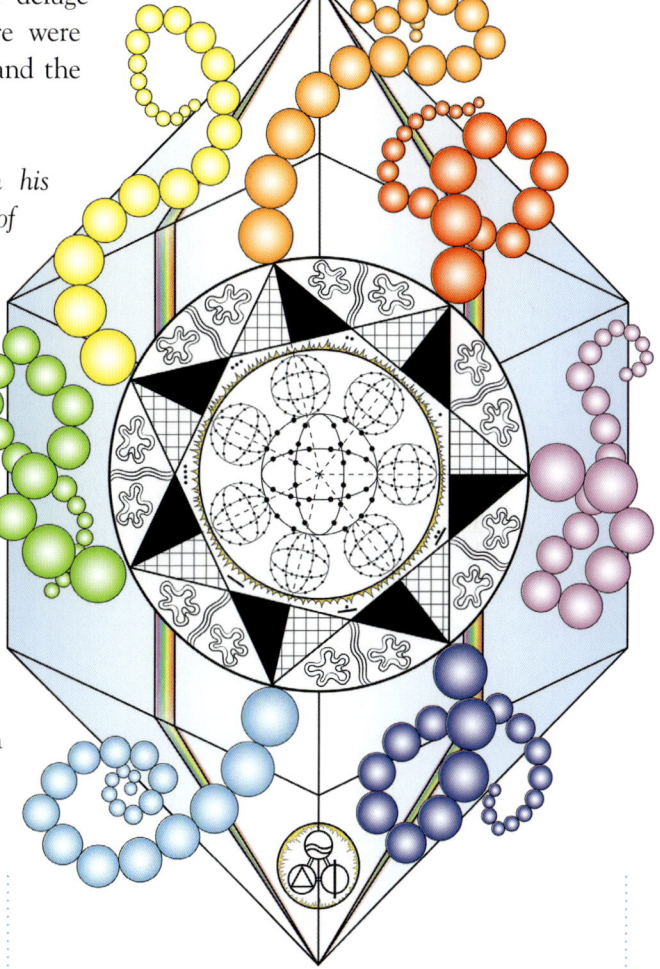

HEPTONOOGENESIS
The mind-generated power of seven is the root of all cosmology and symbolic systems. Number is the ultimate symbolic order.

punctuation marks between the development of the different root races, according to *The Secret Doctrine*. This perception is similar to the seven evolutionary stages or sequence of human evolution found in Cosmic Science (see *CHC, Vol. II*).

As mentioned earlier, our present fifth root race represents the compounding of all the previous root races, according to *The Secret Doctrine*. According to the Law of Time, we represent the final complexification of all the previous stages of development. At this point, the human being is a hybrid mutant on the verge of becoming a superman or evolving into the sixth root race, capable of acquiring divine powers. However, we cannot embody the sixth root race until the fifth root race is purified.

The serpent initiates point the way to the fulfillment of our evolutive psychology in order to develop a cosmic personality. With a cosmic personality, we overcome the memory fragments that are often mistaken as the basis of our "personality". These fragments must be flushed out and transcended by means of the third force of intelligence, Cosmic History. The conditioned personality is the remnant, but the essence within is the whole.

The transformative psychology of spirit instructs us to exert in creating a rarified field or state of consciousness that continuously dissolves or transmutes the fragments. The new evolutionary change begins with the conclusion of the cycle in 2012 and continues with the full emergence of the Superbeing after 2013. This Superbeing consciously operates with the third, fourth, and fifth dimensions.

After these dimensions are integrated, then the superhuman—and beyond—can be reached. Once we reach the point of the Superbeing, the karmic tendencies greatly decrease, and by the time we fully embody the *Suprabeing*, the karmic tendencies give way to a continuously enlightened state.

The example of Pacal Votan and the other serpent initiates is a reminder that a path is already laid out for you, wherever you are.

Consider the following practical suggestions given by Mme. Blavatsky for initiates in her pithy book, *Practical Occultism*:

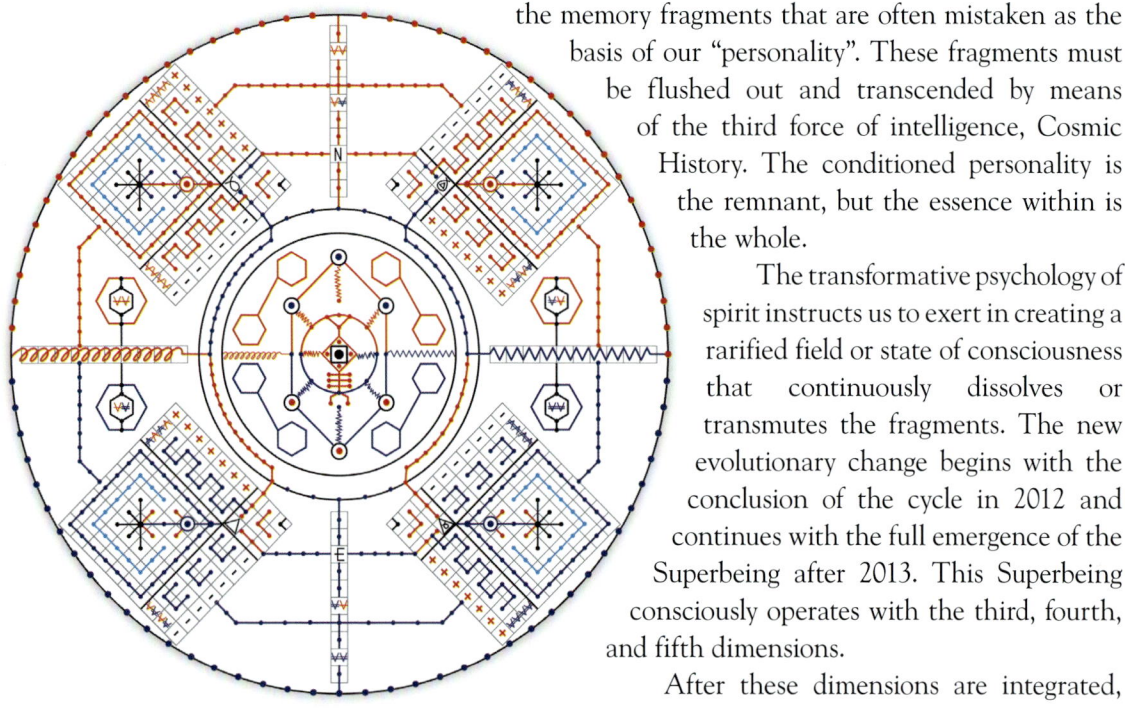

"Mother Board of the Mother Ship"
"... with all the different wirings of all the different aspects of all the different teachers, ascended masters, guardians of the earth, planetary logos, etc."

Part IV • Exploring the Inner Dimensions

1. Learn that there is no cure for desire, for the love of reward, for the misery of longing, save in the fixing of the mind on that which is invisible and soundless.

2. A man must believe in his innate power of progress. A man must refuse to be terrified by his greater nature, and must not be drawn back by his lesser or material self.

3. All the past shows us that difficulty is no excuse for dejection, much less for despair, else the world would have been without the many wonders of civilization.

4. Strength to step forward is the primary need of him who has chosen his path. Where is this to be found? Looking round, it is not hard to see where other men find their strength. Its source is profound conviction.

5. The man who wars against himself and wins the battle can do it only when he knows that in that war he is doing the one thing which is worth doing.

6. "Resist not evil", that is, do not complain of or feel anger against the inevitable disagreeable of life. Forget yourself (in working for others). If men revile, persecute, or wrong one, why resist? In the resistance we create greater evils.

7. The immediate work, whatever it be, has the abstract claim of duty, and its relative importance or non-importance is not to be considered at all.

8. The best remedy for evil is not the suppression, but the elimination of desire, and this can best be accomplished by keeping the mind constantly steeped in things divine. The knowledge of the Higher Self is snatched away by engaging the mind in contemplating with pleasure the objects, which correspond to the unruly sense.

9. Our own nature is so base, proud, ambitious, and full of appetites, judgments, and opinions, that if temptations restrained it not, it would be undone without remedy; therefore are we tempted to the end that we may know ourselves and be humble. Know that the greatest temptation is to be without temptation, wherefore be glad when it assaults thee, and with peace and constancy resist it.

10. Feel that you have nothing to do for yourself, but that certain charges are laid upon you by the Deity, which you must fulfill. Desire God and not anything that he can give. Whatever there is to do, has to be done, but not for the sake of enjoying the fruit of action. If all one's acts are performed with the full conviction that they are of no value to the actor, but are to be done simply because they have to be done—because it is in our nature to act—then the personality

of egotism in us will grow weaker and weaker until it come to rest, revealing the True Self to shine out in all its splendor.

11. Do not allow joy or pain to shake you from your purpose. Until the master chooses you to come to him, be with humanity, and unselfishly work for its advancement. This alone can bring true satisfaction.

12. Knowledge increases in proportion to its use—that is, the more we teach the more we learn. Therefore, with the faith of a little child and the will of an Initiate, give of your store to him who hath not wherewithal to comfort him on his journey.

13. A disciple must fully recognize that the very thought of individual rights is only the outcome of the venomous quality of the snake of self. He must never regard another man as a person who can be criticized or condemned, nor may he raise his voice in self-defense or excuse.

14. No man is your enemy, no man is friend. All alike are your teachers. One must no longer work for the gain of any benefit, temporal or spiritual, but to fulfill the law of being which is the righteous will of God.

[Cosmic History Profile: Cross-section of Self-Perfected Hermetic Personality]

"Radial Genesis: Transcending Binary Conflict"

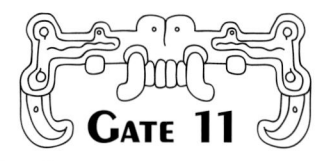

Gate 11
Sex and the Coming Noogenesis

As you approach the next gate, you feel a colossal energy followed by a tingling sensation throughout your entire being. Your body vibrates, your head clears, and your chakras open, dissolving all of the former blockages of the body and psychic centers. Suddenly you feel a flood of indescribable bliss that pulses and circulates throughout your entire body, electrifying your senses in ripples of elated joy that penetrate every cell of your being. You are awake! You are alive!—alive as you have never been—This is the power of sex—the life-force—the most essential dynamic by which the universe maintains itself.

> *All that has existed, exists, or will exist, arises from the union of the masculine and feminine principles. All that which exists, all that which has been formed by the Ancient whose name is holy, can only exist through a male and female.*
>
> —Zohar

> *On the elevation of woman the world's redemption and salvation hinge. And not till woman bursts the bonds of her sexual slavery, to which she has ever been subjected, will the world obtain an inkling of what she really is and of her proper place in the economy of nature.*
>
> —Eliphas Levi

Sex is a vital force of the dynamic of cosmic creation. The power of sexual energy serves as a potent channel to unlock the vibratory energy of the cosmos stored in the psychophysical centers or chakras. This vibratory energy is constantly streaming into us through hidden streams or invisible cosmic showers.

These cosmic showers contain loads of sexually activating energy that flow into us by means of cosmic plasmas. To open to these higher frequencies, our mind must be free from habits and attitudes embedded in historical notions. These potent energies are increasingly working to transmute us at a cellular level as we approach the 2012 event horizon and beyond.

Sexual energy is an electromagnetic fluid force associated with the "kundalini" energy. Kundalini is the source of vital energy and universal life-force inherent in all beings. In the human, the center of the kundalini energy is the base of the spine. As the energy is activated it moves through our chakras and untangles knots and clears blockages, both physical and psychic.

When properly directed, the transmutation of sexual energy, whether with a partner or through yoga/meditation, fills us with a great electrical force that, when radiated out, endows us with a "magnetic personality". The transmuted energy can be turned into new channels of healing for ourselves, for the planet and for the universe.

THE SCIENCE OF SEX

The universe consists of a number of interactions of different energy or force fields such as sonic, thermic, electromagnetic, light (photonic) or breath (prana). Living matter generates itself through these force fields by engaging opposite forces. This engagement of opposite forces, creates a fundamental stratum of cosmic universal forms of behavior, beginning with the interaction of microcosmic electrical charges, solen (–9) and kemio (+6), and also the mertanica vidica lines of force (see *CHC, Vol. II*).

> "ALL THAT HAS EXISTED, EXISTS, OR WILL EXIST, ARISES FROM THE UNION OF THE MASCULINE AND FEMININE PRINCIPLES. ALL THAT WHICH EXISTS, ALL THAT WHICH HAS BEEN FORMED BY THE ANCIENT WHOSE NAME IS HOLY CAN ONLY EXIST THROUGH A MALE AND FEMALE."
> –BOOK OF ZOHAR

Here, the universe begins as a dynamic of electrical charges that create positive and negative fluctuations, as well as relative conditions of stasis. This is an on-going dynamic, where states of disequilibrium further the possibility of new states of being. During conditions of stasis, there is a build-up of charges within the elements that compose a particular condition, entity or dimension. When the charges have built up sufficient pressure, then comes a release or discharge into a new condition that inaugurates an evolutionary level that upgrades the "norm".

This dynamic of opposite charges or forces is built into the very structure of the phenomenal universe and extends to the tenth dimension where the positive/negative charges still occur. *Negative* does not mean something bad, but is rather a counterbalancing force. Negative is a sublimating force and positive is an activating force. The activating force externalizes, and the sublimating force internalizes. These are two primary aspects of energy functions and the basis of understanding sex.

The engagement or regeneration of living matter occurs through an even more conscious process of engagement of opposite elements. For example, consider how crystals produce and reproduce; some crystals have lots of baby crystals on the surface. These are generated through interactive forces of light and heat, but there is also a reproductive mechanism within the chemistry of the crystal that engages the elemental forces to create the baby crystals. There exists a larger process that consists of pressure and elements of light and heat that brings the crystal into manifestation. This process includes the crystal's capacity to proliferate seed crystals. In living matter, self-replication is characterized by a process of dynamic engagement of opposite forces.

At the unicellular level, there occurs the reproduction of the cell itself: mitosis. The cell splits apart and then splits again—it has within it the capacity to reproduce itself. How does this happen? How is it that a cell can split apart and reproduce itself? If the cell is just sitting there breathing and experiencing osmosis taking in certain elements and minerals, then what gives it the urge to split apart? What kind of experience is that cell having?

It appears there is a primary electrifying dynamic consciousness that occurs even at that unicellular level. At its core or nucleus, the cell enters a state of excitation and then splits in two; an internal force causes it to become dynamic. From its point of view it is probably quite exciting. This is one level of sexual excitation.

At another level, the cells combine and create more complex forms. There are certain stages of plants or primary reptilian animals beyond the radiolaria (jellyfish) types; then there are the pre-vertebrates that lay eggs, such as starfish; and on into the insects—a seed is passed from one member to another and an egg is laid. In this process, a regenerative function is fulfilled by a male member impregnating a female member. The female member then develops eggs and lays them. For example, a female spider lays many eggs; same with the ants or reptiles and birds. This is a process of generation and regeneration; a continuum of living matter extending itself, and thus, establishes its own morphogenetic field or medium of domain.

When the eggs hatch, the animal is small, but instinctually well developed, far more than a human baby. It stays close with its mother for a short while, but it basically knows what to do. The animals advance rapidly through stages of maturation, and then they are set on their own. We are talking about a continuum of living matter that takes different forms; reptilian or bird, and so forth. The mammal is a different type of species; it does not lay eggs, but reproduces itself wholesale in the placenta, which is more complex. This is the process of sexual reproduction.

Again, we ask: What is the unicellular paramecium experience? There is obviously some type of primary ecstatic experience occurring. Is it having sex with itself? At this point, the sexual and reproductive impulses are mingled together. But when we reach the human species, then there is a distinction between the reproductive function of sex and some other level of sex. But what is sex?

SEX IN ABORIGINAL SOCIETY AND HISTORICAL SOCIETY

Sex in prehistory or Aboriginal society is vastly different than sex in the historical cycle. In Aboriginal tribes, such as the Xingu in the Amazon, everyone is either naked or minimally covered with simple adornments. All their sexual parts are exposed, though no one is flaunting anything, and there is no apparent shame or lust. In the aboriginal society, the sexual hang-ups seem to minimally exist. Sex is merely understood as a natural function. Every tribe has its own rules and codes of conduct, but generally speaking the feeling is far less fixated on the issue of sex.

Tribes that did not opt for the course of civilization carry on traditions of the *fourth root race*, and are informed by a natural wisdom. The customs and ways of the fourth root race are not embedded in historical consciousness. This is an example of two human choices, two modes of consciousness, and two simultaneously co-existing root races.

The one choice is very conservative with a belief system that has no separation between the human and natural world. The other choice separates the human and the natural environment. The historical element brings with it the evolution of sex apart from the reproductive function. We are certain that there is enjoyment of sex in Aboriginal society, but there is not the fixation, nor perhaps the liberation from procreative function that we find in historical society.

The historical human is increasingly removed from nature and generally has "leisure time" that arises from this separation—this allows the imaginal realm to evolve and develop more addictions and indulgences. Sex in historical society is one of the main indulgences, or rather, preoccupations. Drugs, alcohol, gambling and sports are other indulgences in historical society that are a result of a fundamental physical imbalance caused by a primal deviation of human consciousness from nature. This imbalance can be seen today in the displacement of indigenous and aboriginal societies. When they are removed from natural time, they often fall prey to alcoholism, disease, substance abuse, etc.

The taboos around sex are complex and elaborate in historical society. It is a telling statement that, proverbially speaking, the oldest profession in the world is prostitution. Throughout the male dominated historical process, an oppressive yoke had been placed upon the role of the female. At the beginning of Babylonian history—and the history of empire—sex became a commodity that men were foolish enough to pay for. We can see this at the beginning of Babylon conjured by Biblical images of the "whore of Babylon", where the harlot—the prostitute—becomes a metaphor for materialist society in general.

Some women throughout history have felt there was no choice but to become a prostitute in their given circumstance. Other women chose to become concubines, courtesans or mistresses. In the elite imperialistic class certain women aspired to become a courtesan of a powerful king or ruler. The lead courtesan often had great power and influence over the king or emperor. There are many examples of prominent courtesans throughout history.

In most of the imperial courts throughout history, the ruler possesses some type of harem or "kept" women. Some of these rulers rationalized this by claiming they needed to propagate and create a larger lineage. Existing simultaneously in many of these societies was the institution of laws of adultery. This is to illustrate the contradictory nature and double or multiple standards that develop around this whole issue of sex.

On the one hand, the idea of concubines and consorts is looked down upon by many for apparent reasons; but we must penetrate deeper to understand why, throughout history, there has been a type of separation out of the experience sex for reasons other than reproductive. This is a point that bears a fair amount of contemplation. What does it tell us about sexuality and the world? The women are selling their sex, not to procreate, but because they know men are so driven by their lower instincts that they will do virtually anything for sex. In this regard, sex is associated with sheer materialism based on debased pleasure and instincts.

TANTRA

For initiates and adepts and seekers of truth, sex exists for evolutive purposes or as an evolutionary mechanism. This is the *tantric* perspective.

Tantra is the internal union between masculine (Shiva) and feminine (Shakti) energies. Tantra is also the point of view that experiences the complex of reality as a continuum of distinguishing energies: body, mind and speech (emotive communicative faculty). These three factors represent layers or currents of energy that allow us to participate in and express the phenomenal world at different levels of consciousness. We engage in the phenomenal world with our mind and emotional apparatus as well as with our physical body. Each level of being engages in energies in various ways—activating, stimulating and arousing.

We also have our external sense organs—we live by and through our senses. Then we have internal sensations such as hunger, thirst, sex, sleep and dreaming. If thirst corresponds to liquid and hunger corresponds to food, then sex corresponds to the invisible physiology of our nervous system. Sexual excitation creates electrical vibrations or tingles in the nervous system.

While the apparatus of sex is through the sex organs, the stimulation is not solely focalized in the

SEX IS A POTENT ENERGY THAT WHEN PROPERLY TRANSMUTED CAN CREATE REJUVENATION, HEALING, AND SPIRITUAL DEVELOPMENT

sex organs. Erotic zones are located throughout the body, and when touched or stimulated, create sensual feelings that open the chakras or subtle body, attuning it to higher frequencies.

Sex is an all around pan-neural experience. While touch is the sense most commonly associated with sexual arousal, all the senses play a part. Smells of flowers or different fruits, musky odors, or perfumes can excite the sexual imagination. Different tastes and textures can do the same, just as juicy or succulent textures or sweet flavors can arouse this sexual excitation. Different sounds or music can also create this effect. And then there is the visual element of erotic art or literature as seen in traditions such as the Kama Sutra, but also in Chinese Taoist traditions or esoteric Persian traditions, where there are artistically rendered paintings of people in different sexual positions.

This is to illustrate the power of sexual energy and how it can be aroused through each of the senses. This indicates that sex is more than just a reproductive function, but a potent energy that, when properly transmuted, can create rejuvenation, healing and spiritual development.

Sex in Historical Society

All the present and coming miseries and the cosmic cataclysms to a great degree result from the subjugation and abasement of woman. The dreadful decline of morality, the diseases and degeneration of some nations are also the results of the slavish dependence of woman.
—Helena Roerich

Most of history is male dominated, with a male priest-class, male ruling class, and male hierarchies. The aristocracies often had queens or women like Cleopatra or Queen Elizabeth I, but for the most part it was a male dominated society. This has its repercussions, and the whole of the historical cycle is fraught with sexual melodrama.

Our historical sexual thought traces back to the story of

... sex is more than just a reproductive function, but a potent energy that, when properly transmuted, can create rejuvenation, healing and spiritual development.

Adam and Eve, the progenitors of the fifth root race. Whatever their transgression might have been—eating from the forbidden tree of knowledge prematurely—that deed caused them to experience shame, and thus, they felt the need to cover their sexual organs. In famous Christian paintings, Renaissance artists painted fig leaves over Adam and Eve's sex organs.

> ### Maldek and Sex Taboos
>
> Men and women often have many divisive views on what sexual intimacy is, which can cause discord in their relationships. This is reinforced by the fact that the historical conditioned mind has a confused, contradictory taboo attitude about what sex is—as exemplified by celebrities and mass media.
>
> Sex taboos have their archetypal roots in Maldek where primal disturbances occurred. Maldek is the place of the first Adam archetype in this solar system. The story of Adam in most monotheistic traditions revolves around a primal transgression. Adam actually derives from an androgynous prototype: Adam Kadmon. From the androgynous prototype comes the model of Eve, the primal female. The creation of the primary male and female has everything to do with cosmic universal forces. As the cosmos evolves and complexifies, its self-regenerative process also becomes more sophisticated requiring male and female components, not only to reproduce, but to advance the cause of cosmic consciousness.

When viewed from a pure tantric point of view, the act of sex reproduces the ultimate creative act; the union of the masculine and the feminine cosmic principles. Sex is an evolving and complex instinct that we have hardly begun to explore. As with anything in the nature of duality, some choose to avoid exploring it, but demean it instead.

Society, as a whole, tends to portray sex as a lower instinct, where people take lovers, often in secret, and apart from their "legitimate" existence as husbands to wives or wives to husbands. What does this say about conventional social arrangements? How did this come about? It could only come about if there was a stratum or hierarchy of a male priest class that was making judgments about sex, setting apart the temple virgins, who would then become the temple prostitutes, etc.

Again, this traces back to the theme of Adam and Eve: what feeling or awareness made them suddenly put fig leaves over their "private" parts? Some of the priest class are eunuchs, this means they are self-castrated; they are not sexually reproductive. At the same time, there exists the priest class who are sexually abstinent or who mutilate themselves sexually. Simultaneously, comes the rise of the temple virgins as well as the court prostitutes. This creates a polarizing contrast that gives rise to the creation of sex taboos; from the male eunuch priests come the institution of monasticism or celibacy and also traditions of homosexuality. Asceticism or sexual abstinence, on the one hand, is balanced by libertinism on the other.

Throughout the course of history, some viewed sex as lurid, or lustful and so was introduced the institution of strict monogamy to keep order in society and for the "sake" of the children. Though, in aboriginal tribes the entire clan generally raises the children. In some tribes or religions there exist different arrangements such as polygamy, endogamy, and so forth.

Most historical societies are contradictory in nature. On the surface, there are strict rules

Sex is an evolving and complex instinct that we have hardly begun to explore.

regarding adultery. In some societies, adulterers are stoned or imprisoned. However, in these very same societies there is prostitution and kings with courtesans and concubines, etc. We see much ambiguity throughout history with regard to the attitude of sexuality.

This brings us to the Cycle of Transformation that began with the Industrial Revolution in the eighteenth century. At this stage comes the breaking down of older social patterns and the rise of figures such as the Marquis de Sade in France who promoted a flagrant libertinism. The archetype of the libertine was strong at the time of the French Revolution in the late eighteenth and early nineteenth centuries with an "anything goes" attitude about sex. At this point, the exploration of different forms of sexuality was promoted to the point of sadism—derived from the idea of the Marquis de Sade, whose name gave rise to the very concept of sadism.

Further breakdown of the social patterns continued through the nineteenth and twentieth centuries, as witnessed by the rise of women's rights and feminist movements that sought to break down historical male hierarchical patterns and give women equal social power. This process has yet to be completed on the world stage—but it is sufficiently underway.

In the modern world, all sexual options are now available and are highlighted by a proliferating pornography industry. What is this and why does it exist? The pornography industry is, again, a function of double standards. For instance, many people are upset with pornography, such as pervades the Internet, but on the other hand, society values the freedom of speech more than it abhors pornography, so it continues to proliferate. This is another example of the contradictory nature of human society.

At this stage, pornography industries manufacture exaggerated and artificial images of sex, and thus profane this sacred, natural energy. Historical conditionings use the sexual instinct to exploit, commercialize and market our very life-force. In this sense, pornography exists only because the human is so immersed in dualism—a direct result of the fundamental separation from nature. From the point of view of Cosmic History, these are primitive issues resulting from conditioned reflexes coded into the historical process, which become second nature by the time we reach present civilization.

The social mind of the historical human is so primitive that it commonly views sex as something to get away with when no one else is looking. This way of thinking keeps the human from seeing that sex is a vital electromagnetic force of higher spiritual evolution.

SEX AS VITAL ELECTROMAGNETIC FORCE

The kundalini, in the form of latency is coiled like a serpent; one who impresses this shakti to move will attain liberation.
—Hatha yoga-pradipika, Ch. 3, v. 108

Sexuality exists apart from the need for living matter to reproduce itself. This is well known by tantric practitioners who understand sex as a metaphor of a higher order. Western hermetic traditions speak of "conjunction oppositiorum", the union of opposites—king and queen, sun and moon, etc. This illustrates a cosmic process or mechanism.

Sex is a complete pan-sensory experience that not only affects the nervous system, but the consciousness as well. Sex has the potential to liberate consciousness and release vast amounts of energy. However, the constraints of social conditioning are such that not many people know how to unlock and harness this potent force. This is due to a misunderstanding of sex.

The science and technology of sex is ever-evolving. The science of Kundalini yoga was developed around 70,000 years ago by rishis in India and Tibet. The teachings of Kundalini Yoga were brought to the west and presented as a living practice to the public for the first time in 1969 by Yogi Bhajan.

Yoga texts tell us that the kundalini energy is represented by a serpent coiled at the base of the spine representing dormant energy. It is awakened and released through different yogic techniques and pranayams. This means that while we are taking prana in, what is being stored in the kundalini is another force called *apana*. This is known as "kundalini rising".

The trick is to get the prana to move down through the etheric current or circuits, through the *ida* and the *pinghala*, and to reach and activate the apana (eliminating energy), which is locked beneath the mulabundha in the lower chakras. At this point, the apana and the prana meet to bring the kundalini up the central nerve channel. The pressure of the two forces acting upon each other creates a combustion or inner psychic heat that rises and activates the other chakras.

Sexual energy as an evolutionary force has the power to unlock the plasmas, radion, prana and apana stored primarily in the root chakra. In Hindu tradition, the dynamic aspect of this energy is called *shakti* and is considered the foundation of consciousness. Release of this energy activates the chakras and psychoactive nerve centers that are aligned with the *sushumna* or the central channel of the body.

Wilhelm Reich, a Western psychologist who pioneered the release of sexual energy, talked about the *orgone* as the fundamental dynamic energy released through sex. As such, the orgone is the primary energy of the universe. He saw that the whole of the galaxy was actually a large sexual entity and this universal force or energy exists everywhere—something like a galactic electro-psychic force pervading all of space. Or maybe this orgone is the energy within the prana, the shakti that activates the energy within the apana and creates excitation—psychosexual combustion.

Any type of excitation has a sexual aspect to it. Sex is excitation; a total body sensation. But it is an excitation that pacifies through release. The orgone represents the energy inside that gets excited or that gets activated. Reich believed an enclosure or orgone box could be created to experience that energy.

The United States government said he was not a medical doctor and therefore forbade him to use or promote the orgone box. So threatened were they by Reich and his invention that they jailed him. He was greatly persecuted by the United States government and died in prison for his beliefs in the 1950s. What does this tell us about the repressed power of sexual energy in human society? Is the present social order a mere strait-jacket meant to contain and repress sexual energy—the energy of freedom and liberation?

This brings us back to the question: What is sexual energy? When we experience excitation—and everyone has at some time or another—if we try to identify it, we see that it is not just an activation of sexual organs, but an entire excitation of the nervous system. We might feel a tingle or an arousal, but what is this? It is different from other types of energy and is peculiar and unique unto itself. It makes us feel like we are turning into liquid jelly or becoming more etheric and electrical.

Sexual energy is electromagnetic and can be reduced to two elements, *liquen* and *solen*, according to Cosmic Science. Liquen and solen are primary partons that create a primary electrical activation. These two partons are combined with kemio, the catalyzing radial energy, which has a frequency number of six. So there is kemio (6) and solen and liquen (9). These primary partons are the basis of life, according to Cosmic Science.

> ### Mathematics of Sex
>
> The frequency of the solen/liquen of nine and the kemio of six interact to create a charge of fifteen: 6 x 9 = 54 (5 +4 = 9) + 15 = 69.
>
> 69, the name given to the taboo sex position, is also 6 + 9 = 15 or 1+5 = 6. Numerologically, 6 is the underlying frequency of sex. Six is the law of three doubled and geometrically is a six pointed star, a male upward and female downward triangle conjoined.

Within this fluid-solen-liquen-kemio (orgone or apana), is created the primary impulse of life—the activating agents in the hidden stream of the universal cosmic sexual force. By the time we get to the human species, the sexual energy becomes an evolutionary force. In other words, the human being becomes a medium for the evolution of sex as the vitalizing force of cosmic consciousness.

Cosmic Science also affirms that in the next stages of evolution, sex will be set apart from procreation. We might determine that there is no need to procreate because we have discovered the keys to longevity and immortality. *The Knowledge Book* also confirms this when it says that sex will be totally its own evolutionary spiritual mechanism and driving force and energy that will take us to increasing heights of spiritual awareness.

In the tantric traditions there is an understanding of primary forces referred to as the Shakti force, represented by a downward pointing triangle (6). And then there is the Shiva force represented by an upward pointing triangle (9). Related to these two forces are prakriti (matter) and purusha (spirit). The sexual conjoining of the Shakti and Shiva triangles create the six-pointed star, also known as the seal of Solomon. This is represented in *The Knowledge Book* with the same number frequencies: six and nine.

Shakti is the supramental force that descends (red triangle), and Shiva is the evolutionary spirit in matter that ascends (blue triangle). Shakti is a force of the power and frequency of six, and the Shiva is the frequency of nine. These two elements, Shakti and Shiva; yin and yang; male and female, create an integrated psycho-electromagnetic energy force field: the spark of life.

This force field can occur both through engagement of male and female, and also as a solo androgynous process. In other words, everyone has these elements within in them.

The law of sex can be formulated in the following way:

1. **The infinite universal self-regeneration is a function of an equalization of opposite forces in a self-created unified field.**

2. **This is possible because every element contains its opposite, which is a projective force that can be focalized on a medium of opposite attraction (this is magnetic transmission).**

3. **Once conjoined, all elements dissolve all boundaries, releasing electromagnetic waves in ceaseless radiation.**

The Cosmic History Chronicles • Volume IV

Shakti and Shiva

Universal self-regeneration is a function of the equalization of opposite forces in a self-created unified field. Any element always contains its opposite. If the right-hand side is the Shakti then the left-hand side is the Shiva; the upper part represents the dominant force and the lower part is the opposite force. It is these opposite forces that attract the like force in the other. If these opposite forces didn't exist one within the other, then they would repel, since like attracts like.

Even though man and woman are opposite, they still have a like element in the other. This is a description of the law of sex. Man and woman create the infinity sign. The negative charge of the blue side that is dominant balances the positive red side and vice versa. This creates infinity. This is why it says *infinite universal self-regeneration*. It is always going on. This is also the basis of self-androgyny which we are evolving into—this is a type of angelic realm, where we will become like hyper-enlightened self-excitable paramecium, but without the need to reproduce.

The nature of sexuality is such a powerful, intense energy that it must be harnessed and focused. This is the function of the sex organs. The sex organs can be likened to an electrical circuit: there is a plug and there is a socket. When we put the plug in the socket, then the light goes on. This is an obvious metaphor—but in the case of sex, the hookup creates a micro universe, a unified biocosmic totality.

When we divorce history from sexuality and sexuality from reproduction, then we create an opening. In this opening, we can unite the pure energy so that we become infinitely regenerating beings—regenerating both ourselves and the biosphere. Any unified force field has a powerful effect on the context in which it occurs. When there is a conscious unified force field that is created by two sexual partners who both understand the law of sex, then the consciousness in which they perform the sex act impacts the whole field with magnetic charges. This whole field can be extended into larger contexts from the social context to the planetary context and beyond.

If this kundalini, orgone or hidden stream of sexual energy, is the primary underlying circuit that creates cosmic universal life, then it must be an electromagnetically charged force. In this way, the Earth herself is an electromagnetically charged force of tremendous sexual potency.

If the Earth is electromagnetically charged, then is there

Sexuality will become the principle medium of spiritual evolution ...
We may choose according to twin soul affinities to integrate even further with another being and start another psychosexual chain reaction ...
This is our future.

not a type of geomagnetic Earth kundalini? Yes there is. As we change our perception of ourselves to see that we are actually cosmic electromagnetic entities operating with these different cosmic forces, charging our circuits in different ways, then we can understand the Earth herself is like this. At this point, we can begin to experience a type of Earth sex—a sex that is occurring at etheric or higher-dimensional levels where we are learning how to charge, and be charged by, the Earth.

This occurs at the instinctual level in the prehistoric cultural stages that form a seamless whole—the bonding of mind and nature. We will come to that again at a higher level when we understand sex as a cosmic force and begin to direct it to have interactions with other cosmic forces in our environment. We have restricted ourselves so rigidly from "the bad rap" we have given sex that we do not understand how to begin to open to these energies.

When we understand the different ways that we have sex and the different ways we utilize the sex organs then we can begin to experience our sexuality in a more categorically scientific manner in order to release and

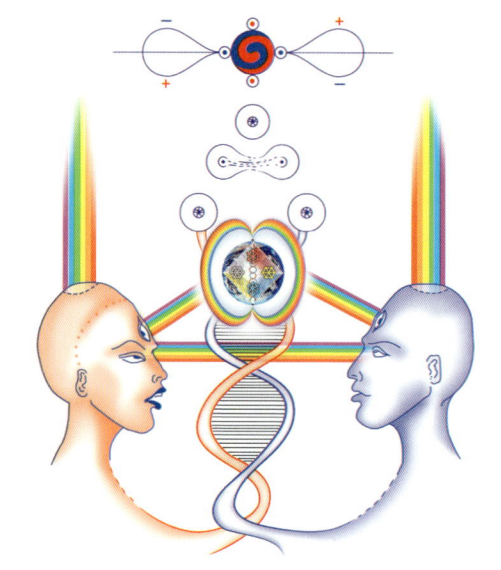

THE FUTURE OF SEX

realize different levels of energy. We know that we exchange energy with each other in many different ways, from a touch, to a word, to a smile. We exchange much magnetic energy through eye contact. When we gaze into they eyes of another, we experience dissolution of ego identity, and recognition of our unity and oneness. Depending on the level of awareness, we can use eye contact to synergize higher levels of cosmic consciousness through a mutually interactive flow of magnetic light beams.

SEX AS COSMIC FORCE/SHAKTI AND SHIVA

Sexual energy is a cosmic evolutionary force. The build-up of excitation releases different plasmas, prana and radion. We must learn to direct this energy in ways that are beneficial to ourselves, to others, and to our environment. When we release the notions of sexuality strictly for reproductive purposes, then we can explore sexuality as a type of environmental interactiveness.

For instance, in the Hindu tantric tradition there are different kinds of Shakti energy. These correspond with different shades of sexual energy released, like the *parashakti* energy (light and heat), or the *jnana* shakti energy (excitation through mind). In *The Secret Doctrine* also mentions these six primary forces of nature (shakti) synthesized by the seventh point in the center. The shakti is the feminine principle and also the principle of the matrix. Mme. Blavatsky refers to the mythic forms or names that correspond to supernatural entities or principles also found in *Cosmic Science*.

The Six Shakti Forces

1. The first primary force is the Parashakti; power of light and heat (or luminic and thermic, according to Cosmic Science).

2. The second force is Jnana shakti; power of intellect or knowledge. This has two aspects which refer to the power of mind and sensation—or the power of memory to recall past ideas. This is the part of the mind that recalls experiences and creates a type of intellectual order. This force has the power of connecting ideas together by mysterious links of memory.

3. The third force is Itcha shakti; power of will. Its most extraordinary manifestation is the generation of certain nerve currents which set in motion the muscles required for the accomplishment of the desired object. This also corresponds to the will or capacity to project charisma.

4. The fourth force is Kriya shakti; the mysterious power of thought that enables the ability to produce external perceptible phenomenal results by its own inherent energy. Any idea will manifest externally if one's attention is deeply concentrated upon it. A yogi generally performs his wonders by means of Itcha shakti and kriya shakti—the point is that all these shaktis are summoned as well in sexual activity.

5. The fifth force is Kundalini shakti; power of force released through the sexual energy. Kundalini is the universal life principle that manifests everywhere in nature. This force includes the two great forces of attraction and repulsion, which has much to do with magnetism. Cosmic Science also affirms this. The partons or six types of cosmic electricity, as well as the electronic lines of force are found throughout nature—everything has in its makeup those partons. Electricity and magnetism are but manifestations of this. So, kundalini is a magnetic force; it is the power that brings about the continuous adjustment of internal and external relations, which are the essence of life; it is the continuous assessment of external relations to internal conditions which is the basis of the transmigration of souls. A yogi has to subjugate this power before he/she can attain moksha or liberation and release—in other words, we must master the kundalini power in order to attain to the higher stages of evolution.

6. The sixth force is Mantrika shakti; the forces or powers of letters, speech or music. The Mantrika shakti has the influence of melody; the power of the ineffable name is the crown of this shakti. Mantrika shakti works through the vibrational power of sound which lead to states of bliss or ecstasy. This is highlighted in the chanting of Bhakti yoga.

These six forms of shakti represent the qualities of being, or powers that reside in—or are latent in—our being. These are the powers available to reach our true potential: Parashakti (power of light and heat), Jnana shakti (power of mind), Itcha shakti (power of will)—the will, the Kriya shakti (power of thought), Kundalini shakti (power of life-force), and the Mantrika shakti (power of sound).

The Cosmic History Chronicles • Volume IV

To these six shaktis, we add magnetism, the cohesive power that unifies. When we consider these shaktis as a spectrum of primal energy activation based on vibration, then we can recognize the focalizing power of pan-sexuality as a means of placing us in complete resonance with the cosmos as a whole.

There is a seventh shakti, *deva prakriti*, the light of the logos. This is a supernal or etheric shakti, the universal force that accomplishes different aspects of the ongoing functioning of nature. This also pertains to our own internal system and its functions—most namely will and thought. In other words, all that is accomplished in the medium of life is actually brought about by channels of different flows of the different kinds of energies required by the spectrum of our thought and actions in an evolving continuum of cosmic evolution.

We must explore new levels of comprehension of sexual energy in the new time. If we view Shakti as the supermental descent and Shiva as the spiritual ascent through matter that engenders this type of union, then the actual process of closing the cycle through two entities, male and female, is also part of a larger cosmic sexual function.

> **Terma/Terton**
>
> The Tomb of Pacal Votan was sealed hermetically. In Tibetan tradition, terma is hidden knowledge and for it to come to light the terton has to have union with the feminine principle. The higher knowledge comes about or is born from the union of masculine and feminine that brings the birth of a new knowledge. Masculine and feminine transform each other, through each other creating a new knowledge base that regenerates and restores the human race.

The activated knowledge of the closing of the cycle, inclusive of the *Cosmic History Chronicles* and the Law of Time is due to a mechanism known as terma and terton. There are two aspects to this. The terma represents a descent of a type of shakti energy (which is the terma of Pacal Votan), and the terton represents the aspiration to discover the terma or the treasure.

For this to be fully facilitated there is an actual human engagement of two avataric forces or principles. The shiva is symbolized by the closer of the cycle, the ascending blue triangle, and the shakti is symbolized by the regenerator of the cycle, the descending red triangle. They come together and form a six-pointed star in a common field. The ouroboric circle around them is Cosmic History. When the union is complete, then the noogenesis occurs and ignites the planetary kundalini that makes the law of sex become a conscious operating factor in human evolution.

The energy is harnessed and focalized through the sex organs. From a higher level, this produces whole other internal imaginal experiences and sensations. One of the finest of these can be represented by the lotus and the vajra. The mantra Om Mane Padme Hung can be translated as: Oh hail, the jewel in the flower of the lotus!

The jewel is the vajra scepter, which represents the male element and the lotus, the female element. When these are brought together and focused at the heart center, then we have a channeling of the sexual energy through an imaginal emblem that radiates out in fields of compassion, sending bliss waves to all beings. These are waves of charged energy that pacify and calm the environment and creatively engage it at subliminal levels.

By 2012 and beyond we will become much more sexually integrated beings and our sexuality will be primarily self-generating and directed toward ourselves in ever-more evolved states. Sexuality will be liberated altogether from procreation, and instead, will become the principle medium of spiritual evolution. In our sexual cultivation we will become brilliant, radiant energy beings and at the same time we may choose, according to twin soul affinities, to integrate further with another being to start a new psychosexual chain reaction. This is our future waiting to be explored.

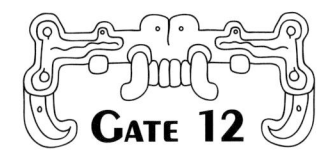

Gate 12
Noospheric Initiation—Becoming a Cosmic Medium

> *As you continue to make your way through the labyrinth, you pause and consider all the gates you have been through. What a journey! What does it all mean? What is it telling you? You reflect on the wave of great occult masters of the late nineteenth and early twentieth centuries. You understand how they began to prepare people for the changing of the aeon—now it is upon you—the great mind shift. You continue to make your way through the labyrinth when you spot Gate 12 all lit up in rainbow lights: Noospheric Initiation. You enter excitedly as you are now ready to wake up and recognize yourself as a cosmic medium—you are ready for the noospheric initiation into galactic harmony.*

December 21, 2012 marks the grand planetary initiation—it is not an end unto itself—but a beginning for those who can make it past the threshold. This major evolutionary shift is known as the *biosphere-noosphere transition*; this is the most tremendous shift in the entire evolution of the human species, and consequently of the whole Earth. This transition crosses us over into a new condition of being, a new condition of knowing and a new condition of consciousness. This level of consciousness is structurally characterized as *galactic hierarchy* and referred to as "noospheric" consciousness. This is the next great epoch for planet Earth.

As we make this transition we are called upon to become cosmic mediums on behalf of the Earth. In order to do this, there are a few things we must keep in mind. The first is that the Universe is designed as a hierarchy or ever-evolving system. This must be thoroughly understood if we are to understand our place in the universe.

Within this system are numerous grades of teachings and initiations that correspond to different levels of energy, dimensions, and intelligence. The momentum of evolution produces streams of cosmic consciousness that are always going through grades of evolvement. The universe is organized through coordinating systems that convey information using various frequency beams. All components of universal evolution are guided by a large governing system or process often simply referred to as the "Plan".

Initiation always occurs within the context of hierarchy. This planetary initiation affects not only human beings, but also all other forms of life in the universe. All the animals, plants, minerals, etc., have their part to play in the Grand Initiation (as will be elucidated in *CHC, Vol. V*). It is the universe becoming conscious through the cosmic consciousness of the planetary logos—the noosphere.

Eliphas Levi points out that equality amongst the human race can only exist by hierarchical grades. There must be great and little, so that people may mutually assist, and have need of each other.

> ### Life as Initiation
>
> The planetary initiation is well underway. The Law of Time and the *Cosmic History Chronicles* provide a sanction, showing which direction the initiatic process might go in order to have a positive outcome. This is the role and function of initiatic systems of knowledge. This knowledge system exists at this point in time so we can distinguish the lifeline of galactic hierarchy that is pulling us through this initiatic process into a moment where we acquire the condition or quality of the noospheric state of mind and consciousness.

Origins of Hierarchy—The Genesis Code

Why is the universe constructed as a hierarchy? Let us look again at the origins of this hierarchical process.

The root of all hierarchical systems and teachings is symbolized by the apple that Adam was told not to eat. By disobeying God's command and eating the apple, Adam created karma. Why? What did that apple represent?

The apple represented higher knowledge for which Adam was not yet prepared. So when he bit into the forbidden apple, he bit into certain knowledge that he was not yet ready to know, and, thus, suffered the consequences.

The first consequence was the feeling of shame for having disobeyed the command of God, and the second was confusion about what it was that he just ate. This new feeling of shame made Adam and Eve, as psychomythic prototypes, feel exposed; this "exposure" is represented by the sexual organs. They covered their sexual organs in an attempt to feel less exposed. This is the fall from innocence.

This scene revolving around the apple, the serpent, the tree, the man and woman, and the feeling of shame, set the whole karmic cycle in motion inclusive of sex taboos. Because of the little knowledge that Adam and Eve gained from biting the apple, ego was born. One could even say that ego was born with the intention to bite the apple. Their consciousness said "Aha! I know something. I'm smart and clever now." This gave way to self-deception and all the games and neurotic rackets that ego has contrived since that moment.

To reiterate, ego was born by ingesting that forbidden bite of knowledge prematurely, giving rise to self-deception. This act had a complex set of karmic consequences, including a whole gamut of sexual misperceptions and taboos. However, the primal error was not the bite of the apple, but the disobedience to the command not to eat the fruit.

At the same time, this event gave birth to the spiritual impulse, which has two aspects: the *moral imperative* and the *religious instinct*. These aspects were ultimately created with two fundamental underlying questions:

1. How do we keep ourselves and our descendents from repeating the same mistakes again?
2. How do we get back to the oneness?

Hierarchy originated in the Fall; for to rise again, we must ascend. The ascent is defined by the ladder of hierarchic consciousness, the original inner structure of all true religious and spiritual systems. To return to oneness, we must follow a process or path—this is what creates the different spiritual systems, which includes first deleting the unnecessary acquired egoic trash.

Forbidden Knowledge

In the Sufi cosmology of Ibn al-Arabi, there are seven heavens that contain seven principle teachers or masters: Abraham, Moses, Aaron, Enoch, Joseph, Jesus and Adam. As the seventh of these, Adam occupies the closest heaven. Adam is transformed into a teacher when God shows him mercy. He is the first to learn that submission is the way to access the Absolute. Adam then transmits his knowledge to Noah, and from Noah to Abraham, etc.

It is of significance that Adam is the *seventh* of the seven principle prophets or messengers, and that he occupies the heaven closest to us. This shows that the knowledge he bit into brought him down to the level closest to Earth. This is because he is now prepared for the seventh day of creation.

It is also interesting to note that one of the major pioneers in the cybersphere is *Apple,* and the logo of Apple is the apple with the bite taken out. What was that knowledge that was bit into? That knowledge was actually the fruit—the fruit is the knowledge that ripens on the seventh day of creation. The essence of the fruit is the knowledge of sexual union that was not yet known, as it would engender a powerful occult energy, setting off a series of unconscious actions for which the human was not prepared or mature enough to handle.

According to Cosmic History, we are just completing the sixth day of creation; the seventh day of creation has yet to dawn. With Apple and the cybersphere, the consequent proliferation of information demonstrated one of the final consequences of that premature bite, resulting in an overwhelming deluge—floodwaters of the collective unconscious.

Apple started in 1976 (April 1, Kin 63) and was a real pioneer of the information revolution. It was then that another bite was taken from the Apple, which helped foment all the information that everyone is drowning in at the closing of the cycle. Less than five months after the founding of Apple on July 25, the primal face of man's Martian Adam was beamed down to Earth. It is also of note that when the archetypal quartet of the Beatles formed their own record company, it, too, was called Apple.

It was also an apple that is responsible for the discovery of the law of gravity. According to legend, as Isaac Newton rested under a tree, he was nearly hit by a falling apple. He wondered if, as the Earth tugged upon an apple, did it also tug upon celestial bodies like the Moon? He conceived that the same force acted on both the Moon and the apple.

The Fall of the apple and the Fall of man to Earth, are both functions of the same psychocosmic law of gravity. The resultant effects of Adam's bite of the apple have played themselves out. The religious/spiritual traditions have played themselves out, and we are now undergoing a collective initiatic process and unprecedented perceptual shifts.

At this stage of initiation, two types of information or knowledge are given: *individual* and *evolutionary*. Knowledge is given to the individual, like meditation or prayer practices, so the individual can climb the ladder of light to the Supreme One, the Source, the dharmakaya. Then there is evolutionary information to prepare, not only the individual, but the whole system for a shift. We are now at the brink of the shift.

Thinkers such as Vernadsky, Pierre Teilhard de Chardin, and Sri Aurobindo helped pinpoint scientifically what that moment of the mind shift might be. Aurobindo perceived the supramental descent creating the stage of super consciousness that will transition us to the next stage of the superman or *superhominization*. This is the stage that we are coming into now—this is planetary whole system knowledge, which is different than the knowledge given just for our own enlightenment.

In the Buddhist system there is a distinction made between the bodhisattvas who are working on behalf of all sentient beings for the total universal salvation of the world soul, and the bodhisattvas who are primarily concerned with their own personal salvation and enlightenment.

We are now at a time where the personal salvation programs merge into the evolutionary/planetary salvation program. This is part of the initiation into the noosphere, which is a stunningly, qualitatively different state of consciousness than we can now imagine. While the individual still exists, the normative consciousness becomes increasingly collective and telepathic so that the kind of privatization that characterizes the process of history is dissolved. The individual, while retaining a sense of his/her body autonomy, will merge into a collective field of consciousness—a telepathic system of communication, knowing and learning.

What is the actual mechanism that facilitates this shift into the new aeon?

Part IV • Exploring the Inner Dimensions

Avataric Transmutation—The Mechanism of the Shift.

After we have properly understood the function of hierarchy, then we can ask: What is the actual mechanism that facilitates this shift into the new aeon? This mechanism is referred to as *avataric transmutation* on behalf of the species. This shift occurs when entitization takes on a dual form to create a particular dynamic of consciousness. This dual entitization serves as a conduit of specific information and energy that triggers this shift.

The twin soul avatars that were written of in *CHC, Volume II* and Gate 7 of this volume, engage in specific forms of interaction with a deliberately designed system of synchronic transformation—the purpose of this is to create increasingly systematic states of superconsciousness on behalf of planetary transformation. In this process emerges a body of radiance. It is through this medium of avataric transmutation that this change is facilitated. Examples of this function can also be found in the *Epic of Gilgamesh* or in the *Popol Vuh* with its story of the mythic Mayan twins.

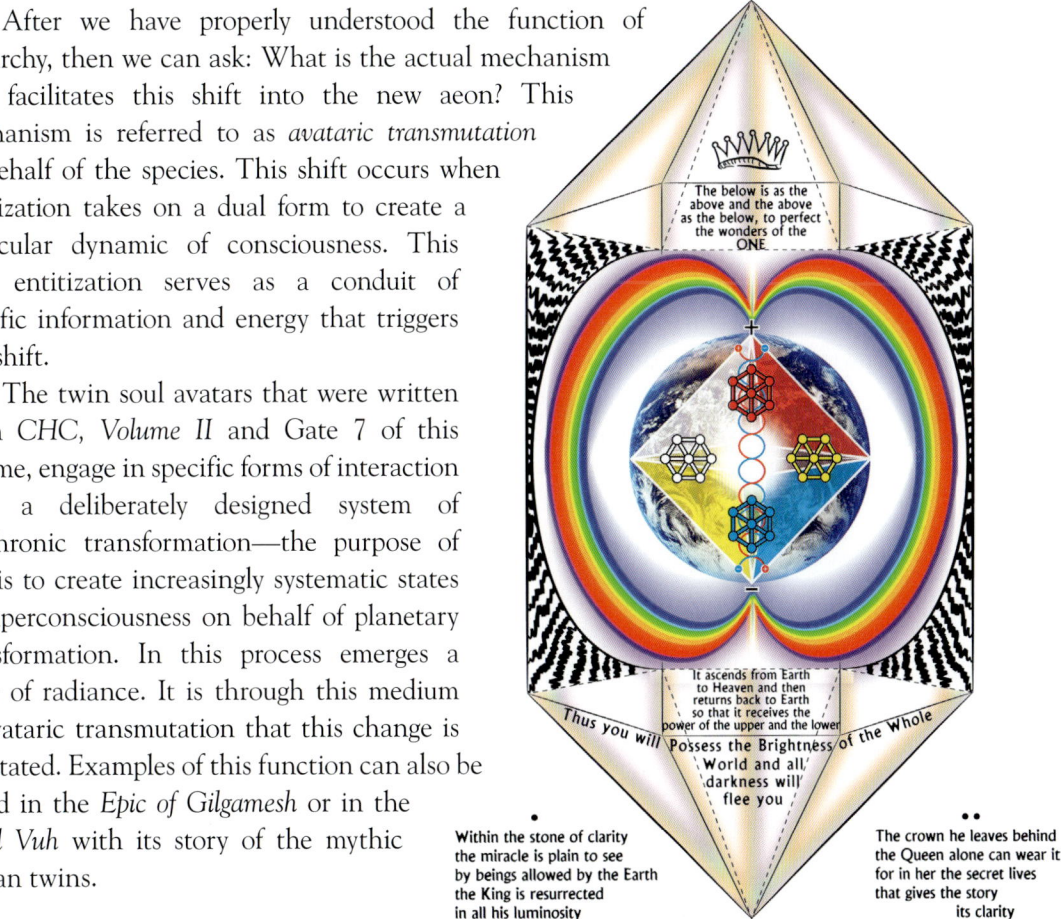

The below is as the above and the above as the below, to perfect the wonders of the ONE

It ascends from Earth to Heaven and then returns back to Earth so that it receives the power of the upper and the lower

Thus you will Possess the Brightness of the Whole World and all darkness will flee you

• Within the stone of clarity the miracle is plain to see by beings allowed by the Earth the King is resurrected in all his luminosity

•• The crown he leaves behind the Queen alone can wear it for in her the secret lives that gives the story its clarity

Cosmic Mediumship

Through the avataric transmutation mechanism the entire field of human consciousness is rapidly changing. The more prepared we are to advance into ego-free states of mind, the more likely it is that we will soon wake up and discover (if we haven't already) that we are all cosmic mediums. All the radio and television channels that we might wish for are actually channels of paranormal mediumship, connecting us with various levels of hierarchical information panels.

Perhaps you have done some channeling before, or you might be aware that all songs are floating in the air awaiting a receptive unit. You also might realize that you have a choice as to what channels you wish to operate with. This is the new normative phase that we are coming into; a new system of order of the homo noosphericus. This is the system being evolved through the avataric transmutation process on behalf of the entire species.

If we follow the thread of history back to 3113 BC, we can contemplate what facilitated this jump in consciousness. Here, we see Krishna, the avatar from India who grounded the necessary consciousness or frequency to survive spiritually through the historical cycle. These are just a few examples of individuals who served to ground the energy of a particular consciousness on Earth that facilitated a qualitative shift into a new condition.

Much exertion and mental concentration is required to transcend the present world system of dominant perceptions. It is hard for most people to think outside the consensual box; for to do this, we must question every aspect of our life. It is only the few who are able to extract themselves from the conditioned perceptual world implanted at birth.

To transcend that world system is the purpose of changing to a plant based diet and living increasingly in a hermetic environment, or with others of the same intent and discipline. One must also decrease the normal, everyday intake of outer influences, of news media and social scenes in order to focus on the purification, preparation and integration of the three bodies: physical, emotional and the mental body (Temple Body, Body of Destiny, Body of Radiance).

The Three Bodies

When entering this new system of order, we must first integrate the three bodies:

1. *Nirmanakaya*—physical, third-dimensional body or body of transformation. Known as the body of the temple in the cosmology of the cube.
2. *Sambogakaya*—emotional, fourth-dimensional astral body or body of destiny.
3. *Dharmakaya*—electronic, fifth-dimensional body. This body is the manifestation of the electronic entity of pure radiance, also known as the rainbow body.

The purpose of physical/emotional purification is to attune with the pure electronic plane of the fifth-dimensional being. Once the physical body is sufficiently purified, then it can open to receive the cellular molecular systems of the fourth- and fifth-dimensional bodies. This creates a precipitation of radiance; a cellular transformation or transmutation.

This is an arduous process that, on one hand, requires tremendous discipline, and on the other hand, is highly guided. As long as the disciplines are maintained, then a channel is formed for divine grace waves to flow in, affecting the two systems. This is a description of the operating mechanism and its components.

The three bodies are suspended on the central axis of the chakra system. The five main chakras govern from the bottom of the physical body—the root—to the top of the mental body—the crown. The center of the mental body is the third eye, and the center of the physical body is the secret center. The center of the emotional body is the heart that extends to the throat chakra for its expressive ability and extends to the solar plexus where emotional energy is received and transmitted.

The heart is the main transducer of energy and is also an organ of knowing. The physical body zone of psychic activation extends from the root chakra to the solar plexus—emotional information from the solar plexus comes into the physical body and the key of the physical body is the root. The heart of the energy is the secret center that contains the life-force. The mental body is organized in the crown which extends into the throat where communication takes intelligible form.

The throat chakra is both with the mental and emotional bodies—it is the center for artistic expression and also for communicating intelligence derived from the mental. This is also true for the solar plexus chakra, where we feel instinctual/intuitive energy and also emotional information. This energy is transferred to the heart chakra where the transduction of the emotional energy occurs.

In the heart, all of the impulses of the innate being or essence nature are exposed to the input from both the physical and the mental bodies. The heart is like a mirror, if the input is unclear or distorted so is the feedback. To truly activate the essence nature there must be a total mental exertion and physical purity.

This is the time of the Earth purification for the closing of the cycle. This is the time of the soul purification—the total purification—we want to be cleaned out and have a well functioning, strong physical body, a stress-free emotional body and a logical/consistent mental body. There are regimens and disciplines to cultivate each of these bodies—asanas, mudras, pranayams, cleansing and fasting for the physical body; practices of meditation and artistic expression help channel the emotional energy into higher states; and meditation, visualization and telepathic exercises for the mental body. Find what works for you.

Cosmic Function of Chakras

The five principle chakras are: root, solar plexus, heart, throat and crown. The minor chakras are the secret center and third eye. In many ways these are the most significant for cultivating the cosmic being. While the five main chakras focus on the integration of the three bodies, the two minor chakras revolve around the transcendental functions of being.

The third eye is associated with wisdom and the secret center is associated with sex. These two minor chakras are connected by the kundalini third eye wisdom channel (paranormal powers). The sexual activity has significance when it is consciously coordinated with the opening of the third eye; this is the purposive function of sex as an evolutionary activity and process.

As we get to the point of transforming the three bodies into a body of radiance, we will experience cellular transmutation and a new quality of radiance that enters into the whole three-bodied program. At this point, we will begin to have openings in the secret center, heart center and third eye. When the third eye opens then we gain true insight. The slogan of this program is: *In sight, I see.*

The Cosmic History Chronicles • Volume IV

As Christ said, "If thine eye be made single, then thy whole body will be filled with light." When we are able to open and one-pointedly focus that pinpoint beam of the third eye—the pineal gland just above the brow—then the light energy from both the crown chakra, as well as the exterior higher-dimensional light universe, floods into the third eye and fills the physical and astral nervous system with light.

In sura 57 and 66 of the Quran, it says we will see the believers with "light radiating from their right hand"—like a beam or a headlight coming from the right hand palm of the vritris. This is the radiance program we are evolving into.

When that third eye is finally opened, then a complete vision of the homo noosphericus as the fulfillment of the body of the temple of the New Jerusalem becomes activated, creating a permanent opening in the heart—*in sight, I see*. Then the flooding of the light and the heart opens and says: *In God, I am*.

The heart is the seat of the memory of God or the face, or the throne of God. Then the kundalini opens the secret center and says: *In Sex, We are*.

These three bodies are united in the secret kundalini third eye wisdom channel, and together project the noosphere membrane of the fourth body. This is what allows everyone to be a channel. A channel is one who is able to project his/her noosphere membrane, or resonating auric membrane of the fourth body—this is the cosmic medium on Earth. Through this medium, we can channel the seven planes of hierarchy: the planetary logos, the solar logos, the galactic logos, the cosmos logos and then three universe levels higher, and feel how these impact the membrane.

Descending through the top are the three higher levels: 1) the plane of the Absolute 2) the Lords of Creation, the Oxlahuntiku (13), and 3) the Lords of Time and Destiny, the Bolontiku (9).

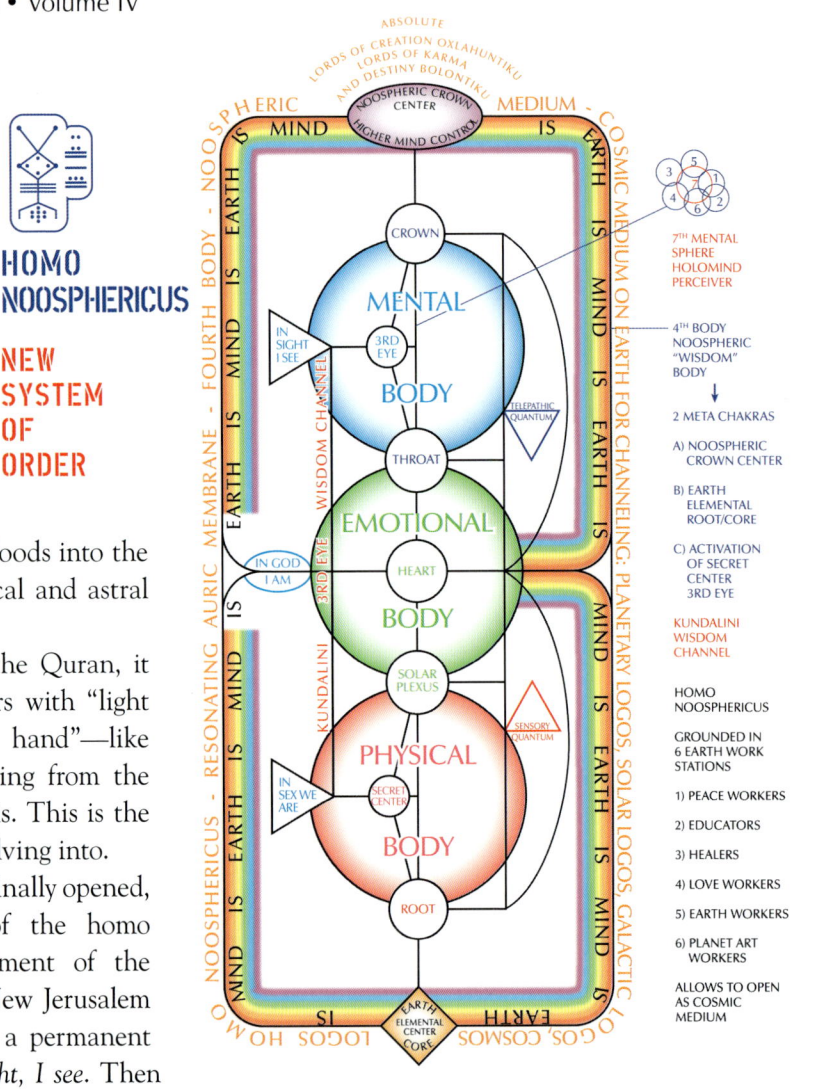

218

Part IV • Exploring the Inner Dimensions

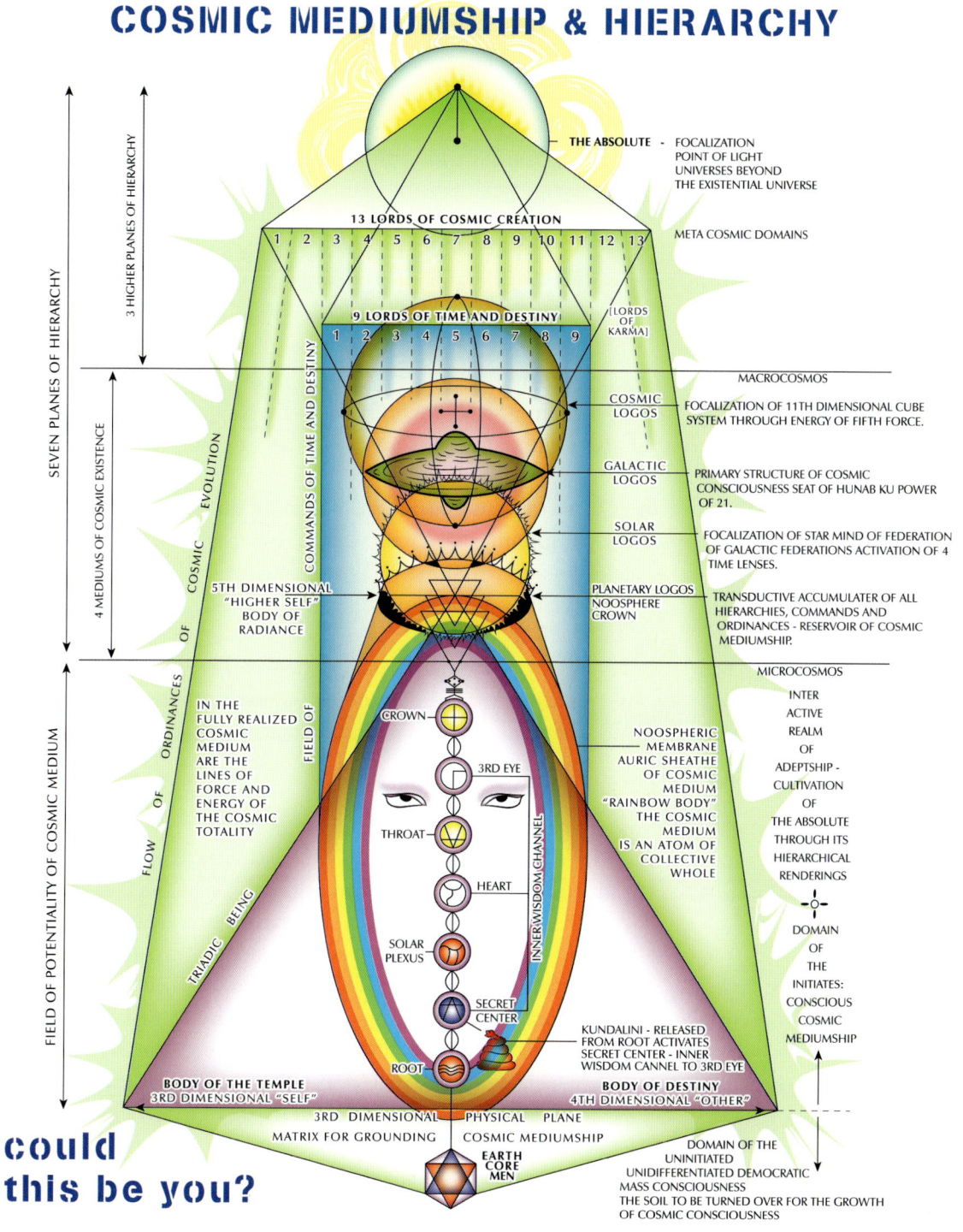

COSMIC MEDIUMSHIP & HIERARCHY

SEVEN PLANES OF HIERARCHY

3 HIGHER PLANES OF HIERARCHY

THE ABSOLUTE — FOCALIZATION POINT OF LIGHT UNIVERSES BEYOND THE EXISTENTIAL UNIVERSE

13 LORDS OF COSMIC CREATION
1 2 3 4 5 6 7 8 9 10 11 12 13

META COSMIC DOMAINS

9 LORDS OF TIME AND DESTINY
1 2 3 4 5 6 7 8 9 [LORDS OF KARMA]

4 MEDIUMS OF COSMIC EXISTENCE

COSMIC EVOLUTION

COMMANDS OF TIME AND DESTINY

MACROCOSMOS

COSMIC LOGOS — FOCALIZATION OF 11TH DIMENSIONAL CUBE SYSTEM THROUGH ENERGY OF FIFTH FORCE.

GALACTIC LOGOS — PRIMARY STRUCTURE OF COSMIC CONSCIOUSNESS SEAT OF HUNAB KU POWER OF 21.

SOLAR LOGOS — FOCALIZATION OF STAR MIND OF FEDERATION OF GALACTIC FEDERATIONS ACTIVATION OF 4 TIME LENSES.

PLANETARY LOGOS NOOSPHERE CROWN — TRANSDUCTIVE ACCUMULATER OF ALL HIERARCHIES, COMMANDS AND ORDINANCES - RESERVOIR OF COSMIC MEDIUMSHIP.

5TH DIMENSIONAL "HIGHER SELF" BODY OF RADIANCE

FIELD OF POTENTIALITY OF COSMIC MEDIUM

FLOW OF ORDINANCES

FIELD OF TRIADIC BEING

IN THE FULLY REALIZED COSMIC MEDIUM ARE THE LINES OF FORCE AND ENERGY OF THE COSMIC TOTALITY

CROWN
3RD EYE
THROAT
HEART
SOLAR PLEXUS
SECRET CENTER
ROOT

INNER WISDOM CHANNEL

NOOSPHERIC MEMBRANE AURIC SHEATHE OF COSMIC MEDIUM "RAINBOW BODY" THE COSMIC MEDIUM IS AN ATOM OF COLLECTIVE WHOLE

MICROCOSMOS

INTER ACTIVE REALM OF ADEPTSHIP - CULTIVATION OF THE ABSOLUTE THROUGH ITS HIERARCHICAL RENDERINGS

DOMAIN OF THE INITIATES: CONSCIOUS COSMIC MEDIUMSHIP

KUNDALINI - RELEASED FROM ROOT ACTIVATES SECRET CENTER - INNER WISDOM CANNEL TO 3RD EYE

BODY OF THE TEMPLE
3RD DIMENSIONAL "SELF"

BODY OF DESTINY
4TH DIMENSIONAL "OTHER"

3RD DIMENSIONAL PHYSICAL PLANE
MATRIX FOR GROUNDING COSMIC MEDIUMSHIP

EARTH CORE MEN

DOMAIN OF THE UNINITIATED UNDIFFERENTIATED DEMOCRATIC MASS CONSCIOUSNESS THE SOIL TO BE TURNED OVER FOR THE GROWTH OF COSMIC CONSCIOUSNESS

could this be you?

219

Those are the three that immediately impact the membrane: the planetary, solar, galactic and cosmic logos.

The logoi refers to aggregate entitizations that have a locus within a hierarchy of celestial bodies of planets and star galaxies. The activity of the logoi is to coordinate evolutionary functions or processes within the celestial body in which they hold their energy field. For the planetary noosphere is a manifestation of mind and of the planetary logos.

The logoi act on every aspect and facet of conscious evolution through the mental spheres; this opens up a diverse range of possibilities of consciousness, perception, sensation, etc. Beyond the logoi are laws of destiny, laws of creation and the Absolute. This is the realm of cosmic design that defines the infrastructure of the universe we live in. The non-manifest realms of the absolute open to yet other universes, including the seven light universes.

This is a hierarchy of levels of information that impact the functioning of cosmic consciousness and the construction of cosmic civilization. This will be a major theme to be developed in later volumes.

In each of these seven planes are hierarchies of differentiation. The information of these planes act upon each other, creating a descending ripple effect that descends through the different logoi, finally reaching the designated cosmic medium on Earth. The incoming hierarchical information affects the auric field of the cosmic medium, causing interactions within the etheric system of the three bodies.

The fourth body, the resonating auric membrane, opens as a result of the integration of the three bodies and the opening of the wisdom eye, secret center and heart center—this entrains the two metachakras—the noospheric crown and the elemental Earth core chakra. The noospheric crown is the higher mind control that tunes us into the higher telepathic collective consciousness, the field of the planetary logos. The Earth core chakra is what gives us the ability to talk to angels, devas, fairies and birds. This will be further explored in *CHC, Vol. V and VI*.

We may also experience our body, from the heart through the three lower chakras, continuously generating sensory quanta, and from the upper three chakras, how we are generating

At this next level, the very nature of what we think of as reality is viewed as a function of frequency beams that are projected subliminally to different sections of the brain.

Part IV • Exploring the Inner Dimensions

telepathic quanta. We will experience in our brain the creation of the seventh mental sphere, the holomind perceiver. This will allow the central channel to open fully to the seven planes of hierarchy while at the same time radializing our sensory perceptions into supermental states of consciousness.

When we open past the world system of the conditioned perceptions, then we enter into a vastly different level, where a whole new cosmos dawns. This new cosmos is actually a dynamic of energies, dimensions, force fields, frequency beams, and projecting beams as well as systems of projections and their receivers.

At this next level, the very nature of what we think of as reality is viewed as a function of frequency beams that are projected subliminally to different sections of the brain. These frequency beams register and cause certain types of responses that create the pictures of the world we believe to be real; we then create the world according to those pictures and images.

The larger mother beam is the 13 baktun synchronization beam. This beam synchronizes certain portions of the brain to be activated to receive other frequency beams that create alternative pictures of reality, allowing the soul different possibilities of response. The point is to give the soul various options while creating a complex and rich psycho-spiritual environment.

The reason for religious and spiritual traditions is to help us remember there is a way of moral conduct. Once we have established a moral safety net, then there is a possibility of ladders of ascent that tune into hierarchies as they are defined in the historical system. Many of these hierarchies are based on the septenary system which was very elaborately developed by Madame Blavatsky and Alice Bailey, and is also referred to by Gurdjieff as the *heptaparaparshinokh*—the system of seven, which is also very prevalent in the Law of Time.

As we move into the noospheric system, the hierarchical system rearranges and simplifies key aspects of what was hierarchically perceived, and as defined in the late historical cycles by different occult masters that we have alluded to.

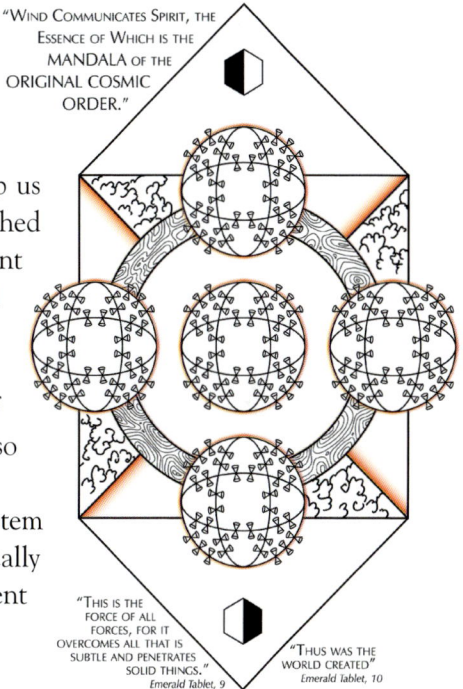

"Wind Communicates Spirit, the Essence of Which is the Mandala of the Original Cosmic Order."

"This is the force of all forces, for it overcomes all that is subtle and penetrates solid things."
Emerald Tablet, 9

"Thus was the world created"
Emerald Tablet, 10

New System of Order

When we reach the Galactic Seed in 2013, a new long term synchronization beam will come into play: the intergalactic cosmic consciousness beam. This beam will establish the noosphere systems of order. In the homo noosphericus' new system of order, we evolve into the seventh mental sphere: the holomind perceiver, which radializes our consciousness. Through cultivation of the seventh mental sphere, we experience the fourth body: the noospheric wisdom body, which is the auric membrane

221

that resonates with the rainbow Earth.

At this stage, we receive two new *metachakras*, the noospheric crown center, which functions higher mind control, and the Earth root, the elemental center or the core (see *CHC, Vol. I*). These superhuman centers are effectively the antennas and grounding rods of cosmic consciousness, amping the frequency of the other seven chakras. We then receive the activation of the secret center, the third eye and the heart chakras; the connection of these three centers creates the *kundalini wisdom channel*. This is the fundamental blueprint for the galactic operating system of order.

As this activation emanates out from the transmutational base, then people will begin to "get it" and will, in turn, apply themselves to disciplines that further activate these new evolutionary organs. For this system to work smoothly, it must be grounded in different types of activities. In noosphere consciousness, human activity is always organized according to six stations or types of activities (work stations).

The following are the six work activities that maintain the noosphere as a positive self-generating, self-evolving field of consciousness. All the activities assume that the practitioner has attained the level of non-egoic cosmic mediumship. You can work with one or more of these as your field of activity according to your inclination.

1. **Peace Workers**—These are the ones who understand peace as a fundamental quality of being. They stabilize socio-mental fields with harmonic actions and activities to create programs of mental stabilization for the planet. These programs include various meditation methods and stabilization practices and techniques to equalize and balance the emotional body. The peace workers begin with communities and then expand out to continuously stabilize the social well-being in harmonic perceptions using various programs and skills. They pass these teachings onto others, extending even to the animal, plant and mineral kingdoms.

2. **Educators**—These are the ones who understand the cycles of time and the new system of order. They understand and are able to transmit the Law of Time, the synchronic order, Cosmic History and the nature of the noosphere. Educators are very important for setting in place the programs of new knowledge and new systems of measure that correspond with cosmic harmonic standards, rather than shifting third-dimensional standards. Educators will travel to different bioregions to transmit knowledge. Their job is to ensure that everyone is operating with the highest single unifying cosmic information base in resonance with the one mind of the Earth, the noosphere.

3. **Healers**—These are the ones who know the art of self healing; how to heal the body, how the body regenerates itself, etc. Their job is to transmit this knowledge to others, so that eventually, the human race enters the realm of deathlessness. The healers are those who are advanced in radiating cosmic light through their bodies to others and to the planet. They will teach others about the regenerative powers of the body, inclusive of knowledge about the plant

kingdom. They will ensure that self-healing is restored to the human species and that everyone understands the system of the three bodies and techniques of healing—down to food intake, breath control, the attitude and perceptions of the body and how to maintain it at a level of self-generative radiance. In this way, they will assist in the collective realization of the one body of the noosphere.

4. **Love Workers**—These are the people who are concerned with spreading the highest mental well-being throughout the species which is based on the cosmic force of love. They teach others, by example, how to spread love and compassion to all beings. They operate with a great range of techniques for arousing universal compassion as a condition of externalizing and universalizing continuing consciousness. This is the basis of mental health and radiant well-being. The Loveworkers also teach how to activate principles of self-love so that one learns how to generate his/her own love and light without taking energy from others. In this way, self-generating compassionate love becomes the normative value of relation in the universe; the bonding agent of the noosphere.

5. **Earth Workers**—They are the gardeners growing the food and tending the orchards. They also regulate the commerce thereof. They liberate the animals, plant the gardens and trees, and in general, create increasing harmony between the biosphere and noosphere. The fourth body, generated from the noosphere center has the phrase "mind is" and from the Earth core, "Earth is". The Earth workers transmit thoughtforms such as: Mind is Earth is Mind is Earth is Mind is Earth, etc. This is the mantra of the Earth workers. Through their work, the biosphere and the noosphere become integrated. This leads to a whole new level of perception of the Earth—of Earth caretakers. Those who understand the Earth as a living being and living mind, not only elevate other humans, but elevate the Earth Herself. This defines the Psychozoic Era—it is not just the humans—it is everything that is spiritually alive. This is the knowledge that the Earth workers transmit. Every cell of the Earth must become enlightened. The Earth workers assist in entering us into the hyperorganic phase of evolution. In this way, the new economy is a form of spiritual ecology.

6. **Planet Art Workers**—These beings help create the whole planet as a total work of art. This again has to do with developing networks and weavings of artistic forms and harmonies that integrate the human social and perceptual systems with nature's systems. Through these art and nature weavings, new forms are created of living art, and forms of art as radiance. All senses are utilized and synthesized into even more inclusive forms of synaesthesia. The Planet Art Workers see to it that the whole of the Earth is transformed and realized as a galactic art whole, a medium for the artistic transformation of every range of cosmic energy and radiation. Grounding these activities is what gives you the license to be a cosmic medium. You have to be doing something worthwhile to activate your cosmic mediumship.

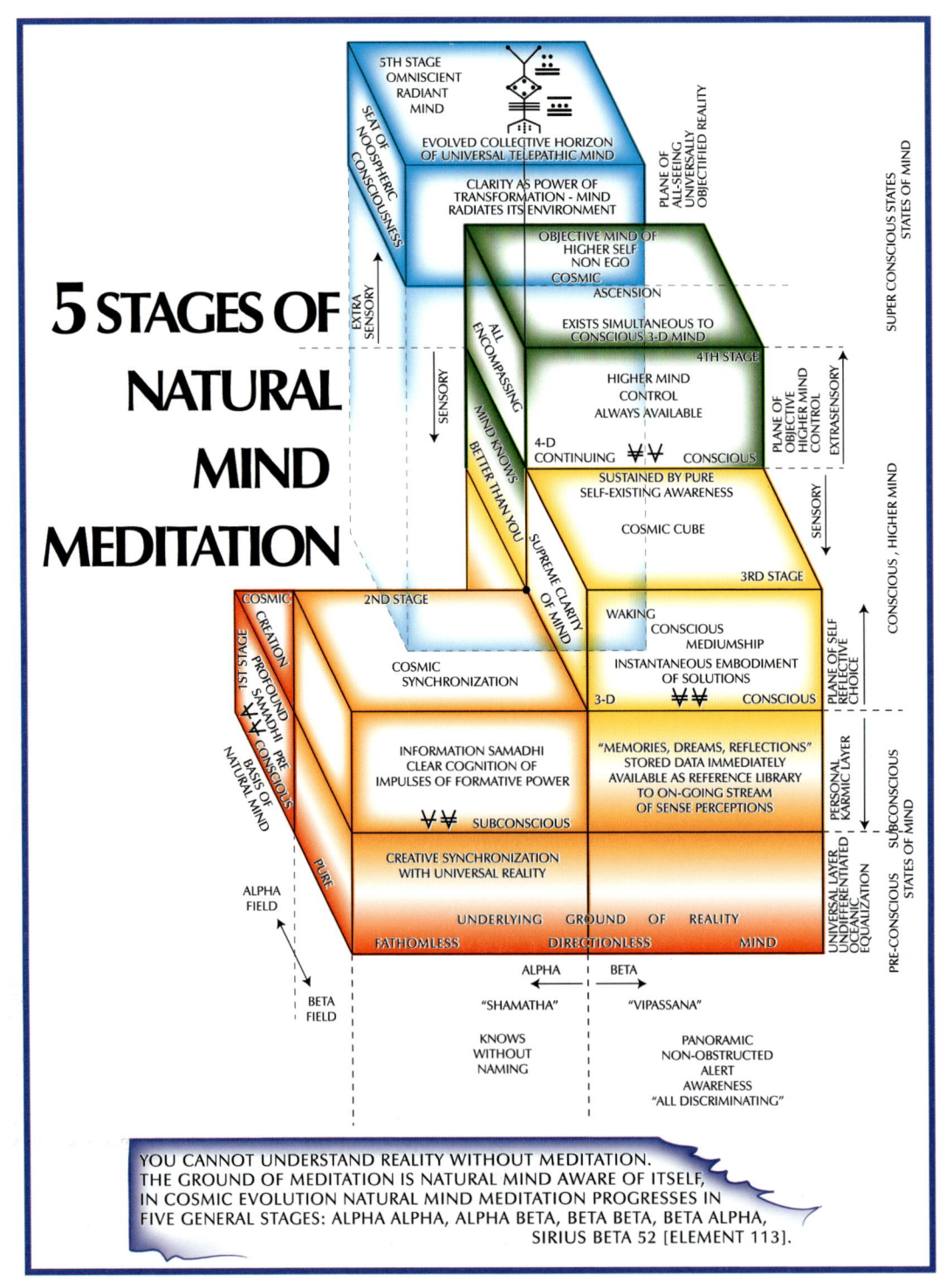

The Cosmic History Chronicles • Volume IV

5 STAGES OF NATURAL MIND MEDITATION

5TH STAGE OMNISCIENT RADIANT MIND
EVOLVED COLLECTIVE HORIZON OF UNIVERSAL TELEPATHIC MIND
CLARITY AS POWER OF TRANSFORMATION – MIND RADIATES ITS ENVIRONMENT
SEAT OF NOOSPHERIC CONSCIOUSNESS
PLANE OF ALL-SEEING UNIVERSALLY OBJECTIFIED REALITY
SUPER CONSCIOUS STATES / STATES OF MIND
EXTRA SENSORY

OBJECTIVE MIND OF HIGHER SELF NON EGO
COSMIC ASCENSION
EXISTS SIMULTANEOUS TO CONSCIOUS 3-D MIND
4TH STAGE
HIGHER MIND CONTROL ALWAYS AVAILABLE
4-D CONTINUING ¥¥ CONSCIOUS
ALL ENCOMPASSING
PLANE OF OBJECTIVE HIGHER MIND CONTROL
EXTRASENSORY

SUSTAINED BY PURE SELF-EXISTING AWARENESS
COSMIC CUBE
3RD STAGE
MIND KNOWS BETTER THAN YOU
SUPREME CLARITY OF MIND
SENSORY
CONSCIOUS, HIGHER MIND

2ND STAGE
COSMIC SYNCHRONIZATION
WAKING CONSCIOUS MEDIUMSHIP
INSTANTANEOUS EMBODIMENT OF SOLUTIONS
3-D ¥¥ CONSCIOUS
PLANE OF SELF REFLECTIVE CHOICE

COSMIC CREATION
1ST STAGE
PROFOUND SAMADHI ¥ PRE CONSCIOUS
BASIS OF NATURAL MIND
INFORMATION SAMADHI CLEAR COGNITION OF IMPULSES OF FORMATIVE POWER
"MEMORIES, DREAMS, REFLECTIONS" STORED DATA IMMEDIATELY AVAILABLE AS REFERENCE LIBRARY TO ON-GOING STREAM OF SENSE PERCEPTIONS
¥¥ SUBCONSCIOUS
PERSONAL KARMIC LAYER
SUBCONSCIOUS

PURE
CREATIVE SYNCHRONIZATION WITH UNIVERSAL REALITY
UNDERLYING GROUND OF REALITY
FATHOMLESS DIRECTIONLESS MIND
UNIVERSAL LAYER UNDIFFERENTIATED OCEANIC EQUALIZATION
PRE-CONSCIOUS STATES OF MIND

ALPHA FIELD
BETA FIELD

ALPHA — "SHAMATHA" — KNOWS WITHOUT NAMING
BETA — "VIPASSANA" — PANORAMIC NON-OBSTRUCTED ALERT AWARENESS "ALL DISCRIMINATING"

> YOU CANNOT UNDERSTAND REALITY WITHOUT MEDITATION. THE GROUND OF MEDITATION IS NATURAL MIND AWARE OF ITSELF, IN COSMIC EVOLUTION NATURAL MIND MEDITATION PROGRESSES IN FIVE GENERAL STAGES: ALPHA ALPHA, ALPHA BETA, BETA BETA, BETA ALPHA, SIRIUS BETA 52 [ELEMENT 113].

These are the noosphere activities that everyone can participate in, in one way or another. As you become consciously engaged in these activities, then through your mediumship, or your resonating auric membrane, you can tune into the necessary channels to benefit the whole.

In *CHC, Vol. III* we speak about the community of the cube and the four specific intergalactic channels: Cosmic Creation, Cosmic Ascension, Cosmic Synchronization and Cosmic Cube. Any one of these channels can be hooked up in the brain and utilized to connect with different levels of the planetary or galactic logos. The messages received are specific for different areas of activity that take on different emphasis depending on whether you are working in the Community of the Cube or the Community of Cosmic Ascension, etc.

As we begin to study the entire noosphere social program, we begin to see that there are many varieties of activities and different perspectives required that utilize different channels. This leads to different levels of information that need to be channeled to accomplish the Great Mission of Planetary Evolution into the Noosphere. Eventually, everybody will function as a cosmic medium.

If the biosphere is the surface on the Earth for the transformation of cosmic energy, then the noosphere is the region on the Earth for the cultivation of cosmic mediumship. The purpose of cosmic mediumship is for the transformation of the Earth into a planetary/galactic art whole. This gives a working context for realizing that we are a cosmic medium as well as participants in the galactic hierarchy as it informs the cosmic civilization on Earth.

This is the future.

NEW ARK OF THE COVENANT: CONTAINING RADIOGENETIC
TRANSMISSION CODES FOR ESTABLISHING GALACTIC LIFE WHOLE
AND STRUCTURING GALACTIC ART WHOLE

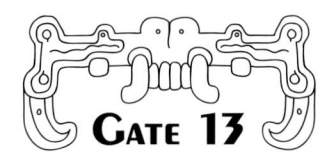

Gate 13
Seven Planetary Initiations
Galactic Invocations for Planetary Consciousness

For untold millennia we have been traveling through the great starry time space in search of ourselves. Many great teachers have come to us—seers, shamans, mystics, poets, visionaries, occult masters, prophets and messengers of every kind have arisen amongst us, to give comfort, to point the way, to deliver a vision of what might be.

Today we approach the end of the great cycle. No one is free who claims to be free. Our thoughtless addictions, slavery to our machines, and our erroneous perceptions of time have caused us to all but destroy our world.

Surely some great change is at hand; surely a new state of being, a new mind and consciousness are about to be revealed. All of the great masters and teachers, prophets and seers of every culture and of every time have pointed to this great moment, the changing of the aeon, the closing of the cycle, the beginning of the great return, the flowering of the rainbow tree of prophecy.

Now we have passed beyond the shores of history into the great galactic ocean of cosmic time. We open ourselves to new and higher forces of life and dimensions of knowing. To these higher galactic forces we cry out:

WE ARE ALL ONE! These simple words have been proclaimed and glorified by our dreamers and martyrs for millennia. This is the meaning of the noosphere—the planetary mind—WE ARE ALL ONE.

In offering these galactic invocations on behalf of the one planetary mind, may we come to know ourselves as one planetary being, a single destiny, a single vision unifying us! May fear and suffering be relieved! May all hindrances and impediments of the mind be dissolved! May the glory of the noosphere shine forth in resplendent power around the planet as the rainbow bridge to the higher dimensions of mind and spirit! May galactic consciousness flourish on Earth! WE ARE ALL ONE!

1

INVOCATION OF THE GALACTIC FORCE
FIRST INITIATION OF PLANETARY CONSCIOUSNESS
POLAR HARMONIC OF KNOWLEDGE
OPENING THE GALACTIC CHANNEL ZENITH

From the Star Channel *Sirius*
Great Being Power of the Galactic Knowledge
Extending the wisdom of the Nine Lords of Time and Destiny
From the universes of light beyond the universe we know,
Inspire us with the self-healing power of galactic knowledge
Open within us the evolutionary channels of the greater dream
Give birth within us to the expanded powers of our own life-force
And seal the gates of death with the nectar of immortality
That we may forever be One in the Galactic Knowledge of Being

11

INVOCATION OF THE GALACTIC FORCE
SECOND INITIATION OF PLANETARY CONSCIOUSNESS
POLAR HARMONIC OF PROPHECY
RECEIVING FROM THE GALACTIC CHANNEL NADIR

From the Star Channel *Canopus*
Bright Heavenly bestower of the magical force
Grant us the power of being aligned with the truth
And of causing our words and our actions to be undeviating
From the Great Will of the Galactic Spirit force
Grant that our little wills be magnetized into the greater breath of spirit
That we may be accepted as enlightened prophets of the galactic order
Time travelers awake to the cause of universal ascension
Spreading waves of truth throughout the planetary time space cube!

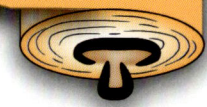

111
INVOCATION OF THE GALACTIC FORCE
THIRD INITIATION OF PLANETARY CONSCIOUSNESS
THERMIC FORCE FIELD OF LOVE
CENTRIFUGAL FORCE OF THE HEAT OF COMPASSION

From the Star Channel *Arcturus*
Guide of the seven eternal sages who bestow the cosmic wisdom
The bearers of galactic culture forging the great federation of light
Into the single force of love
Forever determined and defined by art
May we be granted the galactic vision to transform all matter
Into the purifying radiance of the higher dream
May the abundance of the galactic power of the higher dream
Generate forever the compassionate heat of cosmic love!

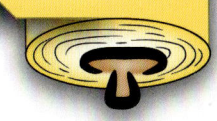

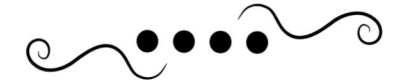

IV
Invocation of the Galactic Force
Fourth Stage of the Ascent of Planetary Consciousness
Luminic Force Field of Intelligence
Centripetal Force of the Light of Wisdom

From the Star Channel *Antares*
Great guiding light of higher intelligence
Born of the flowering of cosmic awareness
Illumined in the galactic star-realm of vision
May we be transformed into wizards of the higher law
Seeing with the eyes of the cosmic eagle
Knowing with the mind of the warriors of light
That we may easily trace the billion blazing paths of Return
Throughout the ever-evolving matrix of cosmic synchronicity

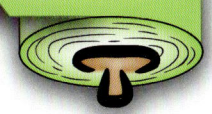

V

INVOCATION OF THE GALACTIC FORCE – THE HUNAB KU
FIFTH INITIATION OF PLANETARY CONSCIOUSNESS
POWER OF THE FIFTH FORCE
INTEGRATING POWER OF THE COSMIC TOTALITY – HEART OF RADIANCE

From within the *Galactic Center* – Heart of radiance
May we be encompassed by the fifth force power of Hunab Ku
The Call to the One realized by the prophets and singers of galactic time
Those who know how to invoke
The 72 dimensional energies of the 18-dimension universe
Spinning the matrix creation force throughout the great dominion of time
O you One Giver of Movement and measure
By the power of the 13 galactic tones of endless creation
Bestow on us now your unitive force of the presence of Cosmic Totality!

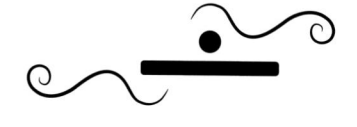

VI
INVOCATION OF THE GALACTIC FORCE
SIXTH INITIATION OF PLANETARY CONSCIOUSNESS
TELEPATHIC FORCE OF THE TRANSCENDENT MIND
SUPERMENTAL POWER OF TRANSCENDENT ORDER – CROWN OF RADIANCE

From the Star Channel *Vega*
Extending in a rainbow beam from the Galactic Center
The transcendent force of the supermental crown of radiance
May the vision of the star elders of the great councils of light and wisdom
Descend upon us that we may ascend to the sublime grace
Of the dimensions beyond manifestation
May the light of those universes of pure light
Infuse our soul journeys with the telepathic power of the infinite
That the planetary noosphere may become the crown of pure radiance

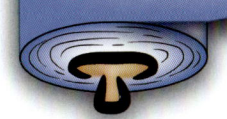

VII
Invocation of the Galactic Force
Seventh initiation of Planetary Consciousness
Attainment of the Supramental Reality
Radialized Order of the Supramental Source of Radiance

From the Star Channel *Pleiades*
Origin of the time travelers mission to Earth
Galactic Mayan star base where the commands are received
May the supramental forces gather their great structures
Of spiritual evolution and release them into the noosphere
May the higher yogic force within the planetary consciousness
Direct all manifestation to its fulfillment
May our perceptions be organized into a cosmic whole
That we may all become One with the radialized order of the Primal Source!

Ah yum Hunab Ku evam maya eh ma ho!
Ah yum Hunab Ku evam maya eh ma ho!
Ah yum Hunab Ku evam maya eh ma ho!

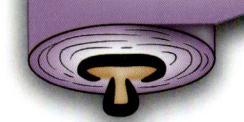

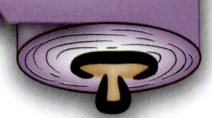

Prayer of the Seven Galactic Directions

From the East, House of Light,
May wisdom dawn in us so we may see all things in clarity!

From the North House of Night,
May wisdom ripen in us so we may know all from within!

From the West, House of Transformation,
May wisdom be transformed into right action so we may do what must be done!

From the South, House of the Eternal Sun, may right action reap the harvest
so we may enjoy the fruits of planetary being!

From Above, House of Heaven where star people and ancestors gather,
May their blessings come to us now!

From Below, House of Earth,
May the heartbeat of her crystal core bless us with harmonies to end all war!

From the Center, Galactic Source, which is everywhere at once,
May everything be known as the light of mutual love!

Ah yum Hunab Ku evam maya eh ma ho!
Ah yum Hunab Ku evam maya eh ma ho!
Ah yum Hunab Ku evam maya eh ma ho!

Appendix:
Synchronic Order as Symbolic Construct

Synchronic Order as Symbolic Construct

Synchronicity is the operation of a higher moving template of mathematical order that coordinates all phenomena telepathically. The synchronic order is the fourth-dimensional order of reality; it is the realm of universal synchronization. The synchronic order and the Law of Time govern all manifestations of the third-dimensional physical plane. Its frequency, 13:20, codes in numerous ways the patterns of fourth dimensional time.

The 13:20 frequency constitutes recurring sets of cycles; the smallest cycle being the four-day pattern of the harmonics. In this pattern, we see that the 20 solar seals are coded by four colors to create the five sets: red, white, blue, yellow. One set of these is called a harmonic, the four-day cycle that establishes the first pattern of meaning: Red initiates, White refines, Blue transforms, and Yellow ripens. The next pattern is the chromatic (5 units for five-day cycles)—starting and ending with the same color.

The fundamental cycles of the synchronic order are:

4-day cycles
5-day cycles
7-day cycles
13-day cycles
20-day cycles
28-day cycles

Chromatics
Each chromatic set has four chromatics each. The chromatics are essentially three types: 1. Clan chromatics, 2. Overtone chromatics 3. Wisdom chromatics.

Within the 28-day cycles, there are four seven-day sub-cycles. Everything is patterned, organized and harmonized in the seven-day pattern. The seven days are coded by the seven radial plasmas, the psychotelepathic plasmas that govern and organize the sequence of the seven-day cycles.

We are also following a 260-day cycle or galactic spin; there are 73 of these 260-day cycles to every 52 years. There are 73 five-day chromatics to every 52 weeks. There are five 52-day castles to each 260-day spin. In contemplating these cycles, we feel the rich complex of interactions and overlays, or harmonic patterns:

4-day harmonic/time cells,
5-day chromatic,
7-day week (heptad),
13-day wavespell (tones 1-13),
20-day vinal (five harmonics/time cells),
28-day moon,
52-day castle,
260-day spin (five castles),
364 + 1 Day Out of Time = 13 Moons.

The Cosmic History Chronicles • Volume IV

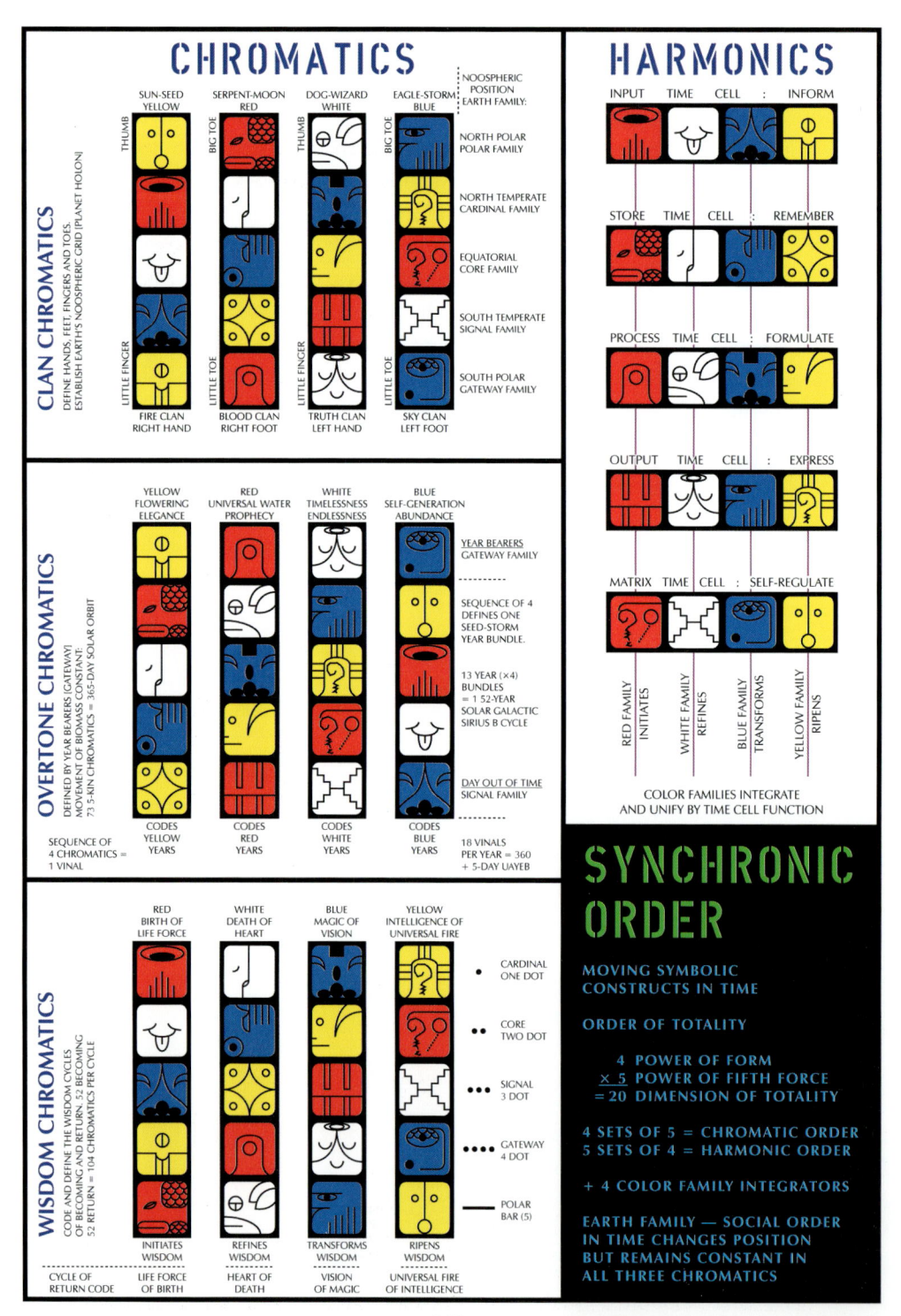

Appendix • Synchronic Order as Symbolic Construct

We are dealing with fractal patterns and symbolically coded constructs, inclusive of moving patterns of symbols: 20 solar seals, 7 radial plasmas, 24 Futhark runes, etc.

The synchronic order is the immediate elaboration of the primal pattern of number as it is projected from mind into time. There is void mind, then there is mind with the primary self-arising qualities of sound, light and fire; then there is mind that logically discriminates and creates a dimension of pure number.

The Law of Time is made up of primary symbolic constructs, the first being 13 galactic tones. Each tone or symbol has a unique quality that defines a *wavespell* of time. The 20 solar icons or symbols describe the movement of space in time. The 13-tone wavespell coordinates the 20 units of the movement of space in time to create a pattern of 260 different symbolic constructs, referred to as *galactic signatures*.

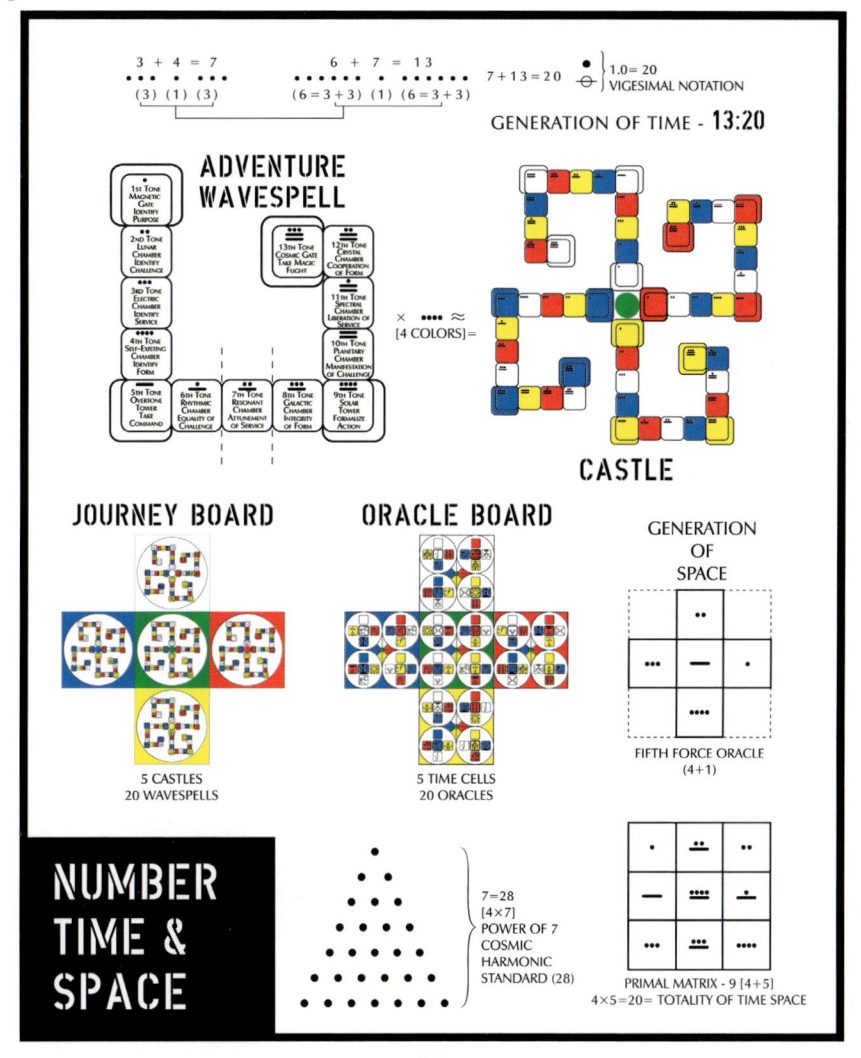

Each of these galactic signatures corresponds to one of the 13 galactic tones or numbers and also to one of the 20 solar seals and one of the four colors. These permutations create 260 possibilities. This is the primary symbolic set of the synchronic order. With their affirmations, the 260 galactic signatures constitute the *Book of Kin*.

The 20 "solar seals" each have their own fifth force pattern called a *fifth force oracle*. These fifth force oracles combine to create a larger fifth force pattern, which is the fifth force oracle board that shows the coordination of the movement of space in time. This creates a fractally repeating fifth force pattern with its own numerological constructs. These patterns move in time according to shifting color patterns.

Everything is a harmony of fractally repeating patterns projected from the fourth-dimensional higher mind. This higher mind receives its imprint from the center of the fifth dimension that projects a specific program into the fourth-dimensional space of the evolving mind of whatever particular point in space might need and be receptive to such a program. The projecting fifth-dimensional mind is the "Sirius B program". The fourth-dimensional mind, in this case, is Earth's noosphere.

The 20 seals, with their fifth force oracle patterns, are organized by the wavespell in time to create a *fractally repeating pattern* of 20 wavespells (13 x 20 = 260). These 20 wavespells are contained within five castles; four wavespells per castle, with different colors, directions and functions: the red castle (East), white castle (North), blue castle (West), yellow castle (South) and green castle (Central matrix). There are five harmonics of time with 20 seals, and five castles of time with 20 wavespells. This defines the basic patterns of the synchronic order, but it is well to note that when placed on the boards they create genuinely moving symbolic constructs in time. The fifth force oracle, as well as the journey board can also be folded into a cube.

There is a sequence of 260 coded patterns that interact with a sequence of 365 (364 + 1) coded days. The 364 + 1 coded days reduce to the simple pattern of thirteen repeating sets of four seven-day weeks. Each week is based on one of four color patterns. The first week is red, the second white, the third blue and the fourth yellow. Each of the seven days is also coded by one of the radial plasmas. Each of the seven radial plasmas has its pattern, color and meaning that forms the seven-day week into a *heptad* for recapitulating the primal cube of creation.

Even the pattern of the orbit, which we think of as a 365-day cycle, is a construct of 13 sub-cycles—moons—coded by the four colors and seven radial plasmas. These 13 sub-structures, based on the multiplication of four and seven, are coordinated by the wavespell pattern. All the frequencies are resonant with each other and fit into the code and pattern of the annual wavespell, which, again, is a symbolic construct. Just as there are thirteen 28-day moons, there are also 28 thirteen-day wavespells.

There are also four-year harmonic cycles that consist of a set of red, white, blue, and yellow years.

If we coordinate the 13 moon/28-day pattern plus the 365th day (Day Out of Time) with the 260-day pattern, we arrive at a cycle of 18,980 days, or 52 years, or 73 of the 260-day patterns.

Appendix • Synchronic Order as Symbolic Construct

The mentioned cycles are all coordinated by yet another symbolic construct known as the *galactic compass*. Note that the 52-year solar galactic cycle corresponds to the orbit of Sirius B around Sirius A.

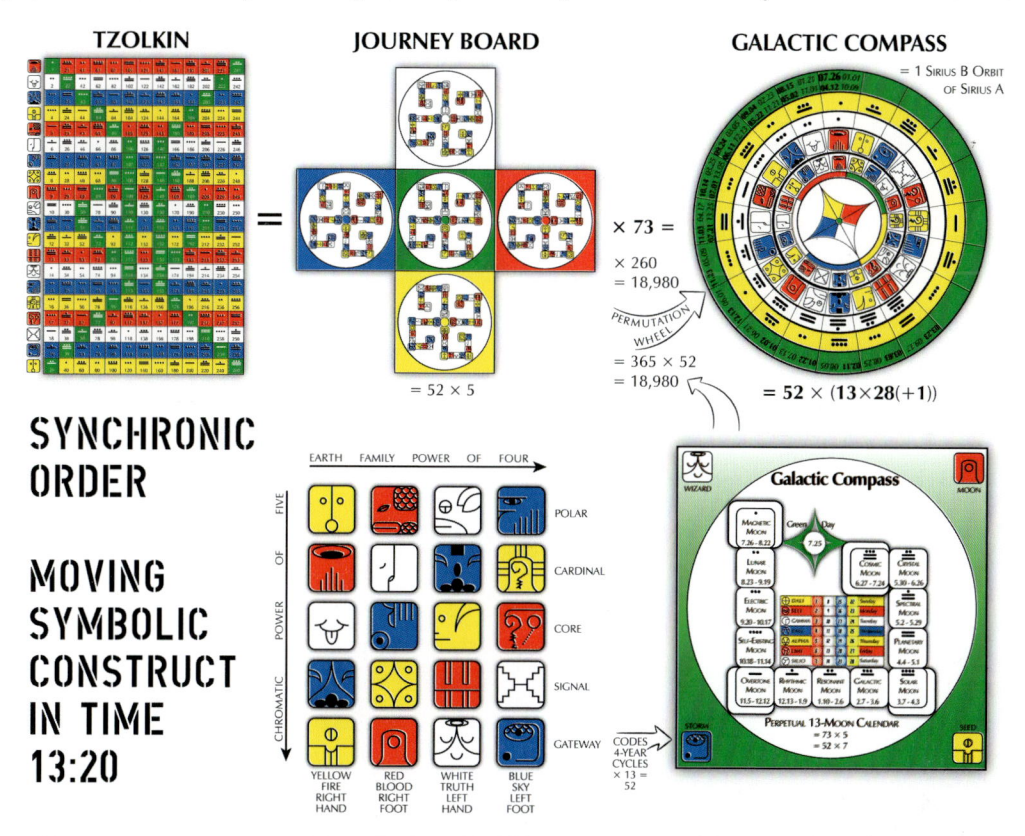

SYNCHRONIC ORDER

MOVING SYMBOLIC CONSTRUCT IN TIME 13:20

Galactic Compass

The galactic compass is comprised of five moving parts with different relationships of patterns, such as the four-color pattern at the center; the five-castle pattern in the ring around that; the 20-wavespell pattern with the seals of the wavespells; the 20-day pattern, which is not the same order as the wavespell pattern; and the 13 tones that go with the 20 days. Every year is coordinated by one of four seals from what is called the Gateway Family: Red Moon, White Wizard, Blue Storm or Yellow Seed year. Those seals recur every 20 days. There is a yellow ring here that corresponds to the pattern of the tones that occur every 20 days for any given seal. On the outermost ring is the frequency of those 20 day cycles. This frequency is coded into the Gregorian calendar to translate the old time into the new time.

All these moving parts on the galactic compass constitute a permutation frequency of 18,980 days, of which no two days are the same. These cycles repeat as 52-year patterns; every 52 years is itself a component of a whole different set of patterns. For instance, there are 260-year cycles of five 52-year cycles each—a chromatic of solar galactic time; there are also 260 52-year cycles and on and on …

The Cosmic History Chronicles • Volume IV

How the Synchronic Codes Function

The symbolic construct of coordinates is projected into the layer of the fourth-dimensional consciousness from the "Sirius B" control center—projection of the 52:73 ratio. This ratio is projected down in such a way that the whole of the fourth-dimensional noospheric field is enlivened by the different permutations and patterns created by this ratio. Once we have attuned our consciousness to the 13:20 frequency, then those pattern structures become obvious.

The basic timing frequency patterns are coded by what is called the *Dreamspell*, 13 moon/28-day frequency. This, as we said, is coded into the 260-day frequency matrix with its 65 sets of four radial units (or occult quartets), the tones of each set equaling 28. All the cycles are built into this matrix with its pattern of 52 galactic activation portals. The Dreamspell is the main significant symbolic structure. The Telektonon is the next symbolic structure in this unfolding and ever-evolving system.

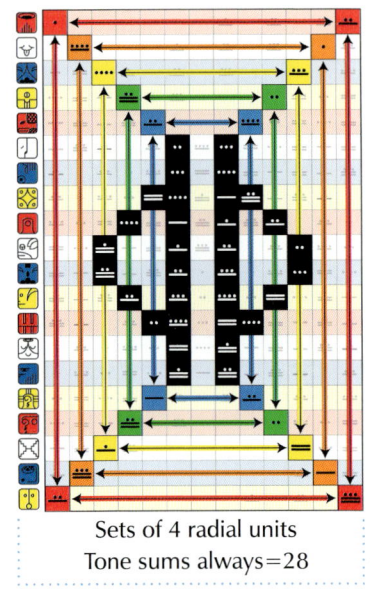

Sets of 4 radial units
Tone sums always=28

The Telektonon shows the coordination of the 28-day cycle within the framework of the fourth-dimensional construct of the solar system. From this dimension, it is the planetary orbits that are of most significance, rather than the planetary bodies. A planet is viewed as an "atomic nucleus" (or electron) that holds a particular frequency in place; the frequency pattern is the orbit. The planetary orbits are the resonant frequency constants of the heliosphere.

The Telektonon is based on showing where the 28-day pattern occurs, which is in the circuit that connects the third and eighth orbits. The Telektonon also shows the structure of the 20 solar seals, broken down into a sequence of 10 each that correspond with the 10 planetary orbits of the galactic/karmic (GK) sequence, which goes from outer (galaxy) to inner (sun); and the ten orbits of the solar/prophetic (SP) sequence which goes from sun out to galaxy.

The 28-day cycle corresponds to the Earth sequence connecting to the Uranus sequence. This forms one circuit. The fifth force power in the Telektonon is seen as the five circuits that connect the planetary orbits. The first circuit connects Mercury and Pluto as the outermost (36 units). The second circuit connects Venus and Neptune (32 units), and the third circuit connects Earth and Uranus. The third circuit consists of 28 units which translates as the 28-day lunar orbital cycle. In this way, we are able to track the 28-day cycle as a planetary circuit. This is a unique and distinguishing pattern.

We are not only following a pattern of four weeks in a schematic coordinated by the wavespell, but we are also following a pattern that coordinates the orbital frequencies of the third planet, Earth, and the eighth planet, Uranus. This is the third circuit. The fourth circuit connects Mars and Saturn (24 units); and the fifth, the innermost circuit, connects the Asteroid Belt/Maldek with Jupiter (20 units).

250

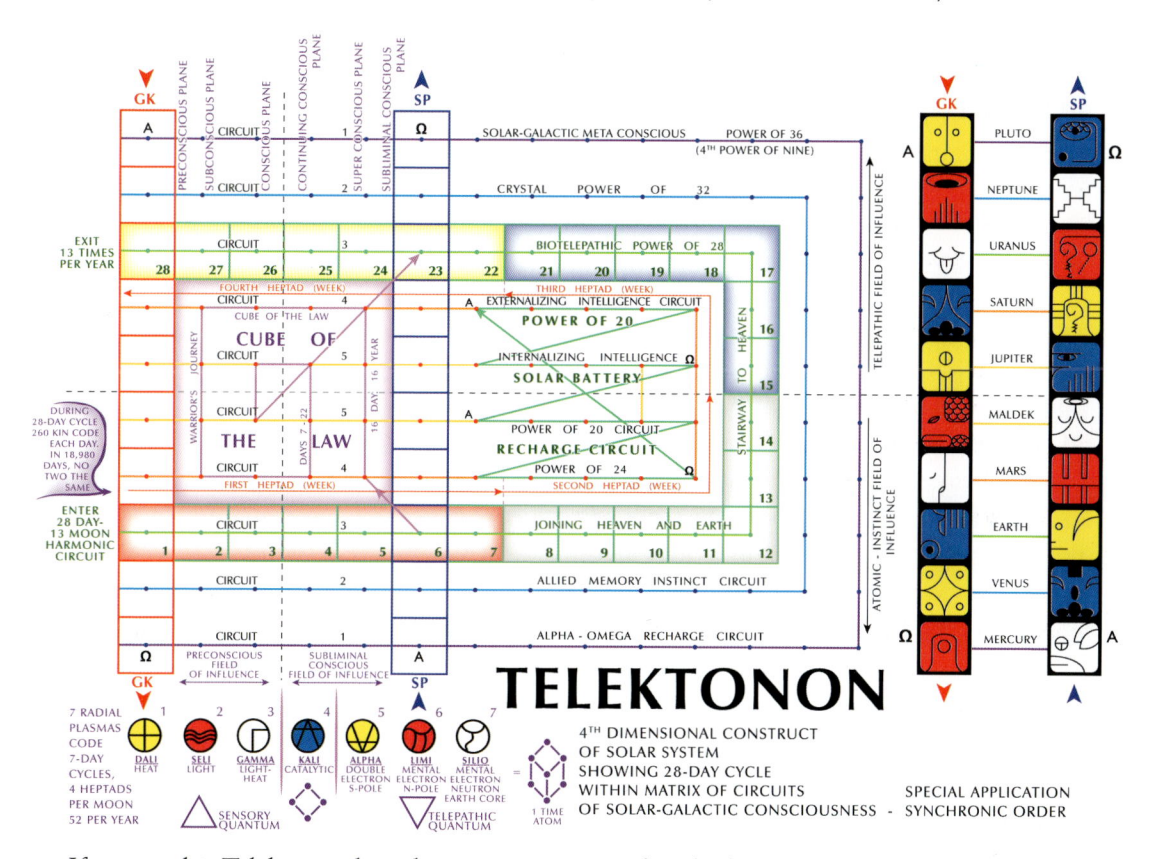

Appendix • Synchronic Order as Symbolic Construct

If we use this Telektonon board as an instrument of study then we see it is a matrix or template that shows the constituents or qualities of consciousness as functions of planetary orbits. Each of the planets is afforded two of the solar seals or symbols. For instance, Mercury has the symbols Moon (GK) and the Dog (SP). The Earth is represented by the symbol of the Hand (GK) and the Human (SP). Those symbols are perfect for the Earth since this is where the hand and the human reside. The symbols for Uranus are Wind (GK), which represents spirit, and Earth (SP) with the power of navigation, for Uranus is the other Earth navigating our Earth.

The Telektonon board, as a symbolic construct, is a fourth-dimensional map of the solar system with a sequence of five circuits that coordinate 140 nodal points of consciousness. The number of units of these five circuits is 140 (5 x 28 or 7 x 20).

This number 140 is the frequency "Telektonon" and defines Telektonon as a cosmic unit of measure. The Telektonon template also indicates that there are two basic fields of consciousness: the telepathic (five outer planetary orbits) and instinctual (five inner planetary orbits or fields of consciousness. It also shows that there are six different instinctual and telepathic alignments from preconscious to subliminal conscious. This is a fundamental tool for following the synchronic order.

The Telektonon board also consists of many internal matrices—the most significant of which is the *Cube of the Law*, first introduced in the cosmic structure of the Dreamspell color cube.

The Cube

The cube structure is essential to the synchronic symbology. In the Telektonon, the cube structure represents 16 units between the 28-unit third circuit and the two planetary flows. These 4 x 4 = 16 units establish the construct of the plane of mind which is a perfect cube matrix. The horizontal line across the center defines the plane of spirit and the vertical line through the center of the cube defines the plane of will. These three planes define the three internal planes of the cube: The plane of mind, which is the two-dimensional plane (the cube's top and bottom sides); and perpendicular to that, the plane of will (the cube's left and right sides); and the plane of spirit (the cube's front and back sides). It is this cube structure as well as the 28-day structure that create the possibility of numerous other coordinating patterns within the synchronic structure of the Telektonon.

One of these possibilities is the 16-year Cube of the Law program of the *20 Tablets of the Law of Time* within the synchronic structure of the Telektonon: The 16-year Cube of the Law is based on the 16 units occurring from day 7 through the three planes to day 22. This is an elaborate and evolved symbology which incorporates every single permutational sequence of the 64 codons or hexagrams of the I Ching.

Each of these hexagrams goes through a 13-week permutation process. 64 x 13 = 832. This is the same number of weeks as in a 16-year cycle. 16 x 52 is 64 x 13. This is one of the special applications of the Telektonon. Every line and codon in the I Ching is accounted for in a permutation sequence over an 832-week cycle which began on July 26, 1997 and concludes July 25, 2013. For each of the 832 weeks, the first six days are for placing the six lines on the six sides of the cube, and the seventh day is for "cubing the codon".

The cube takes on increasing significance in the synchronic order as one of the principle coordinating constructs. In the higher-dimensional reality, the cube represents the complete integration of the time space. From the point of view of the fourth and fifth dimensions, time space is a cube. We often think of the universe as patterns of moving spheres in space creating the megasphere as the ultimate defining geometrical form of the synchronic order. The sphere represents the perfection of consciousness and mind—there are no corners. It is an utter perfection, everything has been equalized. This is why in the Padmasambhava Dzogchen meditation practices it speaks about the ultimate sphere. The ultimate sphere is the primordial, pristine consciousness in which there is no differentiation. In this regard we can say that the sphere is the absolute of the absolute.

The cube, on the other hand, represents the sum potentialities of time space realized as being perceptible and sensible to the different sense organs. The cube also represent the evolution of all the possible constructs of mind in the third dimension on up.

All permutational number constructs and whole number matrices are summarized and/or accommodated by the cube. The sphere, in some sense, is the realm beyond number. Insofar as we are dealing with evolving constructs, the cube is the perfect symbol. The cube has an invisible center point and everything is equidistant from the center: the top and bottom are equidistant to the front and back and the two sides.

The dimensions of the cube are in absolute equality. All the ratios are equal to each other. In the cube there are eight points or vertices, eight corners and six sides. From the point of view of the Law of Time the seven is represented by the center point. So the seventh day of the week is called the day of the cube. Each week, the six-line codon is cubed, that is, it is coordinated in a sequence with six sides—as are the different radial plasmas.

SEEDS OF THE KNOWLEDGE OF THE LAW OF TIME

The seeds of the knowledge of the Law of Time have been left by the Galactic Maya. Because of this, the Law of Time was able to be discovered, resurrected and constructed from the information left here (see *Discovery of the Law of Time*).

The key to this information existed in a single template called the Buk Xoc—the template of divination or permutation of the numbers 13 and 20. These numbers were first decoded by Tony Shearer and then passed on to Valum Votan—this is the matrix of the 13:20 timing frequency. Every aspect of the Law of Time, in one way or another, is embedded in this frequency matrix.

As we know, the 13:20 matrix is a function of the frequency 13:20 which is a universal constant of synchronization. Every four sets of numbers radially opposite of each other within the matrix adds up to 28, and that sum of 28 appears 13 times in the Loom of Maya or 52 galactic activation portals of the 260-day matrix. This demonstrates that embedded within this matrix is the 13 moon/28-day cycle as well as the 260-day cycle. These two cycles create the patterns of synchronization, the fundamental basis of the synchronic order.

The synchronic order was not discovered and formulated until the final three decades of the cycle, beginning with the codes of *Earth Ascending* and *The Mayan Factor* and the full explanation of these codes in *Dreamspell: Journey of Timeship Earth 2013*, including the 13 Moon/28-day calendar. *The Treatise on Time Viewed from its Own Dimension* explains the Law of Time articulated as *T(E)=Art*: energy factored by time equals art.

LAW OF TIME AS SYMBOLIC STRUCTURE

All harmonic mathematics are coordinated by the Law of Time. As mentioned earlier, a key factor of the 28-day cycle is the I Ching DNA hexagram/codons. These 64 codons are coordinated by the permutations of the 16 stages of the Cube of the Law, located at the center of the Telektonon interplanetary template. The 64 hexagrams coordinate with the 64 UR runes, and are organized into 16 sets of four within the 16 positions of the cube.

The 24 runes of the Elder Futhark are also placed in the 28-day cycle, where again we have a sequence of 24 runes, 6 runes for six days and on the seventh day we cube the rune sequence or *psi plate*. These runes also correspond to the different plates of the psi bank. In this way, we coordinate different symbolic structures on a daily basis and also create a construct of the planetary noosphere, inclusive of the psi bank.

As the thinking band of the planet, the noosphere contains within it the universal future memory. The psi bank contains all evolutionary programs and preserves every motion, every thought, all the slightest nuances and feelings that ripple throughout the waves of undifferentiated nature, of the human and the universe. Everything is recorded and nothing is lost.

These practices that evolved, particularly from the Telektonon, integrate consciousness in time with biopsychology, as in the example of the codons with the psi bank, to create the dawning noosphere.

We also have the 7:7::7:7 practices, where the patterns of the daily 28-day sequence coincide with the pattern of the four weeks, and the seven radial plasmas. As with the 16-year Cube of the Law, the 7:7::7:7 also includes fractal time constructs to create different heptagonons of mind, which are actually constructs of time. These are cubed within the Earth.

This is merely to illustrate that the Law of Time is an ever-evolving system of symbolic correspondences that, when practiced, telepathically rearrange the mind. If practiced daily, the synchronic codes place the components of consciousness into different fractal geometrical constructs of time. Ultimately, when the planetary consciousness is fully in the noosphere then these codes will rearrange reality as well.

For example, in the 7:7::7:7 practices, these constructs of time get placed in the Earth every week by the daily practice of creating a time atom of seven parts. There are four time atoms, which create the master 28-unit *time molecule* that coordinates the octahedron at the center of the Earth. These are very interesting adaptations of symbolic constructs, utilizing them to co-evolve with consciousness and various organizing factors of the Earth as a whole system.

We can also place the 22 Major Arcanum of the Tarot into the Telektonon, spanning the 22-day cycle from day 7, the first day of the cube journey, through the 28th day. The 28-day cosmology of the great Sufi Ibn al-Arabi also fits perfectly into the Telektonon. This is all to underscore that the synchronic order exists as a symbolic coded pattern for the organization of knowledge as a program in time.

Once we understand that we are working with a harmonic matrix, then we can begin to take other symbolic constructs and place them within the ongoing synchronic order—the time sequences: the four-day, the seven-day, the thirteen-day, the twenty-day the 28-day, the 52-day, the four quarters, etc. All systems are contained within these cycles.

For example, the Mystery of the Stone practice works with symbolic constructs based on the fifth force oracles that integrate the nine great Lords of Time into the noosphere and into the planetary orbits of the solar system. These are moving symbolic constructs of time. By participating in the synchronic order and codes, we are actually participating in a creative order that descends from the fourth to the third dimension. By seizing the opportunity to engage the symbolic constructs of the synchronic order, we are slowly rearranging our consciousness and perceptions, and thus our third-dimension reality as well. This is the basis of our becoming participants in the Second Creation.

It is an evolutionary step to even begin to engage the Thirteen Moon calendar, the Dreamspell, and the Telektonon codes.

Appendix • Synchronic Order as Symbolic Construct

The 22 Major Arcana Adapted to the Thirteen Moon 28-day Telektonon. A 22-day journey every moon between days 7 and 28 - an entire 16-day Cube Journey plus the Heaven Walk between the Navigation and Spirit Towers. Become the Fool of Time redeemed and learn anew the Play of Time

Table of Correspondences

Arcana	Day	Seal	Planet
0	Day 7 Cube 1	Dragon	GK Neptune
1	Day 8 Cube 2	Wind	SP Uranus
2	Day 9 Cube 3	Night	GK Saturn
3	Day 10 Cube 4	Seed	GK Jupiter
4	Day 11 Cube 5	Serpent	GK Maldek
5	Day 12 Cube 6	World Bridger	GK Mars
6	Day 13 Cube 7	Hand	GK Earth
7	Day 14 Cube 8	Star	GK Venus
8	Day 15 Cube 9	Moon	GK Mercury
9	Day 16 Cube 10	Dog	SP Mercury
10	Day 17 Cube 11	Monkey	SP Venus
11	Day 18 Cube 12	Human	SP Earth
12	Day 19 Cube 13	Skywalker	SP Mars
13	Day 20 Cube 14	Wizard	SP Maldek
14	Day 21 Cube 15	Eagle	SP Jupiter
15	Day 22 Cube 16	Warrior	SP Saturn
16	Navigation Tower	Earth	SP Uranus
17	Heaven Walk 1	Mirror	SP Neptune
18	Heaven Walk 2	Storm	SP Pluto
19	Heaven Walk 3	Sun	GK Pluto
20	Heaven Walk 4	Dragon	GK Neptune
21	Spirit Tower	Wind	GK Uranus

Major Arcana Sequence

21 World/Universe — Great One of the Night of Time — Day 28

20 Aeon/Judgement — Spirit of the Primal Fire — Day 27

19 Sun — Lord of the Fire of the World — Day 26

18 Moon — Ruler of Flux and Reflux; Child of the Sons of the Mighty — Day 25

17 Star — Daughter of the Firmament; Dweller between the Waters — Day 24

16 Tower — Lord of the Tower Hosts of the Mighty — Day 23

5 Hierophant — Magus of the Eternal — Day 12

4 Emperor — Sun of the Morning, Chief Among the Mighty — Day 11

3 Empress — Daughter of the Mighty ones — Day 10

2 High Priestess — Priestess of the Silver Star — Day 9

1 Magician — Magus of Power — Day 8

0 Fool — Eternal Innocent Child of Free Will — Day 7

6 Lovers — Children of the Voice, Oracles of the Mighty Gods — Day 13

7 Chariot — Child of the Powers of the Waters, Lord of the Triumph of Light — Day 14

8 Strength — Daughter of the Lords of Truth, Ruler of the Balance — Day 15

9 Hermit — Magus of the Voice of Power, Prophet of the Eternal — Day 16

10 Wheel of Fortune — Lord of Fate, Forces of Life — Day 17

11 Justice/Lust — Daughter of the Flaming Sword — Day 18

12 Hanged Man — Spirit of Man, Mighty Waters — Day 19

13 Death — Child of the Great Transformers, Lord of the Gates of Death — Day 20

14 Art — Daughter of the Reconcilers, Bringer forth of Life — Day 21

15 Devil — Lord of the Gates of Matter; Child of the Forces of Time — Day 22

Days 1-6 = Six Days of Creation. Day 6: Free Will Tower. On the Seventh Day when God assumes the Throne. Choose to Enter the Cube as the Fool and initiate the experience of the 22 Major Arcana Days 7-28 every Moon.

Day 1	Day 2	Day 3	Day 4	Day 5	Day 6
Day 1 - Tower of accomplishment. Enjoy the power of the first day of creation	Days 2, 5 - Earth walk one to four walk with the mighty majesty of the second to fifth days of creation				Day 6 - Free will tower. Sixth Day of creation. It's your choice to be the Fool

Special thanks to Kin 52, Yellow Cosmic Human, the Great Beast, AC 1875-1947 of the Brotherhood of the Golden Dawn for his inspiration in giving new, amplified meaning to the archetypes of the Major Arcana